THE AMERICAN
DINER COOKBOOK

THE AMERICAN DINER COOKBOOK

ELIZABETH MCKEON

and

LINDA EVERETT

Cumberland House
Nashville, Tennessee

Published by
  Cumberland House Publishing, Inc.
  431 Harding Industrial Drive
  Nashville, TN 37211

Cover design: Gore Studio, Inc.
Text design: Lisa Taylor

Library of Congress Cataloging-in-Publication Data

McKeon, Elizabeth, 1962–
    The American diner cookbook / Elizabeth McKeon and Linda Everett.
        p. cm.
    ISBN 1-58182-345-2 (pbk.)
  1. Cookery, American. 2. Diners (Restaurants)—United States. I. Everett, Linda, 1946– II. Title.
    TX715 .M13984 2003
    641.5973—dc21

                                                                    2002154010

Printed in the United States of America
2 3 4 5 6 7 8 — 08 07 06 05 04 03

This book is dedicated to all those
road-weary travelers who will always enjoy the
comforts of home at their nearest roadside diner.

SUNRISE DINER, JIM THORPE, PENNSYLVANIA

A special thanks to Jacqueline Merlino
for her gracious permission to include her
1957 menu for Mel's Diner on pages 100-103.

PANCAKES AT HENRY'S

When I walked into Henry's Diner in Allston, Massachusetts, for the first time in 1986, I did so with a great deal of reluctance. This was only my fourth visit to a diner in twenty-five years.

Until Henry's, when I ate out I was only concerned with finding a decent cup of coffee and a good breakfast. The last place I expected to find them was in a diner, a place I had long associated with belching truck drivers. To this day I am thankful for my friend who insisted that I go inside and give it a try. I envy those who have known the charm of diners all their lives.

Now—seventeen years later—I am a spokesman for this beloved institution, and I am pleasantly surprised to discover that I love diners more with every visit I make. One cannot fall in love with those venerable ladies of the roadside without having a passion for their history.

As I look at the old photos of the proud grill men behind the counter in their white shirts and ties, I realize that these men and women could not possibly have foreseen the imprint they were making on our culture. It was a job, a way to pay the mortgage or maybe send their children to college. But in their own ways they were making a difference in their communities.

Quietly and unceremoniously, with every cup of coffee and every piece of pie, they were adding to the lore we now cherish so dearly. We are amazed by the grill man who could slide plates of food the length of the marble counter to the ordering customer. We are enchanted when we hear about the waitress who always remembered your name and how you took your coffee. We are wistful when we hear stories of when you could go down to the diner at any time of the day and run into someone, probably someone you knew well enough to have a chat with over a sandwich.

We are nostalgic for this time because we realize that in our mad rush to the twenty-first century we threw away and paved over many of the good and simple things in life. For many, all that is left is some Disneyesque diner wannabe in a barren strip mall. The large restaurant corporations are under the impression that if they spend enough on their marketing campaigns, they can fool us into thinking that any one of their thousand outlets re-creates a "down-home" atmosphere.

We have handed the stewardship of our commercial culture over to those machines of homogenization that roll across the landscape, flattening whatever sense of creativity and cultural diversity we still have. They think they are doing us a favor by making every place an exact copy of all others to ensure consistency.

Certainly there is comfort in consistency, but the damage it inflicts upon our communities is staggering. We lose something not only when another diner is lost, but also when we lose any business that is owned and operated by a local family and is a part of our neighborhood.

And yet, after all this "progress," we are beginning to see that we do not have to give up simple pleasures that add quality to our lives. The diner endures, not because of a sense of nostalgia or because the 1950s were necessarily better than today or because of *Roadside* or the exuberant enthusiasm of diner fanatics. It endures, quite simply, because it is still a great idea. Today we appreciate good service, good food at reasonable prices, and a clean, homey atmosphere. These things never will go out of fashion, provided that we stop trying to rush, package, or process them into oblivion.

The diners that we all love and cherish are run by hardworking men and women who strive to make life better for themselves and for the people they serve. No secret formulas or magic is involved. They are successful because they work hard and find their greatest rewards in the smiles on the faces of their customers as they walk out the door, not in the cash register at the end of the day.

Not every diner is perfect, and not every diner owner is able. The quality of food varies from place to place, but there is joy in finding that diner in the middle of nowhere. There you will find big warm biscuits, like at the Avoca Diner in Avoca, New York, or onion rings, like I found recently at the Midway Diner in Rutland, Vermont. Either way, after you finish eating, you will return home with something to add to your lore of the diner.

I'll never forget that first breakfast at Henry's. I had two blueberry pancakes, two eggs, bacon, coffee, and juice, all for about three dollars. If, indeed, diner owners find a reward in the smiles of their customers, then Henry got very rich that day in 1986.

Randy Garbin
Roadside Magazine
Worcester, Massachusetts

BREAKFAST AT THE COUNTER

beverages, breakfast breads,
pancakes, French toast, waffles,
eggs, omelettes, etc. 5

ON THE SIDE

French fries, onion rings, potatoes,
corn bread, biscuits, chili, baked beans,
vegetables, etc. 39

SOUPS OF THE DAY & SALADS
served with crackers, bread & butter

chicken noodle, chowders, minestrone,
house salad, seafood salads,
potato salad, coleslaw, etc.. 65

SANDWICH PLATTERS
served with French fries, potato salad, or salad

corned beef, roast beef, Philly cheesesteak,
chili dog, patty melt, BLT, clubhouse,
egg salad, tuna melt, etc. 105

THE AMERICAN DINER MENU
breakfast · lunch · dinner
Open 7 Days

FROM THE GRILL
served with soup, house salad, or French fries

chili burger, Texas-style burger, grilled
spareribs, green pepper steak, Santa Fe
chicken, grilled vegetables, etc.. 127

BLUE PLATE SPECIALS
*served with soup or house salad, potatoes,
fresh vegetables, bread & butter*

chicken fried steak, meat loaf, pot roast,
fish and chips, pork chops, baked ham,
veal cutlets, shepherd's pie, etc. 151

FOUNTAIN ALLEY

cherry cola, caboose chaser,
black & white sundae, black cow, banana
split, alleyway parfait, etc. 191

WHAT'S FOR DESSERT?

velveteen cake, chocolate cake, diner
cheesecake, applesauce cake, banana
cream pie, raspberry pie, etc.. 215

THE AMERICAN
DINER COOKBOOK

THE AMERICAN DINING ADVENTURE

Their names are magical: the Miss Albany, the Mayfair, or the Nite Owl, and they draw us in with their warmth and their great food. The American roadside diner is a place like no other.

More than booths and stools, more than homey, personal service, more even than tasty, satisfying food, the diner offers an adventure. Outside, the flash of neon welcomes passersby to stop in for a home-cooked meal. Inside, a long, narrow counter wraps around a hot grill, and stainless-steel Formica tables stand between red Naugahyde booths. A waitress greets you with a smile and a freshly brewed cup of steaming coffee. A short-order cook stands at an open grill ready to prepare your breakfast, lunch, or dinner anytime of the day. The food is served fast, fresh, and made to order.

The local diner is often the focal point of a community. Here conversation mixes with soft music from a corner jukebox. Friends discuss the day's events over cups of coffee. Businessmen consider their latest investment over the house special. Couples relax into their Sunday morning over plates of ham and eggs. Romances begin and end over a chocolate malted milk and a slice of apple pie.

Whether tucked away on a quiet side street or plunked down beside a busy thoroughfare, diners come in an endless variety of shapes and sizes. Generally speaking, diners are pre-fabricated structures, pieced together in a factory and then shipped to their places of business by truck or rail. Like automobiles, the classic diners came in all makes and models: from the sleek Sterling Streamliner to the twelve-stool Pollard. They were built by manufacturers such as Bixler, Kullman, O'Mahoney, Sterling, or the Worcester Lunch Car Company.

Diners and diner-going peaked in the 1950s, when an estimated six thousand of these small, family-owned businesses were in operation across the United States. By the early 1960s, however, diners began to decline as fast-food chains became the newest sensation. For a while it seemed the roadside diner was an endangered species, but things have changed. Renovated, restored, and rebuilt, diners are on the comeback trail, and hungry people are flocking to them once again.

If you have not tried the diner experience lately, you should. You'll find the food delicious, the service excellent, the prices reasonable, and the conversation as plentiful as the coffee. All you need to do is sit back, relax, and enjoy America's foremost dining adventure. And for those who would like to try out their diner favorites at home, this book offers another way to enjoy the adventure. Just keep turning the pages of *The American Diner Cookbook*, and you are sure to find what you want right there on the menu. Come on in! Everyone is welcome.

BREAKFAST AT THE COUNTER

Glazed Doughnuts

1	cup scalded milk
½	cup butter
½	cup sugar
½	teaspoon salt
2	eggs plus 1 egg yolk, beaten
2	envelopes active dry yeast
4	cups all-purpose flour, sifted
	Cooking oil

♦ ♦ ♦

1	cup confectioners' sugar
3	tablespoons water
½	teaspoon vanilla extract

In a mixing bowl pour the scalded milk over the butter, sugar, and salt. Cool slightly. Add the eggs. When the temperature reaches between 105 and 115°, add the yeast. Let the mixture stand for 5 minutes.

Blend in the flour a little at a time. Mix into a soft dough. When smooth, turn the dough out onto a well-floured board. Knead gently for about 2 minutes.

Place the dough in a greased bowl, turning to coat all sides. Let rise for 1 hour.

Punch the dough down, and divide it in half. On a lightly floured board roll each section to ½-inch thickness. Cut with a floured doughnut cutter. Place on waxed paper. Set in a warm place. Let rise for 30 minutes.

In a deep skillet heat the oil to 375°. Using a slotted spoon gently slip each doughnut into the oil. Fry for 2 minutes or until golden brown, turning once. Drain on paper towels.

In a small mixing bowl blend together the confectioners' sugar, water, and vanilla. Drizzle over the doughnuts while they are still warm.

MAKES 2 DOZEN

Plain Doughnuts

4	cups all-purpose flour
4	tablespoons baking powder
½	teaspoon salt
¼	teaspoon nutmeg
½	teaspoon cinnamon
2	tablespoons shortening
1	cup sugar
2	eggs
1	cup milk
	Cooking oil

In a mixing bowl sift together the flour, baking powder, salt, nutmeg, and cinnamon. In a separate bowl cream together the shortening, sugar, and eggs. Add the milk to the dry mixture alternately with the egg mixture. Blend thoroughly.

Roll the dough out on a lightly floured board to ½-inch thickness. Cut with a floured doughnut cutter. Let stand for 20 minutes.

In a deep skillet heat the oil to 375°. Fry each doughnut for 3 to 5 minutes or until they turn a light golden brown, turning them as they rise to the surface. Drain on paper towels.

MAKES 2 DOZEN

Unless otherwise stated, a mixing bowl indicates a large bowl.

SALEM OAK DINER, SALEM, NEW JERSEY

Raised Doughnuts

1 envelope active dry yeast
¼ cup warm water
¾ cup scalded milk
4 cups all-purpose flour
¾ cup sugar
½ teaspoon nutmeg
½ teaspoon salt
2 eggs, well beaten
2 teaspoons grated lemon rind
½ cup shortening, melted
Cooking oil

In a mixing bowl soften the yeast in the warm water. Add the slightly cooled milk. Add 2 cups of flour and 2 tablespoons of sugar. Beat until smooth. Cover and let rise in a warm place for 30 minutes.

Sift the remaining flour with the remaining sugar, the nutmeg, and salt. In a separate bowl blend together the eggs, lemon rind, and shortening. Add the yeast. Add the flour mixture and mix until a soft dough forms. Turn onto a floured surface and knead for 5 minutes or until bubbles appear on the surface. Cover and let rise for 1 hour.

Roll the dough out onto a lightly floured board to 1-inch thickness. Cut with a floured doughnut cutter. Cover and let rise for 1 hour or until doubled in size.

In a deep, heavy skillet heat the oil. Fry the doughnuts for 2 to 3 minutes, turning once. Drain on paper towels.

MAKES 2 DOZEN

Jelly or Custard–Filled Doughnuts

Raised Doughnut dough (see recipe at left)
Fruit jelly (any flavor) or custard

Prepare the recipe for Raised Doughnuts. Roll out to ½-inch thickness. Cut into rounds, 4 inches in diameter.

Place 1 tablespoon of jelly or custard filling on the center of each piece of dough. Turn up the edges and pinch to seal. Place the smooth side on a board. Cover and let rise. Cook as for Raised Doughnuts.

MAKES 2 DOZEN

PAUGUS DINER, LACONIA, NEW HAMPSHIRE

Chocolate Doughnuts

3¾ cups all-purpose flour
4 tablespoons baking powder
½ teaspoon salt
6 tablespoons cocoa powder
½ teaspoon cinnamon
2 tablespoons shortening
1 cup sugar
2 eggs
1 cup milk
1 teaspoon vanilla extract
Cooking oil

♦ ♦ ♦

1 cup confectioners' sugar
3 tablespoons water
½ teaspoon vanilla extract

In a mixing bowl sift together the flour, baking powder, salt, cocoa powder, and cinnamon.

In a separate bowl cream the shortening with the sugar and eggs. Blend together the milk and vanilla. Add the milk to the flour mixture alternately with the egg mixture. Blend thoroughly.

Roll the dough out onto a lightly floured board to ½-inch thickness. Cut with a floured doughnut cutter. Let stand for 20 minutes.

In a deep skillet heat the oil to 375°. Fry for 3 to 5 minutes or until the doughnuts are a light golden brown. Turn the doughnuts as they rise to the surface.

In a small mixing bowl blend the confectioners' sugar with the water and vanilla. Drizzle over the doughnuts while they are still warm. Cool on paper towels.

MAKES 2 DOZEN

Cinnamon Rolls

¼ cup active dry yeast
4 cups warm milk
1 cup sugar
1½ tablespoons vanilla extract
4 eggs
1 teaspoon salt
1 cup vegetable oil
14 cups all-purpose flour

♦ ♦ ♦

½ cup unsalted butter, melted
1 cup sugar
¼ cup cinnamon
1 cup chopped walnuts
1 cup chopped pecans
1 cup chopped raisins

♦ ♦ ♦

6 tablespoons butter, softened
3 cups confectioners' sugar
3 tablespoons cream
1 teaspoon vanilla extract

In a large bowl dissolve the yeast in the warm milk with the sugar. Add the vanilla, eggs, salt, and oil. Beat for 1 minute. Blend in the flour a few cups at a time. Mix until moist but not sticky.

Turn the dough onto a lightly floured board. Knead until smooth and elastic. Use flour as needed to keep the dough moist and soft. Place the dough in a large greased bowl. Cover with a cloth. Let rise in a warm place until doubled in bulk.

In a medium bowl mix together the melted butter, sugar, and cinnamon.

Punch down the dough, and divide it in half. Roll one half into a rectangle. With a pastry brush spread the butter mixture evenly over the dough. Sprinkle with chopped nuts and raisins. Roll up the dough lengthwise into the shape of a log. Cut into 1-inch-thick slices.

Lightly oil a large shallow baking dish.

Arrange the sliced dough in the pan so that the rolls are touching. Let the dough rise until it has doubled.

Bake at 350° for 15 to 20 minutes or until light golden brown.

In a mixing bowl combine the butter with the confectioners' sugar. Add the cream and beat briskly. Blend in the vanilla and beat until smooth. Drizzle the icing over the warm cinnamon rolls.

MAKES 4 DOZEN

At-the-Counter Coffee Cake

1	cup all-purpose flour
1/2	cup sugar
1/4	teaspoon salt
1/2	teaspoon cinnamon
1 1/2	teaspoons baking powder
1/2	cup milk
1	egg, beaten
2	tablespoons butter, melted

♦ ♦ ♦

1/3	cup sugar
1/4	cup all-purpose flour
1	teaspoon cinnamon
1/8	teaspoon allspice
1/2	cup chopped walnuts
1/4	cup butter, melted

In a mixing bowl sift 1 cup of flour with ½ cup of sugar, the salt, ½ teaspoon cinnamon, and the baking powder. In a separate bowl blend together the milk, egg, and 2 tablespoons of melted butter. Add the milk mixture to the flour mixture. Blend just until moist. Do not overmix. Spread the batter into an 8-inch round pan.

In a small bowl blend together the remaining sugar, flour, and cinnamon, and the allspice. Add the chopped walnuts. Blend thoroughly. Spread evenly over the top of the batter. Drizzle with the remaining melted butter. Bake at 400° for 20 to 25 minutes.

SERVES 6

Blueberry Coffee Cake

1/4	cup shortening
3/4	cup sugar
2	cups all-purpose flour
3/4	teaspoon salt
2 1/2	teaspoons baking powder
1	egg
3/4	cup milk
2	cups blueberries

♦ ♦ ♦

1/4	cup butter, softened
1/3	cup all-purpose flour
1/2	cup sugar
1/2	teaspoon cinnamon

Grease a 9-inch square pan.

In a mixing bowl cream together the shortening and ¾ cup of sugar. In a separate bowl combine 2 cups of flour, the salt, and baking powder. Add the egg and milk, and mix well. Add the sugar mixture, and mix thoroughly. Gently add the blueberries. Spread the batter into the prepared baking pan.

In a mixing bowl mix together the remaining butter, flour, and sugar, and the cinnamon with a fork until the mixture begins to crumble. Sprinkle over the top of the batter. Bake at 375° for 45 minutes or until the cake tests done.

SERVES 6

Sour Cream Coffee Cake

½	cup butter
1	cup sugar
2	eggs
1	teaspoon vanilla extract
2	cups all-purpose flour
1	teaspoon baking powder
1	teaspoon baking soda
½	teaspoon salt
1	cup sour cream
½	cup chopped walnuts
⅓	cup packed brown sugar
1	teaspoon cinnamon

In a mixing bowl cream together the butter and sugar until light and fluffy. Beat in the eggs and vanilla.

In a separate bowl sift together the flour, baking powder, baking soda, and salt. Add to the butter mixture alternately with the sour cream.

Mix together the walnuts, brown sugar, and cinnamon.

Spoon half the batter into a 9-inch square pan. Sprinkle the top with half of the walnut filling. Spoon the remaining batter over the filling. Sprinkle the remaining filling over the top. Bake at 350° for 45 minutes.

SERVES 6

JULE'S DINER, BOLTON LANDING, NEW YORK

Banana-Nut Bread

5 medium bananas
1 egg, beaten
¼ cup shortening, melted
1 cup bran
½ cup chopped walnuts
1½ cups all-purpose flour
2½ teaspoons baking powder
½ teaspoon baking soda
½ teaspoon salt
½ cup sugar

Grease a 9x5-inch loaf pan.

In a mixing bowl mash the bananas. Add the egg, shortening, bran, and chopped walnuts. Mix thoroughly.

In a separate bowl sift together the flour, baking powder, baking soda, salt, and sugar. Add to the banana mixture.

Pour the batter into the prepared loaf pan. Bake at 350° for 65 to 75 minutes or until a toothpick inserted in the center comes out clean. Serve warm.

MAKES 1 LOAF

Blueberry Muffins

¼ cup butter
2 cups less 2 tablespoons all-purpose flour
1 tablespoon baking powder
½ teaspoon salt
1 tablespoon sugar
1 cup milk
2 eggs, beaten
1½ cups blueberries

Grease a 12-cup muffin pan.

In a small saucepan melt the butter. In a mixing bowl combine all but ¼ cup of flour with the baking powder, salt, and sugar. In a separate bowl blend together the milk with the eggs.

In a small bowl toss the blueberries with the remaining ¼ cup of flour. Add the melted butter to the egg mixture. Mix the dry ingredients into the batter. Gently stir in the blueberries.

Spoon equal amounts of batter into the prepared muffin cups. Bake at 400° for 15 to 20 minutes or until a toothpick inserted in the center of a muffin comes out clean. Remove the muffins from the pan and let cool.

MAKES 1 DOZEN

Cranberry-Nut Muffins

¼ cup shortening
¼ cup sugar
1 egg
1 teaspoon grated orange rind
1 cup bran
1 8-ounce can whole cranberry sauce
½ cup chopped walnuts
½ cup milk
1 cup all-purpose flour, sifted
1 tablespoon baking powder
½ teaspoon salt
3 tablespoons sugar
½ teaspoon cinnamon

Grease a 12-cup muffin pan.

In a large mixing bowl cream together the shortening and ¼ cup of sugar. Add the egg. Mix thoroughly. Add the grated orange rind, bran, cranberry sauce, chopped walnuts, and milk. Blend together until well mixed. Set aside.

In a separate bowl sift together the flour, baking powder, and salt. Pour the dry ingredients into the cranberry mixture, blending just until moistened. Pour the batter into the prepared muffin pan.

Mix together the sugar and cinnamon. Sprinkle over the batter. Bake at 400° for 20 minutes or until a toothpick inserted into the center of a muffin comes out clean.

MAKES 1 DOZEN

English Muffins

1 cup milk, scalded
3 tablespoons butter
1½ teaspoons salt
2 tablespoons sugar
1 envelope active dry yeast
¼ cup warm water
1 egg, beaten
4 cups all-purpose flour, sifted

In a large mixing bowl pour the milk over the butter, salt, and sugar. Stir until all are dissolved. Set aside until the milk has cooled.

Soften the yeast in the warm water.

Add the yeast to the milk mixture. Add the beaten egg and half of the flour. Blend thoroughly, making sure there are no lumps. Add the remaining flour. Make sure that the dough is elastic. Cover and let stand in a warm place until the dough has doubled in bulk.

Divide the dough into ¾-cup portions. Knead until smooth. Roll to ½-inch thickness. Let rise once more until doubled in bulk. Bake on a griddle over low heat. As the muffins rise, turn to brown the other side.

MAKES 1 DOZEN

Jelly Surprise Muffins

2 cups all-purpose flour
3 teaspoons baking powder
½ teaspoon salt
2 tablespoons sugar
1 egg, beaten
1 cup milk
¼ cup shortening, melted
Strawberry jelly

Grease a 12-cup muffin pan.

In a mixing bowl sift together the flour, baking powder, salt, and sugar.

In a separate bowl cream together the beaten egg with the milk and shortening. Add the creamed mixture to the flour mixture, blending just until moistened.

Fill each muffin cup one-third full with the batter. Place 1 teaspoon of strawberry jelly on the center of each. Pour the remaining batter over the top of the jelly until two-thirds full. Bake at 425° for 25 minutes. Serve warm.

MAKES 1 DOZEN

Red Flannel Hash

3 cups ground beef
4 medium potatoes, cooked and chopped
¼ cup chopped onion
4 medium beets, cooked and chopped fine
1 teaspoon salt
¼ teaspoon black pepper
½ teaspoon dry mustard
1½ teaspoons butter
4 slices bacon
½ cup cream

In a mixing bowl combine the ground beef, potatoes, onion, beets, salt, pepper, mustard, and butter. Blend thoroughly.

Pat evenly into the bottom of a 9-inch square pan. Top with bacon slices. Pour the cream over the entire mixture. Bake at 350° for 40 minutes or until the bacon is crisp. Cut into squares.

SERVES 6

Corned Beef Hash & Eggs

6 medium potatoes, peeled and cubed
¼ cup butter
1 small onion, chopped
1 pound corned beef, chopped
¼ teaspoon black pepper
8 eggs

In a large saucepan cook the potatoes in boiling, salted water until slightly soft but still firm. Drain and set aside.

In a heavy skillet melt the butter, coating the bottom of the pan. Add the onion and sauté for 1 minute. Add the corned beef and potatoes, and season with pepper. Cook until the bottom begins to brown. Turn occasionally so that it does not scorch.

Make 8 wells in the hash. Crack an egg into each. Cover and reduce the heat to low. Continue cooking for 3 minutes.

SERVES 6

Texas-Style Hash

1 pound ground beef
2 cups sliced onions
½ cup chopped green bell pepper
½ cup uncooked rice
2 teaspoons chili powder
½ teaspoon salt
1 16-ounce can whole tomatoes

In a heavy skillet brown the ground beef with the onions and green pepper. Cook, stirring often, until all of the vegetables are tender. Drain the fat.

Add the rice, chili powder, salt, and tomatoes. Blend thoroughly. Bring to a boil, then reduce the heat. Cover and simmer for 25 minutes or until the rice is tender. Stir twice while simmering.

SERVES 4

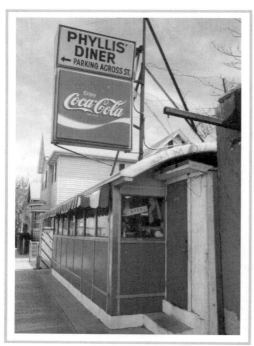

PHYLLIS' DINER, EVERETT, MASSACHUSETTS

Biscuits 'n' Gravy

1¼ cups all-purpose flour
½ teaspoon salt
2 teaspoons baking powder
¼ cup unsalted butter, softened
⅓ cup plain yogurt
½ cup milk

♦ ♦ ♦

1½ pounds lean pork sausage
⅛ teaspoon coarse black pepper
1 teaspoon dried sage
¼ teaspoon salt
½ teaspoon paprika
¼ teaspoon allspice

♦ ♦ ♦

¼ cup unsalted butter
¼ cup all-purpose flour
¼ cup water
2¼ cups milk
Salt and pepper to taste

In a large mixing bowl sift the flour with the salt and baking powder. Using your fingers blend in the butter until the texture resembles coarse meal. Gradually mix in the yogurt and milk. Do not overwork the dough.

Turn the dough out onto a lightly floured board. Knead for 30 seconds. Roll out to 1¼-inch thickness. Cut into 2-inch rounds to make 8 biscuits. Place on a baking sheet. Bake at 425° for 18 minutes or until golden brown.

In a large mixing bowl blend the

MISS WAKEFIELD DINER, WAKEFIELD, NEW HAMPSHIRE

sausage with the pepper, sage, salt, paprika, and allspice. Shape into 8 patties. In a heavy skillet over medium heat cook the sausage for 8 minutes per side. Set the sausage patties aside.

In the same skillet used for the sausage, melt the butter. Stir and scrape the skillet to release the browned pieces from the pan. Reduce the heat.

Blend the flour with the water. Add the mixture to the skillet, stirring constantly. Cook until the flour mixture turns golden brown. Slowly add the milk. Continue stirring until the gravy thickens. Season with salt and pepper. Serve over biscuits with a sausage patty.

SERVES 4

Diner Scramble

6	tablespoons butter
1/2	cup chopped red bell pepper
5	green onions, chopped fine
8	eggs
1/8	teaspoon salt
1/8	teaspoon pepper
2	tablespoons milk

In a medium skillet melt the butter. Add the red pepper and onion, and sauté until the onion is soft but not brown. Remove the skillet from the heat.

In a small mixing bowl beat the eggs. Add the salt, pepper, and milk. Place the skillet over medium heat. Pour in the eggs. Stir slowly until the eggs become creamy and have set.

SERVES 4

Diner Skillet

6	eggs
	Salt and pepper to taste
1/4	cup milk
1/4	teaspoon Tabasco sauce
1	teaspoon Worcestershire sauce
2	tablespoons cooking oil
1	onion, chopped
1/4	cup chopped green bell pepper

In a mixing bowl beat the eggs with salt and pepper. Add the milk and beat thoroughly. Blend in the Tabasco and Worcestershire sauces. Set the bowl aside.

In a skillet heat the oil and sauté the onion and green pepper until tender.

Add the egg mixture. Cook slowly, stirring constantly, until scrambled.

SERVES 4

Potatoes & Eggs

1/4	cup cooking oil
4	cups diced potatoes
2	tablespoons all-purpose flour
1	onion, chopped
1/2	teaspoon salt
	Pepper to taste
1	teaspoon Worcestershire sauce
2	cups water
6	hard-boiled eggs, sliced

In a large skillet heat the oil and cook the potatoes until brown. Remove the potatoes from the pan. Set aside.

In the same skillet brown the flour, stirring constantly. Add the chopped onion and sauté until transparent.

Add the salt and pepper, Worcestershire sauce, and water. Return the browned potatoes to the skillet.

Bring the mixture to a boil. Reduce the heat, cover, and simmer for 12 minutes. Add the sliced eggs, heat, and serve.

SERVES 4

Eggs Benedict

1/2	cup butter
4	egg yolks
1/2	teaspoon salt
	Juice from one lemon
1	cup hot water
	♦ ♦ ♦
1	2-inch ham steak, cooked
	♦ ♦ ♦
3	English muffins, halved
	Butter
6	eggs, poached
	Salt and pepper to taste

In a mixing bowl cream the butter. Add the egg yolks, salt, and lemon juice, and blend thoroughly. Slowly add the hot water. Pour the mixture into the top of a double boiler. Cook over simmering water, stirring constantly, until smooth and thick.

Cut the ham into 6 equal portions. In a skillet fry the ham until brown.

Lightly toast the muffins. Butter each muffin. Top each half with a slice of ham and a poached egg. Pour sauce over the egg. Season with salt and pepper.

SERVES 6

CONNIE'S DINER

Connie's Diner in Waterloo, New York, is a throwback to the era of bobby socks and ducktail haircuts. Records, pictures, and posters from the 1950s cover the walls. "People just love that stuff," says owner Connie Cartizola.

A 1965 Manno, the diner is not quite as old as the decade it celebrates, but the decorations are all original. Connie says people enjoy details, but she knows it's the food that keeps her customers interested.

"Our lasagna is one of the best around," she says, without a hint of false modesty. "We also have our Connie's Cookies, a ham-burger and French fries with gravy poured over everything. Believe me, we sell a ton of those." The diner is also well known for its chili and Sloppy Joes.

"We get a lot of travelers," says Connie. "People who know where we are and just keep coming back. When we first opened, we would get mostly youngsters. Now we get both young and old. It has turned into a real family restaurant. Parents bring their children with them. And of course we get couples who come in, sit in the corner, and hold hands. Nothing's really changed."

Eggs Florentine

2	tablespoons butter
2	tablespoons all-purpose flour
1	teaspoon salt
1/4	teaspoon pepper
2	cups milk
2	cups grated Cheddar cheese
1/2	teaspoon Worcestershire sauce

♦ ♦ ♦

	Butter
1/2	cup cooked spinach, chopped
4	eggs
1/2	cup grated Cheddar cheese

In a saucepan melt the butter over low heat. Add the flour, salt, and pepper. Blend thoroughly. Remove the pan from the heat.

Slowly add the milk. Return the pan to the heat, and stir until well blended and smooth. Add 2 cups of Cheddar cheese and the Worcestershire sauce. Continue stirring until the cheese has melted and the sauce thickens.

Butter 4 individual baking dishes. Place 2 tablespoons of the chopped spinach in each. Break an egg over the spinach. Top with cheese sauce. Sprinkle the grated Cheddar cheese over the sauce.

Bake at 350° for 15 minutes or until the eggs are cooked.

SERVES 4

Ham & Eggs

2	pounds ham steak, cut 1/2-inch thick
	Butter
12	eggs
	Salt and pepper to taste

Cut the ham steak into thirds. In a skillet fry the ham steak for 3 minutes per side. Remove the ham from the skillet, and set it aside.

Add a small amount of butter to the skillet. Fry the eggs to the desired degree of doneness. Remove and serve with sliced ham. Season with salt and pepper.

SERVES 6

Hogwaller

6	sausage links, chopped
1/4	cup chopped onion
1/4	cup chopped green bell pepper
6	eggs, beaten
1	large potato, cooked and cubed
1/4	cup cubed cooked ham
4	slices bacon, cooked and chopped
1	chile pepper, chopped
1/2	cup chopped spinach

In a heavy skillet cook the sausage until brown. Add the chopped onion and green pepper, and sauté until the onion is transparent. Add the eggs, potato, ham, bacon, chile pepper, and spinach.

Cook over low heat, stirring constantly, until the eggs are scrambled. Do not overcook. Serve over toast or English muffins.

SERVES 4

Hush Puppies

1½   cups cornmeal
1½   cups water
⅓   cup milk
1   tablespoon cooking oil
2   teaspoons grated onion
2   eggs
1   cup all-purpose flour
3   teaspoons baking powder
1   teaspoon salt
1   teaspoon sugar
   Cooking oil

In a saucepan combine the cornmeal and water. Cook over medium heat, stirring constantly, until the batter becomes thick and begins to take the shape of a ball.

Remove the pan from the heat. Add the milk, oil, and onion.

In a large mixing bowl beat the eggs. Pour the batter into the eggs. In a separate bowl sift together the flour, baking powder, salt, and sugar. Add the dry ingredients to the batter and mix well.

In a heavy, deep skillet heat the oil to 350°. Drop the batter by the teaspoonful into the oil. Fry for 5 minutes or until light golden brown. Drain on paper towels.

SERVES 6

Spiced Eggs

2   tablespoons butter
¼   pound cooked ham, sliced thin
6   eggs
2½   cups canned tomatoes, chopped
1   teaspoon chili powder
1½   cups grated Cheddar cheese

In a skillet melt the butter. Add the ham and fry until lightly browned. In a mixing bowl beat the eggs thoroughly. Add the tomatoes, chili powder, and Cheddar cheese.

Pour the egg mixture into the skillet. Simmer over low heat. Stir constantly until the eggs have thickened and are set. Remove from the skillet and serve over buttered toast.

SERVES 4

Western Eggs

6   eggs
   Salt and pepper to taste
¼   cup milk
2   tablespoons cooking oil
¾   cup chopped ham
1   onion, chopped
¼   cup chopped green bell pepper

In a mixing bowl beat the eggs with salt and pepper. Add the milk and beat thoroughly. Set the bowl aside.

In a skillet heat the oil and sauté the ham, onion, and green pepper until tender.

Add the egg mixture and cook slowly, stirring constantly, until scrambled.

SERVES 4

Josephine's Special

1	medium potato, cooked
2	tablespoons butter
1	tablespoon olive oil
½	pound lean sausage, crumbled
1	small onion, chopped fine
¼	cup chopped green bell pepper
⅛	teaspoon salt
⅛	teaspoon pepper
⅛	teaspoon Tabasco
1	ripe tomato, chopped
½	cup chopped spinach, cooked
8	eggs, beaten
1	tablespoon chopped parsley
¼	cup grated Parmesan cheese

Peel and cube the cooked potato. In a heavy skillet heat the butter and olive oil. Add the crumbled sausage, and cook over medium heat, stirring occasionally. Add the onion, green pepper, and potato. Cook until the potato is thoroughly heated.

MELROSE DINER, PHILADELPHIA, PENNSYLVANIA

In a mixing bowl blend the salt, pepper, Tabasco, tomato, and spinach. Add the mixture to the beaten eggs. Pour the mixture into the skillet. Gently stir until the eggs become thick and creamy. Top with chopped parsley and Parmesan cheese.

SERVES 4

Bacon Omelette

6	eggs
6	tablespoons milk
½	teaspoon salt
⅛	teaspoon pepper
8	slices crisp bacon, crumbled
1	cup cooked and cubed potatoes
2	tablespoons butter

In a mixing bowl beat together the eggs with the milk, salt, and pepper. Blend until smooth but not foamy. In a separate bowl toss together the crumbled bacon and potatoes.

In a heavy skillet melt the butter. Pour the egg mixture into the skillet. Reduce the heat to medium.

As the egg mixture sets, lift the edges with a spatula and tilt the skillet so the uncooked portion flows to the bottom of the pan. Do not stir. Spoon equal amounts of the bacon filling into the center of each omelette. When the eggs are set but still moist, loosen the edges of the omelette and carefully fold over. Making sure the bottom is loose, slide the omelette onto a serving dish.

SERVES 2

Apple Omelette

4	eggs, separated
2	tablespoons water
1/8	teaspoon salt
1	tablespoon butter
3	large apples, peeled, cored, and sliced
4	sausage links

◆ ◆ ◆

1/4	cup packed brown sugar
1	tablespoon cornstarch
2/3	cup cold water
2	teaspoons fresh lemon juice

In separate bowls beat the egg whites until soft peaks form and the yolks until fluffy. In a mixing bowl blend together the separated eggs with the water and salt. In a skillet melt the butter. Pour eggs evenly into the skillet. Heat quickly and stir constantly until thick. Add the apples and stir gently. Cover and simmer for 5 minutes or until apples are tender. Transfer the omelette to a serving platter.

Using the same skillet fry the sausage links until brown. In a mixing bowl combine the remaining ingredients to make a sauce. Pour the sauce over the eggs. Serve with sausage.

SERVES 2

Cheese Omelette

6	eggs
6	tablespoons milk
1/2	teaspoon salt
1/8	teaspoon pepper
3	tablespoons butter
1/2	cup grated Cheddar cheese

In a mixing bowl beat the eggs with the milk, salt, and pepper. Blend until smooth but not foamy. In a heavy skillet melt the butter. Pour the egg mixture into the skillet. Reduce the heat to medium.

As the egg mixture sets lift the edges with the spatula and tilt the skillet so that the uncooked portion flows to the bottom of the pan. Do not stir.

When the eggs are set but still moist, add the grated Cheddar cheese. Loosen the edges of the omelette and carefully fold over. Making sure the bottom is loose, slide the omelette onto a serving dish.

SERVES 2

Country-Style Omelette

4	eggs
1	teaspoon sugar
2	tablespoons cornmeal
1/2	cup water
1/2	teaspoon salt
2	tablespoons butter

In a mixing bowl beat the eggs. Add the sugar, cornmeal, water, and salt. Let stand about 20 minutes.

In a heavy skillet melt the butter. Pour in the egg mixture. Cover and let cook over medium heat for 5 minutes or until the eggs are firm. Loosen the edges of the omelette and carefully fold over. Making sure the bottom is loose, slide the omelette onto a serving dish.

SERVES 2

MISS ALBANY DINER

Usually, diners are family affairs. Cliff Brown and his family bought the Miss Albany Diner in Albany, New York, during the late 1980s, and since then they have given the business a feeling and flavor all their own.

An engineer, Brown's only prior experience with cooking for the public had come when he served as a scoutmaster. "Cooking for a hundred Boy Scouts is no big deal," says Cliff. "Cooking for adults at a diner isn't a whole lot different."

Brown's son Bill

may take a slightly different view. Bill is a culinary school graduate, and it was he who came up with two of the hottest selling items on the breakfast menu: Mad Eggs and Mad Irish Toast.

"To make Mad Eggs, we take a slightly toasted English muffin, split it in half, and put a poached egg on top of it," says Cliff. "I suppose the eggs could be fried or scrambled. It doesn't matter. Over the egg and muffin we pour a light curry sauce and then a bit of scallion cut real fine. That is probably our most popular regular item."

Apparently, Mad Irish Toast rates a close second. A favorite with droves of Sunday brunch customers, it consists of thick French toast cooked in an egg batter with a pecan-cream cheese filling and served with Irish whiskey sauce.

"When we feature Mad Irish Toast on Sunday, the diner is standing room only," says Cliff. "We will have as many as six or seven groups waiting for a table."

Open seven days a week, the Miss Albany Diner often has customers lined up outside the door, especially at breakfast time. Among its biggest attractions are Cliff Brown's pancakes. "For a while we were serving thick-style pancakes," he says. "Now I make them thin. The first time I made them thin, a customer who ate them caught my eye and motioned for me to come over to his booth. I leaned over the counter, and he said, 'Can I take you home so you can show my wife how to make pancakes?'"

Brown is used to hearing from happy customers. "Often, when they leave, they tell me, 'This was not a meal, this was an adventure.'"

SOME POPULAR ITEMS ON THE MENU AT MISS ALBANY DINER

Dutch Mothers Omelette
A standard three-egg omelette with thinly sliced Granny Smith apples, spicy sausage, and smoked Gouda cheese.

The Bostonian
Two slices of Boston brown bread topped with a cover of bacon (fried until stiff) and two poached eggs, and served with Cheddar cheese and seedless grapes.

Calamity Jane Omelette
A standard three-egg omelette filled with tomato, onion, peppers, Swiss cheese, sausage, and a dash of Tabasco.

Eggs Florentine
Two eggs any style served on a bed of fresh spinach, topped with toasted sesame butter.

Black Bean Eggs
Eggs any style over rice, covered with a spicy black bean sauce.

Smoked Turkey with Eggs
Two eggs any style on a bed of smoked turkey.

Garden Variety Omelette
A standard three-egg omelette with three fresh vegetables (depending on the season), topped with a creamy horseradish sauce.

24

Plain Omelette #1

6   eggs
6   tablespoons milk
1/2 teaspoon salt
1/8 teaspoon pepper
3   tablespoons butter

In a mixing bowl beat together the eggs, milk, salt, and pepper. Blend until smooth but not foamy. In a heavy skillet melt the butter. When a drop of water bounces on the surface, pour the egg mixture into the skillet. Reduce the heat to medium.

As the egg mixture sets lift the edges with a spatula and tilt the skillet so that the uncooked portion flows to the bottom of the pan. Do not stir. When the eggs are set but still moist, loosen the edges of the omelette and carefully fold over. Making sure the bottom is loose, slide the omelette onto a serving dish.

SERVES 2

Plain Omelette #2

6   egg yolks
1/8 teaspoon pepper
6   egg whites
1/4 cup cold water
1/4 teaspoon salt
3   tablespoons butter

In a mixing bowl beat together the egg yolks and the pepper until lemon colored.

In a separate bowl beat the egg whites until thick. Add the cold water and salt. Continue beating until peaks begin to form.

In a skillet melt the butter.

Gently pour the egg yolks over the egg whites and fold together. Pour into the skillet. Smooth out the surface with a spatula. Cook slowly over low heat about 5 minutes or until the bottom is lightly browned.

Place the skillet in a 325° oven. Bake for 12 minutes or until the top is dry but not brown.

SERVES 2

Down South Omelette

6   eggs
6   tablespoons milk
1/2 teaspoon salt
1/8 teaspoon pepper
4   slices crisp bacon, crumbled
3/4 cup peeled and cubed cooked potatoes
1/4 cup chopped onion
3   tablespoons butter
1/4 cup grated Cheddar cheese

In a mixing bowl beat together the eggs, milk, salt, and pepper. Blend until smooth but not foamy. In a separate mixing bowl add the bacon to the potatoes and onion.

In a heavy skillet melt the butter. Pour the egg mixture into the skillet. Reduce the heat to medium.

As the egg mixture sets lift the edges with a spatula and tilt the skillet so the uncooked portion flows to the bottom of the pan. Do not stir. Spoon equal amounts of the bacon-potato filling into the center of each omelette.

When the eggs are set but still moist, add the grated Cheddar cheese. Loosen the edges of the omelette and carefully fold over. Making sure the bottom is loose, slide the omelette onto a serving dish.

SERVES 2

Santa Fe Omelette

6   eggs
6   tablespoons milk
1/2 teaspoon salt
1/8 teaspoon pepper
1/4 cup sausage, cooked and chopped
3   tablespoons chopped onion
1/4 cup chopped green bell pepper
1   mild green chile, chopped
3   tablespoons butter
1/4 cup salsa

In a mixing bowl beat together the eggs, milk, salt, and pepper. Blend until smooth but not foamy.

In a separate mixing bowl combine the chopped sausage with the onion, green pepper, and chile. Mix thoroughly.

In a heavy skillet melt the butter. Pour the egg mixture into the skillet. Reduce the heat to medium.

As the egg mixture sets, lift the edges with a spatula and tilt the skillet so the uncooked portion flows to the bottom of the pan. Do not stir.

Spoon equal amounts of filling into the center of each omelette. When the eggs are set but still moist, loosen the edges of the omelette and carefully fold over. Making sure the bottom is loose, slide the omelette onto a serving dish. Top with salsa.

SERVES 2

Kitchen Sink Omelette

6   eggs
6   tablespoons milk
1/2 teaspoon salt
1/8 teaspoon pepper
1/4 cup cubed cooked ham
1/4 cup chopped green bell pepper
1/4 cup chopped mushrooms
2   tablespoons chopped onion
2   slices crisp bacon, crumbled
1/4 cup grated Swiss cheese
3   tablespoons butter

In a mixing bowl beat together the eggs, milk, salt, pepper. Blend until smooth but not foamy.

In a separate mixing bowl combine the ham, green pepper, mushrooms, and onion. Add the crumbled bacon and Swiss cheese, and mix thoroughly.

In a heavy skillet melt the butter. Pour the egg mixture into the skillet. Reduce the heat to medium. As the eggs set lift the edges with a spatula and tilt the skillet so the uncooked portion flows to the bottom of the pan. Do not stir. Spoon equal amounts of the ham filling into the center of each omelette.

When the eggs are set but still moist, loosen the edges of the omelette and carefully fold over. Making sure the bottom is loose, slide the omelette onto a serving dish.

SERVES 2

Mushroom Omelette

6	tablespoons butter
2	small onions, chopped fine
1/2	pound mushrooms, sliced thin
6	eggs
6	tablespoons milk
1/2	teaspoon salt
1/8	teaspoon pepper
1	3-ounce package cream cheese

In a skillet melt half the butter over medium heat. Add the onions and mushrooms and sauté until the mushrooms are lightly browned. Remove the mixture from the skillet.

In a mixing bowl beat together the eggs, milk, salt, and pepper until smooth but not foamy. Using the same skillet melt the remaining butter. When a drop of water bounces off the skillet surface, pour in the egg mixture. Reduce the heat to medium.

As the eggs set lift the edges with a spatula and tilt the skillet so that the uncooked portion flows to the bottom of the pan. Do not stir. Spoon equal amounts of the mushroom filling into the center of each omelette. When the eggs are set but still moist, loosen the edges of the omelette and carefully fold over. Making sure the bottom is loose, slide the omelette onto a serving dish.

Cut the cream cheese into 1/4-inch cubes and dot each omelette with the cubes.

SERVES 2

Ham & Cheese Omelette

6	eggs
6	tablespoons milk
1/2	teaspoon salt
1/8	teaspoon pepper
1	cup cooked ham, chopped
1/2	cup grated Cheddar cheese
3	tablespoons butter

In a mixing bowl beat together the eggs, milk, salt, and pepper. Blend until smooth but not foamy. Add the ham and grated cheese.

In a heavy skillet melt the butter. Pour the egg mixture into the bottom and reduce the heat to medium.

As the egg mixture sets lift the edges with a spatula and tilt the skillet so the uncooked portion flows to the bottom of the pan. Do not stir. When the eggs are set but still moist, loosen the edges of the omelette and carefully fold over. Making sure the bottom is loose, slide the omelette onto a serving dish.

SERVES 2

Spanish Omelette

1	cup whole tomatoes
3	tablespoons butter
1/2	teaspoon salt
1/8	teaspoon cayenne pepper
1	tablespoon finely chopped parsley
2	cloves garlic, minced fine
1/8	teaspoon cumin
1/8	teaspoon thyme

½ teaspoon all-purpose flour
6 tablespoons diced green bell pepper
6 green onions, chopped fine
½ cup white wine
½ cup sliced mushrooms
½ cup cooked green peas
4 eggs
¼ cup milk
   Salt and pepper to taste
1 tablespoon olive oil
   Parsley

In a small saucepan combine the tomatoes with 1 tablespoon of butter. Simmer for about 10 minutes. Add the salt and cayenne pepper, and cook for 10 minutes. Add the parsley, garlic, cumin, and thyme. Continue to simmer for 15 minutes or until the mixture thickens, stirring occasionally so that the spices do not scorch.

In a separate saucepan melt 1 tablespoon of butter. Slowly blend in the flour. Cook for 1 minute or until thick. Add the green pepper and onions, and brown lightly. Add the wine, stirring constantly until thick. Add the mushrooms and peas.

In a mixing bowl beat together the eggs with the milk, salt, and pepper. Blend until smooth but not foamy. Add the tomato mixture. In a skillet melt the remaining tablespoon of butter with the olive oil over medium heat.

Pour the egg mixture into the bottom of the skillet. Reduce the heat to medium.

As the egg mixture sets lift the edges with a spatula and tilt the skillet so the uncooked portion flows to the bottom of the pan. Do not stir. Spoon equal amounts of vegetable filling into the center of the omelette. When the eggs are set but still moist, loosen the edges carefully and fold over. Making sure the bottom is loose, slide the omelette onto a serving dish. Garnish with parsley.

SERVES 2

M & D DINER, WINGDALE, NEW YORK

Spinach Omelette

1/4	cup plus 3 tablespoons butter
2	small onions, chopped fine
6	eggs
6	tablespoons milk
1/2	teaspoon salt
1/8	teaspoon pepper
4	cups chopped spinach

In a skillet melt 3 tablespoons of the butter over medium heat. Add the onions and sauté until transparent. Remove the onions from the skillet and set aside.

In a mixing bowl beat together the eggs, milk, salt, and pepper. Blend until smooth but not foamy. In the same skillet melt the remaining butter. Pour the egg mixture into the skillet. Reduce the heat to medium.

As the egg mixture sets lift the edges with a spatula and tilt the skillet so the uncooked portion flows to the bottom of the pan. Do not stir. Spoon the onion-spinach filling into the center of the omelette. Loosen the edges and carefully fold over. Making sure the bottom is loose, slide the omelette onto a serving dish.

SERVES 2

Tomato Omelette

6	eggs
6	tablespoons tomato sauce
1/2	teaspoon salt
1/8	teaspoon pepper
3	tablespoons butter
1/2	cup peeled and cubed tomato

In a mixing bowl beat together the eggs, tomato sauce, salt, and pepper. Blend

ZIP'S DINER, DAYVILLE, CONNECTICUT

until smooth but not foamy. In a heavy skillet melt the butter. Pour in the egg mixture. Reduce the heat to medium.

As the eggs set lift the edges with a spatula and tilt the skillet so the uncooked portion flows to the bottom of the pan. Do not stir. When the eggs are set but still moist, loosen the edges of the omelette and carefully fold over. Making sure the bottom is loose, slide the omelette onto a serving dish. Top with cubed tomatoes.

SERVES 2

Vegetable Omelette

6	egg yolks
1/8	teaspoon pepper
6	egg whites
1/4	teaspoon salt
3/4	cup sour cream
1/8	teaspoon dried rosemary
1	large tomato, peeled and chopped
1/4	cup finely chopped sweet onion
1	small ripe avocado, peeled and cubed
3	tablespoons butter

In a mixing bowl beat together the egg yolks and the pepper. In a separate bowl beat the egg whites until thick. Add the salt. Continue beating until peaks begin to form. Gently pour the egg yolks over the egg whites and fold together.

In a saucepan heat the sour cream over low heat. Blend in the rosemary, tomato, onion, and avocado. Set aside.

In a medium skillet melt the butter. Add the eggs. Cook slowly over low heat about 5 minutes or until the bottom is lightly browned.

Place the skillet into a 325° oven. Bake for 12 minutes or until the top is dry but not brown. When a knife inserted in the middle comes out clean, the omelette is done.

Pour equal amounts of vegetable sauce into each omelette. Fold and serve.

SERVES 2

Western Omelette

2	tablespoons butter
1/4	cup chopped onion
3	tablespoons chopped green bell pepper
1/4	cup cubed cooked ham
3	eggs
3	teaspoons milk
1/8	teaspoon salt
1/8	teaspoon pepper
1/4	teaspoon garlic salt

In a medium skillet melt the butter. Add the onion and green pepper, and sauté over medium heat until the onion is tender. Remove the skillet from the heat and add the cooked ham. Remove the mixture from the skillet and set it aside.

In a mixing bowl beat the eggs with the milk. Season with salt, pepper, and garlic salt.

Pour the egg mixture into the same skillet used to cook the onions. As the eggs set lift the edges and tilt the skillet so the uncooked portion flows to the bottom of the pan. Do not stir.

Spoon equal amounts of the ham filling into the center of each omelette. When set but still moist, carefully fold over. Making sure the bottom is loose, slide the omelette onto a serving dish.

SERVES 2

Banana Pancakes

1	cup all-purpose flour
2	tablespoons baking powder
1/4	cup sugar
1/2	teaspoon salt
2	eggs
2	cups milk
1/4	cup cooking oil
2	medium bananas, sliced

In a mixing bowl sift the flour with the baking powder, sugar, and salt.

In a separate bowl blend the eggs with the milk and oil. Pour into the flour mixture. Mix the batter until smooth and creamy. Add the sliced bananas.

Pour equal amounts onto a hot griddle. Flip over when the tops begin to bubble. Pancakes are done when they turn a light golden brown.

Serve with melted butter and maple syrup.

SERVES 5

Blueberry Pancakes

2	cups all-purpose flour
1	tablespoon sugar
1	tablespoon baking soda
1/2	teaspoon salt
1	egg, well beaten
1 1/2	cups buttermilk
2	tablespoons shortening, melted
1	cup blueberries
	Melted butter
	Maple syrup

In a mixing bowl sift together the flour, sugar, baking soda, and salt. In a separate bowl blend together the egg, buttermilk, and melted shortening. Make a well in the center of the dry ingredients. Add the egg mixture. Add the blueberries. Stir just until blended.

Lightly grease the surface of the griddle. Heat until a few drops of water bounces off of it. Pour the batter onto the griddle to make 4-inch cakes. Cook until the tops begin to bubble and become puffy. Turn once.

Serve with melted butter and maple syrup.

MAKES 12

Buttermilk Pancakes

4	eggs, beaten
3/4	cup buttermilk
2 1/2	cups all-purpose flour
3	tablespoons sugar
3	teaspoons baking powder
1/2	teaspoon salt
1/4	cup butter, melted

In a mixing bowl beat together the eggs and buttermilk. In a separate bowl sift together the flour, sugar, baking powder, and salt. Gradually beat the flour mixture into the eggs. Mix thoroughly. Add the melted butter.

Heat a lightly greased griddle. Ladle batter onto the griddle to make 6-inch cakes. Flip over when the tops begin to bubble.

Serve with melted butter and maple syrup.

SERVES 4

LANCASTER DINER

Run by its owner, Frank Savage, for the last six years, the Lancaster Diner is a 1937 Homemade with seating for forty-eight. The diner's decor includes a stainless-steel interior and an old-fashioned jukebox with speakers in every booth.

"But our customers definitely come in for the food," says Frank.

"We offer a lot of specials, and our Homemade Baked Beans and Cinnamon Whirls are out of this world."

Situated on Main Street in Lancaster, New Hampshire, the diner also attracts customers with its friendliness. Waitresses chat with regulars in a relaxed atmosphere, and occasionally even the cook comes out front for a visit with customers.

"But contrary to popular belief," laughs the owner, "here the customer is *not* always right."

32

Cornmeal Pancakes

1   cup all-purpose flour
2   tablespoons baking powder
1/4 cup sugar
1/2 teaspoon salt
1   cup cornmeal
2   eggs
2   cups milk
1/4 cup cooking oil
    Melted butter
    Maple syrup

In a mixing bowl sift the flour, baking powder, sugar, and salt. Add the cornmeal.

In a separate bowl beat together the eggs, milk, and oil. Pour the liquid mixture into the dry ingredients. Mix the batter until smooth and creamy.

Pour equal amounts onto a hot griddle. Flip over when the tops begin to bubble. Pancakes are done when they turn golden brown.

Top with melted butter and maple syrup.

SERVES 5

Cinnamon Pancakes

1   cup all-purpose flour
2   tablespoons baking powder
1/4 cup sugar
1/2 teaspoon salt
1   teaspoon cinnamon
2   eggs
2   cups milk
1/4 cup oil
    Jam or syrup

In a mixing bowl sift the flour with the baking powder, sugar, salt, and cinnamon.

In a separate bowl blend the eggs with the milk and oil. Pour into the flour mixture. Mix the batter until smooth and creamy.

Pour equal amounts onto a hot griddle. Turn once when pancake begins to bubble. The pancakes are done when they turn a light golden brown.

Top with jam or syrup.

SERVES 5

Griddle Cakes

2   tablespoons shortening
2   cups all-purpose flour
1/2 teaspoon salt
1   tablespoon baking powder
1   tablespoon sugar
1   egg, well beaten
1 1/2 cups milk

In a saucepan melt the shortening. Set aside. In a mixing bowl sift the flour with the salt, baking powder, and sugar.

In a separate bowl combine the egg and milk. Add the melted shortening. Make a well in the center of the dry ingredients. Pour the egg mixture into the center and blend just until moistened.

Heat a lightly greased griddle. Ladle batter onto the griddle to make 4-inch cakes. Flip over when the tops begin to bubble.

Serve with melted butter and maple syrup.

SERVES 4

Chocolate Pancakes

1	cup all-purpose flour
2	tablespoons baking powder
1/4	cup sugar
1/2	teaspoon salt
2	eggs
2	cups milk
1/4	cup cooking oil
1	cup semisweet chocolate, grated
1	cup chopped walnuts

♦ ♦ ♦

1	cup confectioners' sugar
1/2	cup packed light brown sugar

In a mixing bowl sift the flour with the baking powder, sugar, and salt.

In a separate bowl blend the eggs, milk, and oil. Pour the liquid mixture into the dry ingredients. Mix the batter until smooth and creamy. Add the grated chocolate and walnuts.

Pour equal amounts onto a hot griddle. Flip over when the tops begin to bubble. The pancakes are done when they turn a light golden brown.

In a mixing bowl mix together the confectioners' sugar and brown sugar with a fork. Sprinkle over pancakes while they are still warm.

SERVES 5

VENUS DINER, GIBSONIA, PENNSYLVANIA

Orange Pancakes

1   cup maple syrup
1   18-ounce can unsweetened orange juice
1   cinnamon stick
2   whole cloves
     Dash nutmeg
2   cups biscuit mix
1   egg
     Butter

In a saucepan combine the maple syrup and 1 cup of orange juice. Add the cinnamon stick, cloves, and nutmeg to taste, and bring to a boil. Reduce the heat, and simmer for 8 minutes. Set aside.

In a separate bowl mix together the biscuit mix, egg, and remaining orange juice. Blend until the batter is smooth.

Pour equal amounts of batter onto a hot griddle. Turn once when the pancakes begin to bubble.

Serve with orange-maple syrup.

MAKES 12

Pancake Sandwich

2   tablespoons shortening
2   cups all-purpose flour
1/2 teaspoon salt
1   tablespoon baking powder
1   tablespoon sugar
1   egg, well beaten
1 1/2 cups milk
     ♦ ♦ ♦
3/4 pound lean pork sausage
1/8 teaspoon coarse ground pepper
1/2 teaspoon dried sage
1/8 teaspoon salt
1/4 teaspoon paprika
1/8 teaspoon allspice
     ♦ ♦ ♦
     Butter
4   eggs
     Salt and pepper to taste

In a saucepan melt the shortening. Remove the pan from the heat. In a mixing bowl sift the flour with the salt, baking powder, and sugar.

In a separate bowl beat together 1 egg and the milk. Add the melted shortening. Make a well in the center of the dry ingredients. Pour the egg mixture into the center. Blend just until batter is moist.

Heat a lightly greased griddle. Ladle the batter onto the griddle to make 4-inch cakes. Flip over when the tops begin to bubble. Place the pancakes on a platter, continuing to make pancakes until all of the batter is used.

In a large mixing bowl blend the sausage with the pepper, sage, salt, paprika, and allspice. Shape into patties. In a heavy skillet over medium heat cook the sausage patties for about 8 minutes per side. Set aside.

Add a small amount of butter to the skillet. Fry the remaining eggs to the desired degree of doneness. Remove the eggs and season with salt and pepper. Place the eggs and sausage between two pancakes.

Serve with maple syrup.

SERVES 4

Pear & Almond Pancakes

5   Bartlett pears
10 ounces light maple syrup
½   cup sugar
1   box buttermilk pancake mix
    Vanilla extract to taste
1   package slivered almonds
10 ounces fig filling
    Whipped butter
    Confectioners' sugar

Peel and core the pears. Chop into ½-inch cubes. In a small bowl blend together half the light maple syrup with half the sugar. Coat the pieces of pears in maple mixture. Refrigerate overnight.

♦ ♦ ♦

Prepare enough pancake mix for four servings, according to the package directions. Add vanilla. Pour the pancake mix over a hot griddle. Immediately add the pears. Add slivered almonds to taste. Flip gently when bubbles appear on the top of the pancakes.

In a saucepan heat the remaining maple syrup with the fig filling. Pour the mixture over the pancakes. Serve with whipped butter and confectioners' sugar.

SERVES 4

Potato Pancakes

3 potatoes
3 tablespoons finely chopped onion
1 beaten egg
1/3 cup all-purpose flour
Salt and pepper to taste
Cooking oil

Peel the potatoes, and cut them into wedges. Grate the potatoes with the onion. Squeeze the potatoes and onion through a vegetable press to remove any remaining liquid. Reserve the juice.

In a small saucepan heat the juice from the vegetables. Cook over medium heat, stirring constantly, until the juice becomes thick. Add the grated potatoes, onion, and egg. Season with salt and pepper.

In a large skillet heat the oil. Spoon large amounts of potato mixture into the bottom and flatten. Fry for 5 minutes or until the potatoes turn a light golden brown. Flip once to cook the other side. Add more oil as needed.

SERVES 5

Thick French Toast

1/2 cup cream
8 eggs, slightly beaten
1/4 cup sugar
1/4 teaspoon salt
14 slices thick-sliced stale bread
3 tablespoons butter
1/4 cup packed brown sugar
Fruit
Syrups
Confectioners' sugar

BLUE DINER, BOSTON, MASSACHUSETTS

In a mixing bowl blend together the cream, eggs, sugar, and salt. Dip the bread slices into the egg batter. Set aside for 10 to 15 minutes, turning at least once.

In a heavy skillet melt the butter. Cook the bread slices over medium heat. Brown gently until golden. Before turning sprinkle with brown sugar. Turn and lightly brown the other side.

Serve with fruit, syrups, and confectioners' sugar.

SERVES 6

Golden Brown Waffles

2 cups all-purpose flour, sifted
3 teaspoons baking powder
1 teaspoon salt
2 tablespoons sugar
2 eggs, separated
1½ cups milk
6 tablespoons butter, melted
 Melted butter
 Maple syrup
 Confectioners' sugar

In a mixing bowl sift together the sifted flour, baking powder, salt, and sugar. In a separate bowl blend the egg yolks with the milk and butter. Pour the liquid mixture into the flour mixture. Mix just until moistened. Beat the egg whites until stiff. Fold the egg whites into the batter.

Heat a waffle iron. Pour the batter onto the hot waffle iron. Cook for 4 minutes or until the waffles are lightly browned.

Serve with melted butter, maple syrup, and confectioners' sugar.

SERVES 6

Fresh Fruit Cup

1 cup seedless grapes
1 small honeydew melon
1 cantaloupe
1 large apple, peeled and cored
1 cup sliced strawberries
½ cup crushed pineapple, drained
½ teaspoon fresh lemon juice
 Sugar
2 medium bananas, sliced
 Fresh mint

Thoroughly wash the grapes under cold running water. Pat dry with paper towels. Cut the honeydew melon and the cantaloupe in half. Remove the seeds from both melons. Scoop out the insides with a melon ball cutter. Cut the apples into bite-size pieces.

In a large mixing bowl toss together the strawberries, grapes, pineapple, and apple. Make sure the fruit does not become bruised. Add the honeydew melon and cantaloupe balls. Add lemon juice and sugar to taste.

Place sliced bananas in the bottom of serving bowls. Place tossed fruit over the bananas. Garnish with fresh mint. Serve chilled.

SERVES 4

FAMILY NIGHT AT THE DINER

The idea of running a diner has always appealed to families who want to own and operate their own business. Since family members can handle the entire operation, from waiting on customers to preparing the food and ringing up orders on the cash register, overhead can be kept at a minimum. Almost from the beginning, diner manufacturers provided everything the owners needed to conduct business—from menu boards to cash registers. But making a success of the business took a lot of hard work.

Owners could avoid the travails of moving their diners from place to place by settling on a permanent location, usually a vacant lot rented by the month. Rooted to one spot, the diners could no longer go to their customers. Instead, hungry customers had to be lured to the diner. To bring them through the door, some owners offered regular house specials such as a single-price soup-and-sandwich combination or a free dessert with every meal.

Some diners accomplished the same thing with styling. Customers were impressed with the newer models rolling off the factory assembly lines. Stylish interiors might include shiny marble counters, colorful porcelain walls, stained-glass windows, and skylights to let in the sun.

One early trademark of the diner was the open grill. Customers could sit at the counter and watch their food being prepared. That way they could be sure of the freshness and quality of the food.

To increase business, diners expanded their hours until some were operating twenty-four hours a day. This contributed to their reputation as "men only" establishments, greasy spoons, or drinking clubs.

To attract more business from their female clientele, owners added flower boxes, comfortable booths, frosted-glass windows for

MISS FLORENCE DINER, FLORENCE MASSACHUSETTS

privacy, and a more varied menu including salads and ice cream. Some gave their diners feminine names, such as "Miss Adams" or "Miss Bellows Falls."

Soon entire families began to enjoy a night out for dinner at the diner. It was much cheaper to go to a diner than to one of the fancier restaurants in a hotel.

ON THE SIDE

Classic Onion Rings

3 large onions
2 eggs, lightly beaten
2 cups buttermilk
2 cups all-purpose flour
1 teaspoon baking soda
  Salt to taste
  Cooking oil

Peel the onions and cut into ¼-inch slices. Divide into individual rings. Soak in a large bowl of ice water for 1 hour.

In a separate bowl beat together the eggs and buttermilk. Add the flour, baking soda, and salt.

Heat the cooking oil in a deep fryer to 350°. Pat the onion rings dry with paper towels, and dip in the buttermilk batter. Fry the onion rings until golden brown, turning once. Cook only a small amount at a time to maintain the temperature.

Drain on paper towels. Season with salt while the onion rings are still hot. Keep warm in a 250° oven.

Serve with ketchup.

SERVES 2 TO 4

Ketchup

2 dozen ripe tomatoes, peeled and cored
1 cup chopped onion
½ cup chopped sweet red bell pepper
1½ teaspoons celery seed
1 cinnamon stick
1 teaspoon allspice
1 teaspoon mustard seed
1 cup sugar
1 tablespoon salt
1½ cups vinegar
1 tablespoon paprika

Sterilize 3 1-pint jars. Set aside.

In a large saucepan cook the tomatoes with the onion and red bell pepper until soft. Press through a sieve. Return to the pan and cook until the mixture is reduced by half.

Tie the celery seed, cinnamon stick, allspice, and mustard seed in a cheesecloth. Add to the tomato mixture. Blend in the sugar and salt. Simmer over low heat for 25 minutes, stirring often.

Add the vinegar and paprika, and cook until the desired thickness. Remove the spice bag. While the ketchup is still hot, pour it into the prepared jars. Leave a ¼-inch space at the top of each. Seal tightly. Process in a boiling water bath for 10 minutes. Let cool. Store at room temperature.

MAKES 3 PINTS

French Fries

8	Russet potatoes
	Cooking oil
	Salt to taste

Scrub the potatoes. Do not peel. Slice to the desired thickness for fries. Place in a bowl of water until ready to cook. Before cooking dry the potatoes thoroughly.

In a deep fryer heat the oil to 375°. Fry the potatoes in small batches to maintain the temperature. Cook until golden brown. Drain on paper towels.

Season with salt while the French fries are still hot. Serve with ketchup or gravy. Keep warm in a 300° oven.

SERVES 4 TO 6

Mustard Pickles

1	quart large cucumbers
1	quart small cucumbers
1	large cauliflower
1	quart water
1/2	cup salt
1	quart peeled pickling onions
1	quart green tomatoes, chopped
2	red bell peppers, minced
1/4	cup dry mustard
1	cup all-purpose flour
2	cups sugar
2	quarts vinegar

Prepare and sterilize 5 1-quart jars. Set aside. Cut the large cucumbers into small cubes. Leave the small cucumbers whole. Break the cauliflower into small pieces.

In a large nonmetal bowl blend together the water and salt. Add all the vegetables. Let the mixture stand for 24 hours.

Pour the mixture into a large pot. Bring to a boil. Drain. In a saucepan mix together the dry mustard, flour, sugar, and vinegar. Cook until thick. Remove the whole cucumbers from the vegetables. Add the vegetables to the saucepan. Heat thoroughly.

Pour the mixture evenly into the prepared quart jars. Seal.

MAKES 5 QUARTS

Red Pepper Relish

12	red bell peppers
3	large sweet onions
1 1/2	cups red wine vinegar
1 1/2	cups sugar
1 1/2	teaspoons salt
1	tablespoon mustard seed

Prepare and sterilize 6 1-pint jars. Set the jars aside. Core the red bell peppers and remove the seeds. Slice the onions. In a food processor finely chop the peppers and onions together.

In a large saucepan blend together the red wine vinegar with the sugar, salt, and mustard seed. Add the puréed vegetables. Simmer for 30 minutes.

Pour the mixture evenly into the prepared pint jars. Seal.

MAKES 6 PINTS

MISS ALBANY FRENCH FRIES

At the Miss Albany Diner in New York, owner Cliff Brown has a passion for French fries. A retired engineer, Cliff devised a system for custom-ordered fries. A sign on the wall reads, "You can have French fries anyway you like them, One's, Two's, or Three's." Pictures illustrate each of the three varieties.

"One's" are cooked until yellowish in color. "Two's" remain in the oil until they turn brown. "Three's" are well done, and they come out of the oil a tasty golden brown all over. To make sure his customers get the idea, Cliff has carved giant fries out of Styrofoam, painted them in shades of yellow and brown, and hung them from the ceiling.

"I know how many French fries the customer wants," says Cliff. "Twelve ounces of fresh cut fries is an order whether they are cooked as one's, two's, or three's."

When it comes to French fries, Cliff can tell the real thing from a cheap imitation. "In France you're served fries with everything, no matter what you order, and the French are very particular about them. They must be a quarter of an inch thick, they must be cooked in peanut oil, and they must be cooked twice."

A real French fry, he explains, is blanched in oil at 225°, just above the boiling point, to get rid of the moisture. After a couple of minutes, they are removed from the oil and spread out to cool at room temperature. Then they are returned to the oil, this time at 325°, for browning. This process of cooking the fries twice makes them soft on the inside and crispy on the outside.

What else has Cliff observed about French fries?

"Well, I find that the biggest consumers of French fries are young women. I notice that when a group of them comes into the diner, they order French fries about 80 percent of the time."

HIGHLAND PARK DINER

Owner Bob Malley is rather proud of his establishment, the Highland Park Diner, in Rochester, New York. A 1948 Orleans model, built on-site rather than at a factory, it operated successfully for years before falling on hard times. For a while it stood vacant and then, for almost ten years, it served as an off-track betting parlor. Bob bought the place in 1986 and has since returned it to its former glory.

"They had gutted the whole thing," says Bob, shaking his head. "When I restored it, I had to replace the counters and all the stainless steel. I was very fortunate that the porcelain was still in such excellent condition since this is a porcelain diner inside and out."

Highland Park Diner is one of the last traditional diners in Rochester, and Bob says this allows him to take advantage of the growing nostalgia craze. "We have a new generation completely unfamiliar with this type of architecture. They are astonished to see this type of restaurant."

The diner is situated in a part of the city long ago saddled with the unpoetic name "Swillburg." As you may have guessed,

pigs were once raised here. Bob laughs at the name. "We call our hamburgers Swill-Burgers," he says.

Bob has a philosophy about how a diner should be run. "We use real food, real potatoes, fresh fruit, and fresh cooked turkeys. We cook our own roast beef. We go the full nine yards. Our motto is: Real Food, Served Real Well."

Running the diner properly takes a lot of effort. "We work seven days a week," he says, and the work pays off. Recently the diner was chosen by the Landmark Society as one of the best restaurants in the region.

The Orleans Diner Manufacturing Company built only three diners in its brief history, the Highland Park being the last. Luckily for citizens of Rochester, it is still around for them to enjoy.

Iowa Hot Wings

½	cup butter
1	large onion, chopped fine
2	garlic cloves, chopped
1	cup Louisiana hot sauce
1	teaspoon ground chile peppers
5	pounds chicken wings

In a heavy skillet melt the butter and sauté the onion and garlic until the onion is tender but not brown. Add the hot sauce and chilies, and simmer for 5 minutes. Let cool.

Cut the chicken wings at the joints. Discard the wing tips or save for broth. Deep fry until crisp. Drain on paper towels. Toss in a bowl with one-fourth of the sauce. Save the remaining sauce for dipping.

SERVES 8

Gravy

¼	cup unsalted butter
¼	cup all-purpose flour
¼	cup water
2¼	cups milk
	Salt and pepper to taste

In a skillet melt enough butter to make ⅛ cup. In a small jar with a lid shake the flour with the water. Add the flour mixture to the skillet and cook until golden brown, stirring constantly. Slowly add the milk. Continue to stir until the gravy thickens. Season with salt and pepper.

Chili Supreme

2	pounds ground beef
2	small onions, chopped
2	garlic cloves, chopped fine
5	cups cooked pinto beans
2½	cups diced tomatoes
2½	cups diced green chilies
½	teaspoon salt
1	teaspoon black pepper
1	cup grated Cheddar cheese

In a skillet brown the ground beef with the onion and garlic until the onions turn brown. Add the pinto beans, tomatoes, and green chilies, and mix thoroughly. Season with salt and pepper. Let simmer for 1 hour.

Top with grated Cheddar cheese.

SERVES 8

WOLFE'S DINER, DILLSBURG, PENNSYLVANIA

Chili Beans

1 pound dry kidney beans
1 small onion, chopped
1 garlic clove, minced
1/4 pound bacon, chopped
2 teaspoons chili powder
1/2 teaspoon salt
1 cup red wine
3 cups water
1 16-ounce can chopped tomatoes
   Crackers or corn bread

Wash the beans, place them in a pot of cold water, and soak overnight. Drain.

Place the beans into a soup pot with the onion, garlic, and bacon. Season with chili powder and salt. Mix thoroughly. Add the red wine and water.

Simmer over low heat for 4 hours or until the beans are tender and the sauce begins to thicken. Add water as needed. In the last hour of cooking add the tomatoes.

Serve with crackers or corn bread.

SERVES 6

5-Spot Chili

1/4 cup vegetable oil
4 medium onions, chopped
12 garlic cloves, chopped fine
5 pounds sirloin steak, cut into 1-inch cubes

3/4 pound lean ground pork sausage
5 tablespoons cumin
2 teaspoons salt
2 tablespoons oregano
3 tablespoons chili powder
1 6-ounce can tomato paste
1 1/2 cups tomato sauce
3 cups beef broth
1 tablespoon chopped chilies
2 cups grated Cheddar cheese
3/4 cup sour cream

In a heavy pot heat the vegetable oil. Sauté the onion and garlic until transparent but not browned. Add the steak, and cook until browned.

In a separate skillet brown the sausage. Drain. Add the sausage to the steak with the cumin, salt, oregano, chili powder, tomato paste, tomato sauce, and beef broth. Cook over medium heat for 30 minutes.

Add the chilies. Reduce the heat and simmer. Cook uncovered for 2 hours, stirring often.

Serve with grated cheese and sour cream.

SERVES 12

Roadside Chili

1/4 cup vegetable oil
4 1/2 pounds lean beef short ribs
1 large onion, chopped
1 large green bell pepper, chopped
1 teaspoon salt
3 large garlic cloves, peeled and chopped
1 28-ounce can whole tomatoes with juice
1 4-ounce can green chilies, chopped
2 tablespoons chili powder

1   beef bouillon cube
¼   cup boiling water
2½   cups cooked kidney beans

In a Dutch oven heat the oil over medium heat and brown the ribs on all sides. Remove the meat and set aside. To the same pot add the onion, green pepper, salt, and garlic. Cook, stirring often, until the onion is transparent but not browned.

Add the canned tomatoes with the juice, green chilies, and the chili powder. Dissolve the bouillon cube in the hot water, and add the mixture to the pot. Add the ribs. Bring the mixture to a boil.

Reduce the heat to simmer, cover, and cook for 2 hours or until the meat is tender. Remove the bones and skim off the fat. Add the kidney beans. Continue cooking until the chili is thoroughly heated.

SERVES 8

Chili Con Carne

1   tablespoon oil
1   medium onion, chopped fine
1   pound ground beef
1   16-ounce can kidney beans, drained
1   16-ounce can whole tomatoes
1   teaspoon chili powder
     Salt and pepper to taste

In a heavy skillet heat the oil and sauté the onion until transparent but not browned. Add the beef to the onions and cook until brown. Add the kidney beans, tomatoes, chili powder, salt, and pepper.

Cover and let simmer for 20 minutes or until the spices are thoroughly blended.

SERVES 4

UNADILLA DINER, UNADILLA, NEW YORK

Sour Milk Corn Bread

1	cup milk
1	tablespoon vinegar
1	cup all-purpose flour, sifted
1½	teaspoons baking powder
½	teaspoon baking soda
1	teaspoon salt
3	tablespoons sugar
1	cup yellow cornmeal
1	egg
¼	cup butter, melted and cooled

Grease an 8-inch square baking pan. Set aside.

In a small cup add the vinegar to the milk. In a mixing bowl combine the flour, baking powder, baking soda, salt, and sugar. Sift the dry ingredients. Add the cornmeal and mix well.

In a separate bowl blend together the egg, milk, and melted butter. Pour the liquid mixture into the dry ingredients. Stir just until moistened.

Pour the batter into the prepared baking pan. Bake at 425° for 40 minutes or until done.

SERVES 4

Corn Bread

1	cup all-purpose flour
3½	teaspoons baking powder
1	teaspoon salt
3	tablespoons sugar
1	cup yellow cornmeal
1	egg
1	cup milk
¼	cup butter, melted and cooled

Grease an 8-inch square baking pan. Set aside.

In a mixing bowl combine the flour, baking powder, salt, and sugar. Sift the dry mixture. Add the cornmeal and blend thoroughly.

In a separate bowl blend together the egg, milk, and melted butter. Pour the liquid mixture into the dry ingredients. Stir just until moistened.

Pour the batter into the prepared baking pan. Bake at 425° for 40 minutes or until done.

SERVES 4

Western Corn Bread

1½	cups cornmeal
3	tablespoons sugar
3	teaspoons baking powder
4	eggs, well beaten
1	cup sour cream
1	cup cream-style corn
1	cup grated Cheddar cheese
1	cup chopped green bell pepper
½	cup chopped onion
½	cup oil
¾	teaspoon salt
½	cup butter, melted

Grease a 9-inch square baking pan. Set aside.

In a mixing bowl blend the cornmeal, sugar, baking powder, and eggs. Add the sour cream, cream-style corn, grated cheese, green pepper, onion, oil, and salt. Mix together thoroughly.

Pour the batter into the prepared baking pan. Bake at 425° for 25 minutes or until the corn bread tests done. Remove from the oven. Pour melted butter evenly over the top. Serve warm.

SERVES 6

Cornmeal Biscuits

1½	cups all-purpose flour
1	teaspoon salt
3	teaspoons baking powder
½	cup yellow cornmeal
¼	cup shortening
¾	cup milk

In a medium bowl sift the flour with the salt and baking powder. Add the cornmeal. Cut in the shortening until the mixture resembles coarse meal. Add the milk and mix until a soft dough forms.

Turn the dough out onto a lightly floured board. Knead lightly. Roll to ½-inch thickness. Cut with a floured biscuit cutter.

Place on an ungreased baking sheet about 1 inch apart. Bake at 450° for 12 to 15 minutes or until golden brown.

MAKES 12

Crunch Biscuits

2	cups self-rising flour
1	teaspoon sugar
½	cup vegetable oil
½	cup milk

In a medium bowl mix the flour with the sugar.

In a separate bowl mix together the vegetable oil and milk. Add the liquid mixture to the dry ingredients. Mix with a fork just enough to moisten the dough.

Roll the dough out between sheets of waxed paper. Cut with a biscuit cutter. Place the dough on a baking sheet. Bake at 450° for 8 to 10 minutes.

MAKES 8

DEMPSEY'S DINER, ALLENTOWN, PENNSYLVANIA

Buttermilk Biscuits

1	envelope active dry yeast
2	tablespoons warm water
2	cups all-purpose flour
1	teaspoon baking powder
1	tablespoon sugar
1	teaspoon salt
2	tablespoons shortening
1	cup buttermilk
1/4	cup butter, melted

In a small bowl dissolve the yeast in the warm water. Set aside. In a large mixing bowl sift the flour with the baking powder, sugar, and salt. Cut in the shortening. Add the yeast mixture. Mix until the dough is the consistency of coarse meal. Add the buttermilk and continue mixing until smooth.

Place the dough on a lightly floured board. Knead lightly. Roll out the dough to 1/2-inch thickness. Cut with a floured biscuit cutter. Place the biscuits on a lightly floured baking sheet. Poke the top of each biscuit with a fork. Brush with melted butter.

Let rise in a warm place for 30 minutes or until the biscuits have doubled in size. Bake at 425° for 15 minutes.

MAKES 12

Dorothy Jean's Drop Biscuits

2	cups all-purpose flour
1/4	cup baking powder
1	teaspoon salt
1/4	cup butter
3	ounces cream cheese
1/4	cup sour cream

In a medium bowl sift the flour with the baking powder and salt. Cut in the butter and the cream cheese. Add the sour cream. Blend until the mixture resembles a soft dough.

When the dough is well blended, drop by teaspoonfuls onto a well-greased baking sheet. Bake at 450° for 15 minutes or until golden brown.

MAKES 12

Heavenly Biscuits

2	envelopes active dry yeast
1/4	cup warm water
4 1/2	cups all-purpose flour
1/3	cup sugar
3	teaspoons baking powder
1	teaspoon baking soda
1	teaspoon salt
2	cups milk
3/4	cup shortening

In a small mixing bowl dissolve the yeast in the warm water. In a separate bowl combine the flour, sugar, baking powder, baking soda, salt, milk, and shortening. Add the dissolved yeast. Cover and refrigerate overnight.

Turn the dough out onto a floured board, and roll to ½-inch thickness. Cut with a lightly floured biscuit cutter. Place on a greased baking sheet. Bake at 375° for 20 minutes or until lightly browned.

MAKES 18

Cheese Bread

2	envelopes active dry yeast
2	cups warm milk
3	tablespoons sugar
1	tablespoon butter
¼	teaspoon salt
4½	cups all-purpose flour
6	ounces sharp Cheddar cheese, cubed

Grease a 1½-quart casserole dish. Set aside.

In a large mixing bowl dissolve the yeast in the milk. Add the sugar, butter, and salt. Stir until well blended. Add the flour. Beat until smooth. Add the cheese and mix thoroughly.

Pour the batter into the prepared casserole dish. Cover with waxed paper and place in a warm area. Let rise for 1 hour or until the dough has doubled in size.

Place the dough in a loaf pan. Bake at 350° for 50 minutes or until the bread tests done. Let cool.

MAKES 1 LOAF

CHARLES DINER, WEST SPRINGFIELD, MASSACHUSETTS

Asparagus with Cream Cheese

2	pounds fresh asparagus
3	ounces cream cheese
1½	cups sour cream
1	teaspoon fresh lemon juice
½	teaspoon salt
	Pepper to taste

Clean the asparagus. Cut into ½-inch pieces. In a pan of boiling salted water cook the asparagus until tender. Drain.

In a saucepan blend together the cream cheese, sour cream, and lemon juice. Season with salt and pepper. Warm slowly over low heat, stirring often. Add the asparagus and cook for 5 minutes.

SERVES 6

Barbecue Beans

¾	cup packed light brown sugar
½	cup ketchup
½	cup dark corn syrup
2	teaspoons Liquid Smoke
	Tabasco to taste
1	onion, diced
3	16-ounce cans lima beans, drained
4	slices bacon

In a large mixing bowl blend together the brown sugar, ketchup, corn syrup, and Liquid Smoke. Season with Tabasco to taste. Add the diced onion. Add the beans and mix thoroughly. Pour the beans into a 2-quart casserole dish. Place the bacon strips over the top of the beans. Bake at 325° for 1 hour.

SERVES 6

City Baked Beans

1	pound dry white beans
6	cups water
½	pound salt pork, cubed
1	onion, chopped
1	garlic clove, minced
1	bay leaf, crushed
2	teaspoons Worcestershire sauce
½	cup tomato sauce
¼	cup dark molasses
1	teaspoon dry mustard
¼	cup packed dark brown sugar
½	teaspoon Liquid Smoke

Wash the white beans and soak overnight. Drain the beans. In a large saucepan bring the water to a rolling boil. Add the beans, pork, and onion, and simmer for 1 hour.

Skim off the fat. Remove all but 1 cup of the liquid. Place the beans and pork in a large pot or Dutch oven. Add the garlic, bay leaf, Worcestershire sauce, tomato sauce, molasses, mustard, brown sugar, and Liquid Smoke. Mix gently. Bake at 400° for about 1 hour and 30 minutes or until done. Add hot Liquid Smoke as needed to keep the beans moist.

SERVES 6

Betty's Baked Beans

2   16-ounce cans baked beans
2   tablespoons mustard
1/4 cup dark molasses
2   tablespoons packed brown sugar
1/2 cup ketchup
1   cup grated sharp Cheddar cheese
1   cup chopped onion
8   slices bacon, chopped

Place the beans in a large soup pot or casserole dish. In a mixing bowl blend together the mustard, molasses, brown sugar, and ketchup. Add the mixture to the beans with the cheese, onions, and bacon. Bake at 350° for 45 minutes. Let stand for 15 minutes before serving.

SERVES 8

Green Beans Extreme

2   16-ounce cans cut green beans
1   14-ounce can sliced tomatoes
1   8-ounce jar sliced mushrooms
1/2 teaspoon salt
    Pepper to taste
1/2 teaspoon basil
1/4 cup butter, melted

Drain the green beans and place them in a large casserole dish. Drain the tomatoes and mushrooms and place them over the sliced green beans.

Season with salt and pepper. Sprinkle the basil over the top. Drizzle with melted butter. Cover and bake at 350° for 45 minutes. Toss gently before serving.

SERVES 8

Green Beans with Mushrooms

1   pound green beans
1/4 pound mushrooms
2   tablespoons butter
1/8 teaspoon onion seasoning
    Salt and pepper to taste
1/2 cup sour cream

Wash the green beans under cold running water. Pat dry with paper towels. Cut the beans into thin strips. Slice the mushrooms.

Melt the butter in a skillet. Add the beans and mushrooms, cover, and cook over low heat until tender. Stir the beans occasionally so they do not burn, adding water as necessary. Add the onion seasoning, salt, and pepper, and blend thoroughly. Add the sour cream, and remove the pan from the heat. Blend thoroughly.

SERVES 4

Prepare the green beans according to the package directions. In a mixing bowl toss the cooked beans with the olive oil, vinegar, onion, salt, garlic, and pepper.

Pour the bean mixture into a greased baking dish. Set aside. In a separate mixing bowl blend together the breadcrumbs, cheese, and butter. Sprinkle over the beans. Top with paprika. Bake at 325° for 15 minutes or until thoroughly heated.

SERVES 6

Supreme Green Beans

2	tablespoons cooking oil
1	onion, chopped fine
1	pound fresh or frozen green beans
1/4	teaspoon salt
3/4	cup boiling water
1/2	cup ketchup
	Pepper to taste

In a skillet heat the oil and sauté the onion for 5 minutes or until tender. Add the green beans, salt, and boiling water. Cover and simmer for 15 minutes or until the beans are tender.

Blend in the ketchup and season with pepper. Do not drain the remaining liquid.

SERVES 4

Broccoli with Almonds

2	tablespoons butter
1/2	cup slivered almonds
1/2	cup sour cream
1/4	teaspoon salt
2	teaspoons fresh lemon juice
1	package frozen broccoli
	Paprika to taste

In a small saucepan melt the butter. Add the slivered almonds and toast over low heat until golden in color. Stir often so the almonds do not scorch.

In a separate saucepan blend together the sour cream, salt, and lemon juice. Place over very low heat. Add the almonds.

Cook the broccoli according to the package directions. Before serving, top with the almond mixture. Season with paprika.

SERVES 4

Roman Green Beans

2	9-ounce packages frozen green beans
3	tablespoons olive oil
1 1/2	tablespoons cider vinegar
2	tablespoons grated onion
1/4	teaspoon salt
1	garlic clove, minced
1/8	teaspoon pepper
2	tablespoons dry breadcrumbs
1/4	cup grated Parmesan cheese
1	tablespoon butter, melted
1/4	teaspoon paprika

ELGIN DINER RESTAURANT, CAMDEN, NEW JERSEY

Bejeweled Carrots

15	carrots, sliced diagonally
1	green bell pepper, chopped
4	celery stalks, sliced
1	medium onion, chopped
1	8-ounce can tomato sauce
1/4	cup sugar
1	teaspoon prepared mustard
1/4	teaspoon salt
1/2	teaspoon pepper
1/2	cup cooking oil
3/4	cup cider vinegar

In a large saucepan cook the carrots in water to cover until tender. Let cool.

In a mixing bowl combine the green pepper, celery, and onion. In a separate bowl blend together the tomato sauce, sugar, mustard, salt, pepper, oil, and vinegar. Pour the tomato sauce mixture over the vegetables. Add the carrots. Refrigerate for 24 hours before serving.

SERVES 6

Baked Carrots

1	small bunch carrots
2	tablespoons butter, melted
	Salt and pepper to taste
1/4	cup seasoned breadcrumbs
1/4	cup water

Clean and peel the carrots. Cut into thin slices. In a mixing bowl place the melted butter and season with salt and pepper. Add the carrots and mix thoroughly so that the carrots are coated in the butter. Mix in the seasoned breadcrumbs.

Place the mixture in a 1-quart baking dish. Add the water. Bake at 350° for 20 minutes or until the carrots are tender.

SERVES 4

Sweet & Sour Cabbage

1   cup water
1   teaspoon salt
1/4 cup vinegar
1   medium head red cabbage, shredded
5   slices bacon
1/2 teaspoon sugar
1/4 cup packed brown sugar
2   tablespoons all-purpose flour
1/4 cup water
1   small onion, sliced thin
1/4 cup thinly sliced green bell pepper

In a saucepan bring 1 cup of water with 1/2 teaspoon of salt and 2 tablespoons of vinegar to a boil.

Add the shredded cabbage, cover, and simmer for about 10 minutes. Drain and discard the water. Set aside the cabbage.

In a heavy skillet fry the bacon until crisp. Drain on paper towels. Discard all but 2 tablespoons of fat. Add to this the sugar, brown sugar, and flour. Blend in 1/4 cup of water, 2 tablespoons of vinegar, 1/2 teaspoon of salt, the onion, and pepper. Cook for 5 minutes, stirring often, or until the mixture thickens.

Add the bacon and sauce mixture to the shredded cabbage. Toss thoroughly.

SERVES 6

Scalloped Corn

2 1/2 cups creamed corn
3   tablespoons butter, melted
1   cup seasoned breadcrumbs
2   tablespoons chopped onion
2   tablespoons chopped green bell pepper
2   tablespoons packed light brown sugar
1/2 teaspoon salt
1/4 teaspoon pepper
1/2 cup milk
2   teaspoons butter, melted

Grease a 1-quart casserole dish, and set it aside.

In a large mixing bowl blend together the creamed corn and 3 tablespoons of melted butter. Add the seasoned breadcrumbs, onion, green pepper, and brown sugar. Season with salt and pepper. Add the milk and mix thoroughly.

Pour the corn into the prepared casserole dish. Drizzle with 2 teaspoons of melted butter. Bake at 350° for 30 minutes or until the casserole is golden brown.

SERVES 6

Scalloped Eggplant

1   medium eggplant
1   cup cottage cheese
1   egg, beaten
3   tablespoons ketchup
1/4 cup minced celery
1/4 cup minced onion

½   teaspoon salt
½   cup seasoned soft breadcrumbs
2   tablespoons butter, melted

Grease a 1-quart casserole dish. Set aside.

Wash and peel the eggplant, and cut into 1-inch pieces. In a pan of boiling salted water cook the eggplant for 5 minutes. Drain thoroughly.

Add the cottage cheese, beaten egg, and ketchup. Blend in the celery, onion, and salt. Add the seasoned breadcrumbs.

Place the mixture into the prepared casserole dish. Drizzle with butter. Bake at 350° for 35 to 45 minutes.

SERVES 4

Broiled Mushrooms

½   pound fresh mushrooms
3   tablespoons butter
3   ounces cream cheese
2   tablespoons sour cream
¼   teaspoon salt
⅛   teaspoon paprika

Wash the mushrooms thoroughly. Remove the stems. In a small saucepan melt the butter. Brush the tops of the mushrooms with the butter.

Place the mushrooms buttered-side-down on a flat baking sheet. Broil for 4 to 5 minutes.

In a mixing bowl blend together the cream cheese and the sour cream. Add the salt and paprika. Fill the mushrooms with the cream cheese mixture. Continue to broil for 5 minutes. Serve warm.

SERVES 5

Au Gratin Potatoes

½   teaspoon salt
    Pepper to taste
¼   teaspoon dill
4   cups potatoes, diced
1   medium onion, diced
¼   pound Cheddar cheese, grated
2   tablespoons all-purpose flour
2   tablespoons butter
2   cups milk

Grease a 1-quart baking dish.

In a small bowl combine the salt and pepper with the dill. Arrange the sliced potatoes and onion in the bottom of the baking dish. Add a portion of the Cheddar cheese. Sprinkle a pinch of the flour over the top. Sprinkle a pinch of the seasonings over the flour. Dot with butter. Continue layering with the potatoes, onion, cheese, flour, and seasonings.

In a small saucepan heat the milk but do not bring to a boil. Pour the warmed milk over the top of the potatoes. Cover and bake at 375° for 30 minutes. Uncover the baking dish and continue baking for 15 minutes or until the potatoes are tender and golden brown.

SERVES 4

Cheese Potatoes

7	medium Russet potatoes
1	10 3/4-ounce can condensed cream of chicken soup
1/4	cup butter
1	pint sour cream
1 1/2	cups grated Cheddar cheese
1/4	cup chopped green onions

Grease a 2-quart casserole dish and set it aside.

In a saucepan boil the potatoes until they are tender. Peel and grate.

In a separate saucepan heat the soup with the butter. Add the grated potatoes. Blend in the sour cream, cheese, and green onions. Pour the potatoes into the prepared casserole dish. Bake at 350° for 45 minutes.

SERVES 6

Delmonico Potatoes

10	red potatoes
1/2	cup sour cream
1	cup milk
1/2	pound sharp Cheddar cheese, grated
1	teaspoon dry mustard
1/8	teaspoon coarse ground pepper

In a saucepan boil the potatoes in salted water until tender. Drain and cool. Peel and slice. Arrange the potatoes in the bottom of a shallow baking dish. Set aside.

In a separate mixing bowl combine the sour cream, milk, cheese, mustard, and pepper. Mix thoroughly. Pour into a double boiler and cook over simmering water until the cheese has melted and the sauce is smooth. Pour the cheese sauce over the potatoes. Cover and refrigerate overnight.

Bake at 325° for 1 hour.

SERVES 8

SHORT-STOP DINER, BELLEVILLE, NEW JERSEY

Golden Brown New Potatoes

1 pound new potatoes
2 tablespoons butter
1 teaspoon salt
  Pepper to taste

In a large pot place the potatoes into boiling salted water. Cook until they are tender. Remove and peel the potatoes, then slice.

In a small saucepan melt the butter. Dip the sliced potatoes into the butter and place the potatoes on a baking sheet. Sprinkle with salt and pepper. Bake at 425° for 12 minutes or until they are golden brown.

SERVES 4

Mashed Potatoes & Gravy

8 large Russet potatoes
  Milk
½ cup butter
¼ cup mayonnaise
  Salt and pepper to taste
  Gravy (see recipe on pg. 53)

Wash, peel, and dice the potatoes. Bring a large saucepan of water to a boil. Add the potatoes and cook until tender. Drain.

In a large mixing bowl mash the potatoes with a fork. Add milk and continue to mash, making a paste. Add the butter. Blend in the mayonnaise, mixing until the potatoes are fluffy. Season with salt and pepper. Serve with gravy.

SERVES 4

O'Brien Potatoes

1 tablespoon all-purpose flour
1 onion, chopped
1 green bell pepper, chopped
¼ pound Cheddar cheese, grated
1 cup milk
  Salt and pepper to taste
2 medium potatoes, cooked and diced
  Seasoned breadcrumbs

In a medium mixing bowl blend together the flour with the onion, green pepper, and cheese. Add the milk and season with salt and pepper.

Grease a 1-quart casserole dish. Pour in the cooked potatoes and the cheese mixture. Blend thoroughly. Sprinkle seasoned breadcrumbs over the top.

Bake at 350° for 20 minutes or until the potatoes are golden and the cheese has melted.

SERVES 4

Potato Cakes

8	large Russet potatoes
	Milk
1/2	cup butter
1/4	cup mayonnaise
	Salt and pepper to taste
I	egg, beaten
I	teaspoon onion seasoning
	Butter

Wash, peel, and dice the potatoes. Bring a large saucepan of water to a boil. Add the potatoes and boil until tender. Drain.

In a large mixing bowl mash the potatoes with a fork. Add milk and continue to mash, making a paste. Add the butter.

Blend in the mayonnaise. Continue to mix until the potatoes are fluffy. Season with salt and pepper. Add the beaten egg. Blend in the onion seasoning.

Shape the potatoes into 8 flat cakes. In a skillet melt enough butter to coat the bottom of the pan. Brown the cakes evenly on both sides, turning so that each side is golden.

SERVES 8

Scalloped Potatoes

4	cups diced potatoes
1/2	teaspoon salt
	Pepper to taste
2	tablespoons butter
2	teaspoons grated onion
2	tablespoons all-purpose flour
2	cups milk

ANGELO'S DINER, GLASSBORO, NEW JERSEY

Grease a 1-quart baking dish.

In a mixing bowl toss the diced potatoes with salt and pepper. Place the potatoes in the baking dish. Add the butter and onion. Mix thoroughly. Sprinkle the flour over the top.

In a small saucepan heat the milk but do not bring to a boil. Pour the warmed milk over the top of the potatoes. Bake, covered, at 375° for 30 minutes. Uncover and bake 15 minutes more or until the potatoes are tender and golden brown.

SERVES 4

Stuffed Baked Potatoes

4	large Russet baking potatoes
6	slices bacon
3	tablespoons melted butter
1	cup grated Cheddar cheese
1/4	cup sour cream
4	teaspoons chopped chives

Wash the potatoes. Bake at 350° for 1 hour or until done.

In a skillet fry the bacon until crisp. Drain on paper towels. Let cool. Crumble and set aside.

Cut the potatoes in half lengthwise. Spoon out the center, leaving one-fourth of the potato next to the potato skin.

In a medium bowl mash together 1½ cups of the potato filling with the melted butter and Cheddar cheese. Add the crumbled bacon.

Refill the potato skins with the filling. Arrange the potatoes in a baking dish.

Bake at 325° for 12 minutes or until the cheese has melted. Serve with sour cream and chives.

SERVES 4

Sweet Potatoes

6	medium sweet potatoes
1/2	cup milk
1/4	cup sugar
1/2	cup chopped walnuts
1/4	cup butter
1/4	teaspoon salt
1/4	cup bourbon
	Marshmallows

Peel the sweet potatoes. In a saucepan cover the potatoes with water and boil until tender. Drain and mash thoroughly.

In a separate saucepan scald the milk. Add the sugar, walnuts, butter, salt, and bourbon. Add the mixture to the sweet potatoes and blend well.

Top with marshmallows. Bake at 350° for 30 minutes or until the marshmallows are golden brown.

 SERVES 6

JAY'S SWEETHEART DINER

Diners are coming back! That's the message co-owners Laurie Kitteridge and Sheri Reece read in the surge of business they are getting at Jay's Sweetheart Diner in Lincoln, New Hampshire.

"Who wants to eat at a chain when you can come to a diner and get a much better hamburger?" asks Laurie. "And tell me, can you get Black Forest Cake or Banana Cream Pie like ours at a chain restaurant?" Not a chance.

Like many other diners, this 1958 Master model has been around. "This diner was originally located in Dover, New Hampshire," says Laurie.

Jay's seats forty and is frequently full. "We serve breakfast and lunch," says Laurie. "People come in for our basic omelettes, which are great, and a lot of people really like our homemade meat loaf. We are probably the only ones in town that make up our own French fries. We get a lot of requests for those."

Candied Sweet Potatoes

4	medium sweet potatoes
2	tablespoons sugar
I	teaspoon cinnamon
⅓	cup maple syrup
2	tablespoons butter

Peel the sweet potatoes and cut lengthwise. Arrange them in the bottom of a 1-quart casserole dish.

In a mixing bowl blend together the sugar and cinnamon. Sprinkle over the top of the sweet potatoes. Pour the maple syrup over the top and drizzle with melted butter. Bake at 350° for 30 minutes.

SERVES 4

Baked Spinach

I	package frozen, chopped spinach
2	tablespoons melted butter
	Salt and pepper to taste
2	eggs, slightly beaten
3	tablespoons seasoned breadcrumbs
½	cup grated Cheddar cheese
½	cup chopped mushrooms
4	slices bacon

Thaw the spinach. Place in a mixing bowl with the melted butter. Season with salt and pepper. In a separate bowl blend the beaten eggs with the seasoned breadcrumbs. Add to the spinach mixture. Blend in the grated cheese and chopped mushrooms.

Place the spinach mixture into a casserole dish. Top with the bacon slices. Bake at 350° for 45 minutes.

SERVES 4

Broiled Tomatoes

½	cup cracker crumbs
I	egg, well beaten
2	large ripe tomatoes, peeled and halved
½	teaspoon salt
¼	teaspoon pepper
2	tablespoons butter
¼	cup grated sharp Cheddar cheese

Spread the cracker crumbs on a plate. In a small bowl beat the egg. Sprinkle the tomatoes with the salt and pepper.

Dip the tomatoes into the cracker crumbs, then into the beaten egg, and again into the cracker crumbs.

Place on a well-greased baking sheet. Broil for 5 minutes or until the tops turn golden brown.

In a saucepan melt the butter. Add the remaining cracker crumbs and brown lightly. Spread the buttered crumbs over the cooked tomatoes. Top with the grated Cheddar cheese.

SERVES 2

MANUFACTURING THE LUNCH CAR

During the early twentieth century, the increasing popularity of lunch cars spawned a whole new industry. As bigger and better models were designed, companies were founded to manufacture them. Pioneers in the field were the Worcester Lunch Car Company and the Jerry O'Mahoney Company.

Founded in 1906 by Philip Duprey, the Worcester Lunch Car Company set out to create a more modern lunch car. In 1907 the American Eagle Cafe became the first Worcester model to roll off the assembly line. It featured windows that opened to help ventilate the car and a separate take-out window for customers on the go.

Another model, the Buffet Lunch, included a kitchen that ran the length of the car behind a long counter instead of being crammed into a corner at the back. Customers sat on stools along the counter, where they could watch as their food was prepared.

In 1913 Jerry O'Mahoney, of Beyonne, New Jersey, decided that he, too, could build a better lunch car. To do so, he resolved to include all the modern conveniences of the day—electricity, for instance.

O'Mahoney's earliest models included a front entrance in the center of each car. Windows adorned the front, and one was of stained glass, spelling out the words, "Pure

Food, Cleanliness, Quick Service, and Popular Prices." This credo would come to symbolize the diner industry. All of the O'Mahoney cars were custom painted and included the name of the business in black lettering on the side.

Soon, other companies were jumping on the diner bandwagon. Manufacturers included Wilson Pollard, who established the Pollard Company in Lowell, Massachusetts, in 1926, J. G. Brill, who built diners in Philadelphia,

GLORY JEAN'S DINER IN RUMNEY, NEW HAMPSHIRE, IS A 1954 O'MAHONEY

and G. C. Kullman, who ran a Cleveland, Ohio, subsidiary of the Brill Company with an eye on midwestern markets.

Kullman models looked much like railroad cars, and this may be how these roadside eateries came to be called diners. Likely coined during the 1920s, the word *diner* is probably a shortened form of "dining car."

Dutch Tomatoes

6   slices lean bacon
1/4 cup butter
1   small onion, chopped fine
3   large tomatoes
1/4 cup packed brown sugar
2   teaspoons cornstarch
1   cup sour cream
1/2 teaspoon salt
2   tablespoons parsley, chopped

In a skillet fry the bacon until crisp. Drain on paper towels. Crumble and set aside.

In a separate skillet melt the butter. Add the onion and sauté until transparent.

Slice the tomatoes ¾-inch thick. Place in the skillet with the onions. Cook for 5 minutes, turning once.

Sprinkle 1 teaspoon of brown sugar on each of the tomato slices. In a small mixing bowl blend together the cornstarch with the sour cream. Spoon onto the tomatoes.

Simmer until somewhat thickened. Sprinkle with salt, parsley, and crumbled bacon.

SERVES 6

Highway Succotash

2   cups green lima beans
1   pound fresh snap beans
1   cup fresh corn
3   large tomatoes, peeled
2   tablespoons butter
2   tablespoons all-purpose flour
1/4 cup cold water
1/4 cup sour cream, room temperature
2   teaspoons sugar
     Salt and pepper to taste

In a large saucepan combine the lima beans and snap beans. Add enough water to cover. Bring to a boil and cook for 20 minutes or until tender.

Add the corn and tomatoes. Cook for 10 minutes more.

In a separate saucepan melt the butter over medium heat. In a covered jar shake the flour with the cold water. Add to the melted butter. Stir for 1 minute or until thick. Add the sour cream. Pour the mixture into the cooked vegetables and gently stir. Return to a boil and add the sugar. Season with salt and pepper.

SERVES 8

Vegetable Medley

1   head cabbage
3   celery stalks
1   small onion
1   cup chopped green bell pepper
1/2 teaspoon salt
     Pepper to taste
1   tablespoon shortening

Wash the cabbage under cold running water and pat dry with paper towels. Remove the outer leaves. Shred the cabbage to make 3 cups. Clean the celery the same as the cabbage. Chop fine to make about 1 cup. Dice the onion.

In a mixing bowl toss the cabbage with the celery, green pepper, and onion. Season with salt and pepper.

In a skillet melt the shortening. Add the tossed cabbage mixture. Cook over medium heat, stirring constantly, for 5 minutes or until the vegetables are tender-crisp.

SERVES 4

MISS PORTLAND

The Miss Portland Diner in Portland, Maine, is a movie star. The 1949 Worcester Lunch Car Company diner has been featured in Mel Gibson's *Man Without a Face* and the *Unsolved Mysteries* television series.

Owned and operated by Randall Chase for more than fifteen years, this forty-by-sixty-foot diner seats about forty people, and its original, mint-condition booths and stools are generally filled with customers. But it's not just the diner's celebrity status that keeps them coming back—the food is great.

Randall's partner and chef, Mae Marx, is famous for her mouthwatering chili, meat loaf, Spanish omelette, and assorted house specials. These and other tempting dishes attract a clientele from all walks of life. "We get truck drivers, doctors, lawyers, blue collar, white collar, you name it," says Randall.

Prices are low. Nothing on the lunch menu, which includes homemade beef stew, real mashed potatoes, hot turkey sandwiches, frightfully good desserts, and much more, is priced over $4.25. And portions are generous.

"We serve dinner portions for lunch," Randall says.

Customers can enjoy it all without choking on

smoke. The Miss Portland was the first restaurant in Maine to go completely smoke-free, a fact that makes the owner especially proud. "I thought we would lose business when we went nonsmoking," he says. "Actually, we've gained some business."

SOUPS OF THE DAY & SALADS

Chicken Noodle Soup

1	4-pound chicken, skinned
2	quarts water
1½	cups finely chopped celery
1½	cups chopped onion
⅛	teaspoon thyme
1	teaspoon salt
3	tablespoons parsley
¼	teaspoon coarse ground pepper
3	carrots, chopped fine
	Homemade Noodles (see recipe on p. 67)

Remove the skin and fat from the chicken. In a large heavy soup pot place the chicken in the water with ½ cup of celery, ¾ cup onion, thyme, salt, parsley, and pepper. Simmer about 1 hour and 30 minutes.

Remove the soup from the heat. Pour the soup through a sieve. Remove the chicken from the bones. Skim the fat from the stock. Return the chicken meat to the stock along with the remaining celery, onion, and carrots. Simmer and cook for 5 minutes. Add the noodles and cook 10 minutes more.

SERVES 6

Chicken Gumbo

2	tablespoons butter
¼	cup sliced onion
2	tablespoons diced green bell pepper
¼	cup diced celery
1	cup fresh okra
1	cup stewed tomatoes
1	teaspoon parsley, chopped
2	cups chicken stock
2	cups cooked chicken
	Salt and pepper to taste

In a large soup pot melt the butter. Add the onion, green pepper, and celery, and sauté for 10 minutes or until the vegetables are lightly browned.

Add the okra, tomatoes, parsley, chicken stock, and chicken to the soup pot. Cover and let simmer for 20 minutes, stirring constantly to blend thoroughly. Season with salt and pepper.

SERVES 6

GIBBY'S DINER

Gibby Wolf is the original owner of the Duanesburg, New York, Gibby's Diner, a Mountain View model built in 1952. He has been running the business in much the same way for more than four decades.

"We make everything here," says Gibby. "All of our pies, breads, sauces, and gravies. We roast our own turkeys. We roast our own beef."

Gibby says that he has created a unique cabbage salad that has proven very popular with his customers. "We serve it every day," says Gibby. Unfortunately, you will not find that particular recipe in this book. Gibby is not quite ready to share it with the world. "It's a secret as to what's in it, you see. Customers can try to duplicate it if they want, but I don't give out the recipe."

Gibby says his diner is one of the last to serve a full, four-course Sunday dinner. The meal may consist of Virginia baked ham with fruit sauce, roasted turkey breast, chicken and biscuits, or a seafood platter of stuffed shrimp and scallops. "Sunday dinner comes with an appetizer, relish tray, entree, homemade dessert, and beverage, all for under $15."

Not surprisingly, Gibby's attracts families. "We are now serving second and third generations of some families," says Gibby. "The mothers ate here when they were young, and now they bring in their kids."

Gibby's not only serves families, but his family serves them. "I have my son-in-law and daughter who have been here for fourteen years. I have other employees that have been with me for thirty years."

Homemade Noodles

1	cup all-purpose flour
1/2	teaspoon salt
1	egg, well beaten
2	tablespoons milk

In a mixing bowl sift together the flour and salt. Add the egg and milk. Turn the dough onto a floured board. Shape into a ball and knead for 5 minutes. Cover with a clean cloth. Let the dough rest for 5 minutes.

Roll out the dough in a rectangle to 1/8-inch thickness, dusting the rolling pin with flour to keep the dough from sticking. Cut into strips 2 inches wide and stack. Cut into strips 1/8-inch wide. Separate and allow the noodles to dry thoroughly before cooking. Cook in chicken broth for 10 minutes before serving.

MAKES ABOUT 1 POUND OF PASTA

Beef Barley Soup

1/2	ounce dried mushrooms
1	cup boiling water
1	tablespoon cooking oil
1	garlic clove, minced
1	onion, chopped
1/2	pound beef round, sliced thin
3 1/2	cups beef broth
4	cups water
2	carrots, sliced
1	celery stalk, chopped
1 1/2	teaspoons salt
1/4	teaspoon pepper
3	turnips, diced
1	small zucchini, diced
1/2	cup quick-cooking barley
2	tablespoons unsalted butter
1/4	cup all-purpose flour
	Parsley

In a small mixing bowl reconstitute the mushrooms in 1 cup of boiling water. Set aside. Coat the bottom of a skillet with the oil. Sauté the garlic and onion until tender but not brown. Increase the heat, and add the sliced beef. Cook so that the beef is brown on all sides.

In a large soup pot combine the beef broth and water. Add the carrots, celery, salt, and pepper. Drain and slice the mushrooms. Add the mushrooms to the soup pot. Bring the soup to a boil. Reduce the heat and simmer for 15 minutes.

Add the turnips, zucchini, and quick-cooking barley. Cover and simmer for 10 minutes.

Melt the unsalted butter in the skillet. Add the flour, blending until smooth. Cook over low heat until the flour turns golden. Remove the skillet from the heat. Add 1 cup of soup, stirring constantly until smooth. Add the mixture to the soup pot. Heat to serve. Garnish with parsley.

SERVES 4

Vegetable - Beef Soup

1/4	cup vegetable oil
1	pound lean short ribs
3	quarts water
1/4	cup chopped fresh parsley
1/4	teaspoon salt
1/4	teaspoon pepper
1	large onion, chopped
3	garlic cloves, minced
3	beef bouillon cubes
1	large soup bone
3/4	cup green split peas
3/4	cup dried baby lima beans
1	cup sliced celery
2	cups raw potatoes, cut into 1/2-inch cubes
1	cup sliced carrots
2	cups peeled and chopped fresh tomatoes
1/2	cup sliced fresh mushrooms

In a large soup pot heat the vegetable oil and brown the short ribs on all sides. Cover with water. Add the fresh parsley, salt, and pepper. Simmer for 5 minutes. Add the onion, garlic, and bouillon cubes. Cover and simmer for 1 hour.

Remove the short ribs from the soup pot and cut them into bite-size pieces. Return the meat to the soup pot. Skim off and discard the fat. Add the soup bone, green split peas, and dried lima beans, and cook for 1 hour. Add water as needed.

Add the celery, potatoes, carrots, tomatoes, and mushrooms. Cover and continue to simmer for 40 minutes more or until all of the vegetables are tender. Serve with corn bread.

SERVES 8

Beef Stock

2	pounds shank bones
1/2	pound stew meat
2	quarts water
5	whole black peppercorns
1/4	cup diced celery
1	bay leaf
1/4	cup sliced carrots
1/4	cup chopped onion

In a large soup pot combine the shank bones, stew meat, and water. Add the peppercorns, celery, bay leaf, carrots, and onion. Simmer for 3 hours.

Strain through a fine sieve. Discard the vegetables and spices. Chill and remove the fat.

Cheese Soup

1	tablespoon butter
1	medium onion, chopped
3	tablespoons all-purpose flour
2	cups soup broth
1 1/4	cups grated Cheddar cheese
1	egg yolk
1/3	cup sour cream
	Chopped parsley

In a soup pot melt the butter and sauté the onion until transparent. Blend in the flour. Pour the soup broth over the top. Simmer over low heat for 5 minutes, stirring constantly until thickened.

EGG PLATTER DINER, PATTERSON, NEW JERSEY

Add the Cheddar cheese. Let the cheese melt slowly, making sure the soup does not come to a full boil. Remove the soup from the heat. Beat together the egg yolk and sour cream, and slowly stir into the soup. Garnish with parsley. Serve immediately.

SERVES 4

Black Bean Soup

1	pound black beans
2½	quarts water
¼	cup diced salt pork
½	cup chopped carrots
½	cup chopped celery
¾	cup chopped potatoes
2	garlic cloves
1¼	teaspoon salt
¼	teaspoon pepper
1	ham bone
1	teaspoon chopped parsley

In a large soup pot soak the black beans overnight in 2½ quarts of water.

In a skillet cook the salt pork for 5 minutes. Add carrots, celery, and potatoes. Continue cooking for 10 minutes or until the carrots are tender. Add the black beans with water. Season with garlic, salt, and pepper.

Add the ham bone to the soup pot. Cover and slowly bring to a boil. Reduce the heat and simmer for 2 hours. Remove the ham bone. Strain the liquid. Press the vegetables through a sieve. Add the vegetable mixture to the liquid. Remove the meat from the ham bone, dice, and return the meat to the soup. Garnish with parsley.

SERVES 6

Navy Bean Soup

1	cup dried navy beans
2	quarts water
1	small onion, chopped
1	tablespoon light brown sugar
1	cup whole tomatoes
1	small ham hock
1/2	teaspoon salt
1/4	teaspoon pepper

In a large soup pot add the beans to the water. Add the onion, brown sugar, tomatoes, ham hock, salt, and pepper. Bring to a slow boil. Cover and cook for 3 hours or until the beans are tender, stirring often so the soup does not burn. Add additional water as needed if the soup becomes too thick.

SERVES 6

Lentil Soup

1	pound dried lentils
2 1/2	quarts water
1/4	cup salt pork, diced
1	ham bone
1/2	cup chopped carrots
1/2	cup chopped celery
3/4	cup chopped potato
2	garlic cloves
1 1/4	teaspoons salt
1/4	teaspoon pepper
1	teaspoon parsley, chopped

In a large soup pot soak the lentils overnight in 2 1/2 quarts of water.

In a skillet cook the salt pork for 5 minutes. Add the ham bone, carrots, celery, and potatoes, and continue cooking for 10 minutes or until the carrots are tender. Add the lentils with water. Season with garlic, salt, and pepper.

Cover and slowly bring to a boil. Reduce the heat and simmer for 2 hours. Remove the ham bone. Strain the liquid. Press the vegetables through a fine sieve. Add the vegetable mixture to the liquid. Remove the meat from the ham bone. Dice and return to the soup. Garnish with parsley.

SERVES 6

Minestrone Soup #1

2 1/2	pounds beef soup bones
4	quarts water
2	teaspoons salt
1	cup dried red kidney beans
3/4	cup chopped onion
1	tablespoon olive oil
1	cup tomato purée
1/2	teaspoon coarse ground pepper
1	teaspoon sage leaves, crushed
2	cups shredded cabbage
3/4	cup frozen peas
1/4	cup parsley, chopped
1/2	cup thinly sliced zucchini
1	garlic clove, minced
1	cup sliced carrots
1	cup finely chopped celery
1/4	cup rice, uncooked
1/2	cup macaroni
	Parmesan cheese

In a large soup pot add the beef soup bones to the water, salt, and kidney beans. Cover and simmer for 2 to 3 hours, or until the meat and beans are tender. Add more water if needed. Remove the soup bones and remove any meat. Discard the bones and return the meat to the soup pot.

In a skillet sauté the onions in olive oil until they become transparent. Add the onions to the soup pot along with the tomato purée. Mix thoroughly. Add the pepper, sage, cabbage, peas, parsley, zucchini, garlic, carrots, and celery. Add the rice and macaroni. Blend thoroughly. Simmer for 30 minutes or until the rice and macaroni are tender. Garnish with grated Parmesan cheese.

SERVES 12

In a large soup pot brown the ground beef. Add the onion and celery. Cook for 5 minutes. Drain.

Add the chopped tomatoes, beans, cabbage, salt, basil, rosemary, tomato sauce, carrots, wine, garlic, pepper, and parsley.

Dissolve the bouillon cubes in the hot water. Add to the soup pot. Simmer for 20 minutes or until the carrots are tender.

Prepare the macaroni according to the package directions. Add to the soup pot.

Continue cooking until the vegetables are tender. Stir constantly to prevent burning. Garnish with grated Parmesan cheese.

SERVES 6

Minestrone Soup #2

2 pounds ground beef
1 large onion, chopped
4 celery stalks, chopped
1 can whole tomatoes, chopped
1 can kidney beans
1/2 small head cabbage, shredded
1 teaspoon salt
1/4 teaspoon basil
1/4 teaspoon rosemary
1 large can tomato sauce
4 carrots, sliced
1 cup red wine
1 garlic clove, minced
1/2 teaspoon coarse ground pepper
1/2 cup fresh parsley, chopped
4 beef bouillon cubes
4 cups hot water
1 cup macaroni
1/2 cup grated Parmesan cheese

French Onion Soup

1/4 cup butter
4 large onions, sliced thin
6 cups beef stock
1/2 teaspoon salt
1/2 teaspoon coarse ground pepper
1/2 teaspoon Worcestershire sauce
6 slices crusty French bread
1/2 cup grated sharp Cheddar cheese

In a large soup pot melt the butter and sauté the onions for 15 minutes or until light brown in color. Add the beef stock, salt, pepper, and Worcestershire sauce, and simmer for 30 minutes.

To serve, place a slice of French bread in the bottom of a serving bowl. Ladle soup over the bread. Top with grated Cheddar cheese.

SERVES 6

Mushroom–Vegetable Soup

6 slices bacon
1 cup chopped onion
1/4 cup all-purpose flour
3 cups water
1 13 3/4-ounce can condensed chicken broth
2 tablespoons chopped fresh parsley
2 tablespoons chopped celery leaves
1 bay leaf
1/2 teaspoon salt
1/4 teaspoon pepper
1 cup sliced celery
3/4 cup sliced fresh mushrooms
1 can evaporated milk

In a large soup pot fry the bacon until crisp. Drain on paper towels. Cool and crumble. Set aside.

Remove all but 3 tablespoons of bacon fat. Add the onion and sauté for 5 minutes. Add the flour and cook for 2 minutes, stirring constantly. Add the water, chicken broth, parsley, celery leaves, bay leaf, salt, and pepper.

Bring to a boil. Cover and simmer for 20 minutes. Add the celery and mushrooms. Simmer 7 minutes more. Blend in the evaporated milk and crumbled bacon. Cook until thoroughly heated. Remove the bay leaf before serving.

SERVES 4

Potato Soup

1 1/2 quarts water
3 cups peeled and diced potatoes
1/2 cup chopped onion
2 tablespoons chopped parsley
1/4 cup finely chopped celery
1 teaspoon salt
1/4 teaspoon garlic powder
1/8 teaspoon pepper
4 slices bacon
1/4 cup water
1/4 cup all-purpose flour
1/4 cup cold water
1 cup sour cream
1/4 teaspoon paprika

In a large soup pot bring 1 1/2 quarts of water to a boil. Add the potatoes, onion, parsley, celery, salt, garlic powder, and pepper. Cook for 20 minutes or until the potatoes are tender.

In a skillet fry the bacon until crisp. Drain on a paper towel. Cool and crumble. Set aside. Strain the potato mixture through a sieve, and return to the stock. Add the 1/4 cup of water. Bring to a simmer, stirring often.

Mix the flour and 1/4 cup cold water together. Pour over the potatoes. Cook for 2 minutes or until thick. Add more flour as needed. Before serving blend together the sour cream with 1 cup of cooled stock. Return to the soup. Garnish with bacon and paprika.

SERVES 6

MEL'S DINER

The bread, rolls, and doughnuts are all home-made at Mel's Diner on Cumberland Street in Lebanon, Pennsylvania. And they are famous.

That's saying a lot for an eatery situated in the heart of the Pennsylvania Dutch Country, where people take good food very seriously.

"We do a Pennsylvania Dutch chicken pot pie," says owner Mel Snaveley. "That's a big one, and it keeps people coming back." Mel's is an institution in Lebanon, and many customers have their own favorite seats. "Especially in the morning, they will come in and sit at certain stools at the counter. They know just where they want to be."

Split Pea Soup

1	large ham hock
2½	quarts water
2	cups dried green split peas
¾	cup chopped onion
½	cup chopped leeks
1	teaspoon salt
⅛	teaspoon pepper
2	carrots, peeled and chopped

In a large soup pot place the ham hock in the water. Slowly bring the water to a boil. Add the peas, onion, leeks, salt, and pepper. Reduce the heat and simmer for 3 hours, stirring occasionally to keep from burning. Remove the ham hock and cut the meat from the bone. Return the meat to the soup and add the carrots. Simmer for 15 minutes more or until the carrots are tender.

SERVES 6

Saturday Night Soup

4	slices bacon
1	cup canned whole tomatoes
1	garlic clove
1	medium onion, quartered
1/4	cup butter
4	cups cooked pinto beans
2	cups chicken broth
2	chicken bouillon cubes
1/2	teaspoon chili powder
1/2	teaspoon salt
1/2	cup cubed Muenster cheese

In a heavy skillet fry the bacon until crisp. Drain on paper towels. Cool and crumble. Set aside.

In a food processor mix together the tomatoes, garlic, and onion for 45 seconds. In a large saucepan melt the butter. Add the blended tomato mixture and cook on high for 5 minutes, stirring constantly. In a blender purée the beans for 2 minutes or until smooth. Add the bean purée to the tomato mixture and continue cooking for 5 minutes. Add the chicken broth, bouillon cubes, chili powder, and salt. Reduce the heat to low and simmer for 10 to 15 minutes.

To serve place a few cubes of cheese in the bottom of a serving bowl. Ladle hot soup on top of the cheese. Garnish with crumbled bacon.

SERVES 4

JENNY'S DINER, RONKS, PENNSYLVANIA

VILLAGE DINER, MILLERTON, NEW YORK

Cream of Cauliflower Soup

½ cup butter
½ cup finely chopped onion
½ cup chopped leeks
½ cup finely chopped celery
¾ cup all-purpose flour
7 quarts chicken stock
3 pounds cauliflower, broken into pieces
½ teaspoon salt
½ teaspoon coarse ground pepper
1 cup heavy cream

In a large soup pot melt the butter. Add the onion, and sauté until light brown. Add the leeks and celery. Stir constantly. Slowly blend in the flour. Continue stirring until the mixture becomes thick and smooth, being careful that the flour does not brown. Blend in the chicken stock. Add the cauliflower, salt, and pepper, and simmer for 1 hour, stirring regularly. Do not let the soup boil.

In a saucepan heat the cream. Blend the cream into the soup.

SERVES 6

Cream of Broccoli Soup

8 cups hot water
3 chicken bouillon cubes
2 10-ounce packages chopped broccoli
2 tablespoons minced onion
1 teaspoon salt
  Pepper to taste
¾ cup dry milk
1 tablespoon dry sherry

In a saucepan bring the water to a boil. Add the chicken bouillon and stir to dissolve. Add the chopped broccoli, onion, salt, and pepper. Return to a full boil. Reduce the heat and simmer for 10 minutes or until the broccoli is tender. Remove the soup from the heat and let cool.

Pour about one-third of the soup into a blender. Add ¼ cup of dry milk and blend until smooth. Pour into a separate saucepan. Repeat until all of the soup and milk is thoroughly blended. Heat through. Before serving, add the dry sherry.

SERVES 6

Cream of Mushroom Soup

1/4	cup butter
1	cup sliced mushrooms
2	tablespoons finely chopped onion
2	cups chicken broth
3	tablespoons all-purpose flour
1/4	cup water
1	cup heavy cream
1/4	teaspoon salt
1/2	teaspoon celery salt
1/8	teaspoon pepper
	Croutons

In a large soup pot melt the butter and sauté 3/4 cup of the sliced mushrooms and the onion until the onion becomes transparent. Add the chicken broth and bring to a simmer.

In a mixing bowl blend together the flour and water. Add the flour mixture to the mushroom-onion mixture. Add the remaining mushrooms, cream, salt, celery salt, and pepper. Continue simmering for 10 minutes, stirring often. Garnish with croutons.

SERVES 6

Cream of Tomato Soup

2 1/2	cups diced and peeled tomatoes
1/4	cup finely chopped onion
1/2	teaspoon salt
1/4	teaspoon celery salt
1/8	teaspoon baking soda
4	slices bacon
2	tablespoons butter
2	tablespoons all-purpose flour
1/4	cup water
2	cups milk
	Sour cream

WOLFFS DINER, STILLWATER, NEW YORK

In a large soup pot combine the tomatoes, onion, salt, and celery salt. Simmer over low for 10 minutes. Press the mixture through a fine sieve and return to the soup pot. Add the baking soda. Reheat.

In a skillet fry the bacon until crisp. Drain on paper towels. Cool and crumble. Set aside.

In a separate pan melt the butter. In a small bowl blend together the flour and water. Slowly blend the flour mixture into the melted butter. As the mixture begins to thicken add the milk. Continue stirring for 1 minute or until the texture is smooth.

Add the melted butter mixture to the tomato mixture. Stir constantly to prevent burning. Garnish with sour cream and crumbled bacon.

SERVES 4

Manhattan Clam Chowder

1/4	pound salt pork, diced
I	onion, sliced
1/4	cup diced celery
2	tablespoons chopped parsley
I	carrot, diced
2	cups diced potatoes
I	teaspoon salt
2	cups water
2	cups chopped clams with liquid
2	14-ounce cans whole tomatoes
1/4	teaspoon basil
	Pepper to taste

In a large soup pot brown the salt pork. Drain all but 2 tablespoons of fat. Add the onion and celery, and sauté until tender. Add the parsley, carrot, potatoes, salt, and water.

Chop the clams. Add with the liquid to the soup pot. Let simmer for 20 minutes or until the potatoes are tender. Add the tomatoes, basil, and pepper. Bring to a boil and simmer for 5 minutes.

SERVES 6

Sea Captain's Chowder

2	pounds whitefish
3	cups water
I	teaspoon salt
4	slices bacon, diced
I	large onion, chopped fine
5	medium potatoes, sliced thin
I	quart milk
1/2	cup Chablis wine
I	cup light cream
	Salt and pepper to taste

In a large soup pot add the whitefish to the water and salt. Simmer over low heat for 10 minutes. Strain, debone, and skin the fish. Reserve the stock.

In a large skillet fry the bacon until crisp. Drain on paper towels. Cool and crumble. Set aside.

In the same skillet sauté the onions in the bacon fat until lightly browned. Add the fish, potatoes, and 2 cups of the stock. Cover and simmer for 10 minutes. Add the milk, wine, and cream, and heat thoroughly, but do not boil. Season with salt and pepper. Garnish with bacon.

SERVES 6

DADDYPOPS DINER

At 6:00 A.M. the doors to Daddypops Diner in Hatsboro, Pennsylvania, open for business. Owner Ken Smith greets the regulars who keep their own coffee mugs behind the counter. They shuffle through the door, grab a mug, and wait for that first cup of freshly brewed coffee.

A classic, vintage 1949, Mountain View diner, Daddypops seats fifty-one people. The music spilling from the Seeburg jukebox in the corner is likewise classic: Patsy Cline and Nat King Cole. Customers can sit in barber chairs if they like, and the cash register is a blessing to anyone shocked by inflation—it won't ring up anything over $1.95.

Ken says that owning the diner was really the dream of his wife, Beth, who passed away in 1994. Before the Smiths bought Daddypops, it had been a Chinese restaurant, and before that a pizza parlor.

The couple spent days replacing broken tables, stripping off the old orange and black paint, and redecorating the interior in green and silver.

Open for breakfast and lunch only, Daddypops offers a variety of house specialties, including breakfast grits, a delicacy rarely tasted in a northern diner. And then there is the Daddypop Duo: two flapjacks, two slices of French toast, two eggs (any style), two strips of bacon, and two pieces of sausage. At lunch Ken serves up homemade soups, salads, sandwiches, and his famous Daddyfries.

The Daddyfries go fast. "This diner will go through 1,400 pounds of potatoes a week," says Ken. "And for a fifty-one-seat diner, that is a lot of potatoes. We serve generous portions because we don't want anyone leaving here hungry."

DADDYPOPS DINER, HATSBORO, PENNSYLVANIA

Daddypops' Clam Chowder

1/2	cup butter
3	medium onions, diced
3	stalks celery, diced
9	medium potatoes, diced
1	6 1/2 -ounce can minced clams
6	tablespoons all-purpose flour
1	cup ice water
3	tablespoons parsley
3	tablespoons basil
3/4	teaspoon pepper
3	teaspoons onion salt
1 1/2	teaspoons celery salt
2	tablespoons chives
9	cups milk
4	cups light cream
	Salt to taste

In a skillet melt the butter and sauté the onion and celery for 20 minutes. In a large pot add the onions and celery to the diced potatoes and the clams with the juice. Bring to a low boil and simmer for 30 minutes.

In a separate saucepan pour the flour over the ice water and stir until it becomes a thick paste. Add the parsley, basil, pepper, onion salt, celery salt, and chives. Mix to a thick paste. Cook over low heat. Once heated, add to the potato and clam mixture. Blend in the milk and light cream. Season with salt. Simmer 30 to 60 minutes or until thick.

MAKES 2 GALLONS

New England Clam Chowder

1/4	pound salt pork, chopped
1	onion, sliced
1	cup diced celery
2	cups clams with liquid
2	cups diced potatoes
1	cup water
3	cups milk
	Salt and pepper to taste

In a large soup pot brown the salt pork. Drain all but 1 tablespoon of fat. Add the onion and celery, and sauté until tender. Chop the clams and add with the liquid to the onion and celery, along with the potatoes and water. Bring to a boil. Cover and simmer for 20 minutes or until the potatoes are tender.

In a saucepan scald the milk. Add the milk to the soup. Season with salt and pepper.

SERVES 6

Chicken Potato Chowder

1/4	cup butter
1/4	cup chopped onion
1/4	cup chopped celery
2	cups chicken stock
1 1/2	cups cooked chicken, cubed
1	teaspoon salt
1/2	teaspoon garlic powder
1/2	teaspoon celery salt
1	cup shredded carrots
4	cups frozen cubed hash browns
3	cups milk
3	tablespoons all-purpose flour
3	tablespoons chopped fresh parsley

In a large soup pot melt the butter. Add the onion and celery and sauté until transparent. Add the chicken stock, cubed chicken, salt, garlic powder, and celery salt. Bring the mixture to a boil. Add the carrots and hash browns, and cook for 5 minutes.

Blend in 2 1/2 cups of milk. Bring the soup to a boil. In a small bowl blend together the flour and remaining milk until smooth. Add to the soup, stirring constantly. Reduce the heat to low and simmer for 10 minutes. Garnish with parsley.

SERVES 6

Croutons

1	loaf day-old French bread
1/2	cup butter
1/2	teaspoon garlic salt

Cut the French bread into thick slices. Remove the crust. Cut each slice into 1-inch cubes. In a skillet melt the butter. Brown the bread cubes in the butter. Season with the garlic salt. Drain on paper towels. Let cool.

Corn Chowder

6	slices bacon
1/2	cup chopped onion
2	cups peeled and diced potatoes
2	10-ounce packages frozen whole corn
1	16-ounce can cream-style corn
1	tablespoon sugar
1	teaspoon Worcestershire sauce
1	cup water
1/2	teaspoon salt
1/4	teaspoon pepper

In a heavy skillet fry the bacon until crisp. Drain on paper towels. Cool and crumble. Set aside.

In the same skillet add the onion and potatoes to the bacon fat. Cook for 5 minutes. Drain well.

In a large saucepan combine the onion, potatoes, whole corn, cream-style corn, sugar, and Worcestershire sauce. Add the water. Blend thoroughly. Add the bacon. Season with salt and pepper. Cover and let simmer over low heat for 1½ to 2 hours.

SERVES 4

Oyster Stew

2	cups shelled oysters
1/4	cup butter
1/4	cup water
4	cups milk
1/4	teaspoon salt
	Pepper to taste
	Parsley

Drain the oysters, reserving the liquid. In a soup pot melt the butter. Add the oysters, reserved liquid, and water. Simmer over low heat until the oysters begin to curl.

In a saucepan scald the milk. Add to the soup and season with salt and pepper. Garnish with parsley.

SERVES 4

Ham Salad

1	head iceberg lettuce
3½	cups cooked ham, cubed
1	cup chopped celery
1	tablespoon fresh lemon juice
½	cup mayonnaise
1	tablespoon mustard
1	tablespoon chopped dill pickle
	Salt and pepper to taste

Wash the iceberg lettuce under cold running water. Pat dry with paper towels. Cut into bite-size strips and pieces. Set aside.

In a mixing bowl blend the ham with the celery, lemon juice, and mayonnaise. Mix thoroughly. Add the mustard and chopped dill pickle. Season with salt and pepper. Refrigerate 2 hours.

To serve, place scoops of ham mixture onto beds of shredded lettuce.

SERVES 6

Chef's Salad

4	cups salad greens
2	cups cooked ham, cut into strips
4	ounces Swiss cheese, sliced
2	cups diced cooked chicken
8	radishes, sliced
1	cucumber, peeled and sliced
2	large tomatoes, diced
4	hard-boiled eggs, quartered
	Salt and pepper to taste
	Favorite salad dressing

Wash the salad greens under cold running water. Pat dry with paper towels. Cut into bite-size strips and pieces.

Place the salad greens in the bottom of a large serving bowl. In the center place the strips of ham, cheese, and chicken.

Place the radishes, cucumber, and tomatoes around the cheese and meat. Top with quartered hard-boiled eggs. Season with salt and pepper. Serve with salad dressing.

SERVES 4

Crab Louis

½	head iceberg lettuce, shredded
1½	cups chilled crab meat
1	tomato, sliced
2	hard-boiled eggs, sliced
1	cup mayonnaise
1½	teaspoons minced onion
1	teaspoon horseradish
1	teaspoon lemon juice
½	cup chili sauce
	Salt and pepper to taste

In the bottom of a serving bowl arrange the shredded lettuce. Top with chilled crab meat. Place sliced tomato and sliced hard-boiled eggs around the crab meat. Refrigerate before serving. In a small bowl combine the remaining ingredients. Pour the dressing over the salad.

SERVES 4

PILGRIM DINER, SALEM, MASSACHUSETTS

Crab Salad

1   6-ounce can crab meat
2   tablespoons fresh lemon juice
1   cup minced celery
1   cup shredded iceberg lettuce
1/2 cup shredded watercress
1/2 cup shredded endive
1/2 cup sour cream
1/2 cup buttermilk
1/4 teaspoon salt
     Pepper to taste

In a mixing bowl drain and flake the crab meat. Pour fresh lemon juice over the top. Let stand.

In a separate bowl toss the celery with the iceberg lettuce, watercress, and endive. In a small bowl blend the sour cream and buttermilk. Add salt and pepper. Mix in the crab meat. Place over the shredded greens. Toss thoroughly. Refrigerate before serving.

SERVES 4

Crab-Stuffed Tomatoes

8   medium tomatoes
2   7-ounce cans crab meat
3/4 cup chopped celery
2   tablespoons chopped green bell pepper
2   hard-boiled eggs, sliced
     Mayonnaise
1/2 teaspoon salt
     Pepper to taste

Wash the tomatoes under cold running water. Slice in half and remove the centers. Place upside down on a plate and refrigerate.

In a mixing bowl drain and flake the crab meat. Add the celery, green pepper, and sliced hard-boiled eggs. Blend in enough mayonnaise to moisten. Add the salt and pepper. Mound the crab mixture into the center of the chilled tomatoes.

SERVES 8

Stuffed Tomato Salad

4	large tomatoes
2	cups chopped spinach
1/4	teaspoon garlic salt
1/4	teaspoon Worcestershire sauce
	Salt and pepper to taste
1	tablespoon butter
1/4	cup grated Parmesan cheese

Cut a slice from the stem end of each tomato. Scoop out and reserve the filling.

In a mixing bowl blend together the chopped spinach and tomato pulp. Add the garlic salt and Worcestershire sauce. Season with salt and pepper.

In a saucepan melt the butter. Blend in the grated Parmesan cheese. Add to the spinach mixture. Stuff the tomatoes with equal portions of the filling. Place the tomatoes in a baking dish. Bake at 350° for about 10 minutes.

SERVES 4

Shrimp & Crab Salad

1	large loaf French bread
1	large sweet onion, chopped
5	hard-boiled eggs, peeled and chopped
2	5-ounce cans shrimp, drained
1	7-ounce can crab meat
1	cup diced celery
1 1/2	cups mayonnaise
1 1/2	cups sour cream
	Lettuce leaves
2	cucumbers, peeled and sliced
1	pound cherry tomatoes

Remove the crust from the French bread and cut into cubes. In a large bowl blend the bread cubes with the onion and eggs. Cover and refrigerate overnight.

Add the shrimp, crab, celery, mayonnaise, and sour cream. Toss gently. Refrigerate for 3 hours. Serve on beds of lettuce leaves. Garnish with cucumber slices and cherry tomatoes.

SERVES 8

Molded Egg Salad

2	tablespoons gelatin
1/2	cup cold water
12	hard-boiled eggs
1	cup mayonnaise
3	tablespoons chopped green bell pepper
1	teaspoon salt
1/4	teaspoon pepper
1	tablespoon fresh lemon juice
	Vegetable oil

♦ ♦ ♦

3/4	cup salad oil
1 1/2	teaspoons salt
1/2	teaspoon dry mustard
1/2	cup chopped parsley
1/8	teaspoon pepper
	Tabasco sauce
2	teaspoons Worcestershire sauce
1/2	cup chili sauce
1	head iceberg lettuce, shredded

In a small bowl blend the gelatin with the cold water. Let stand for 10 minutes. Pour into a saucepan. Bring to a boil, and boil until all of the gelatin has dissolved.

Push the eggs through a sieve. Combine the eggs, mayonnaise, gelatin, green pepper, salt, pepper, and lemon juice. Mix thoroughly.

Coat a gelatin mold with a layer of vegetable oil. Fill with the egg mixture. Chill until the mold is set and firm.

In a mixing bowl blend together the remaining ingredients to make the dressing. Turn the mold out onto a bed of shredded lettuce. Top with dressing.

SERVES 4

Wash the iceberg lettuce under cold running water. Pat dry with paper towels. Cut into bite-sized strips and pieces.

In a mixing bowl combine the lettuce, carrots, cucumber, and scallions. Toss well. Season with salt and pepper. Top with salad dressing. Garnish with sliced radishes.

SERVES 4

Avocado Salad

1	head iceberg lettuce
2	ripe avocados
	Lemon juice
2	tomatoes, sliced
1	hard-boiled egg
1/2	cup chopped celery
	Salt and pepper

In a large bowl shred the iceberg lettuce into bite-size pieces. Peel the avocados. Remove the pits and slice. Sprinkle with lemon juice.

Place the avocados on top of the shredded lettuce. Arrange sliced tomatoes and egg over the avocado slices. Top with celery. Season with salt and pepper.

SERVES 4

House Salad

1	head iceberg lettuce
2	carrots, sliced
1	cucumber, peeled and diced
4	scallions, chopped
	Salt and pepper to taste
	Favorite salad dressing
6	radishes, sliced

Green Goddess Salad

1	head iceberg lettuce
	Watercress, chopped
2	tomatoes, sliced
1	medium onion, sliced
1/2	garlic clove, minced
1/2	cup mayonnaise
1/4	cup sour cream
4	anchovy fillets
1 1/2	teaspoons wine vinegar
1 1/2	teaspoons fresh lemon juice
	Parsley, chopped
2	cups chilled crab meat
	Salt and pepper to taste

Cut the iceberg lettuce into bite-size pieces. Arrange in the bottom of a large serving bowl. Add the chopped watercress, tomatoes, and sliced onion. Refrigerate.

In a separate bowl mix together the garlic, mayonnaise, sour cream, and anchovy fillets. Blend in the wine vinegar, fresh lemon juice, and parsley. Pour the dressing over the chilled salad. Top with crab meat. Season with salt and pepper.

SERVES 6

DAY AND NIGHT DINER

Situated in Palmer, Massachusetts, since 1941, the Day and Night Diner is "known primarily for its food." That's what owner Carl Cartizola says.

"We offer a special seasoned roast beef, whole clams with our fish and chips, and, of course, plenty of regular diner food," says Carl, who has owned and operated this classic Worcester Lunch Car in Palmer for nearly a decade.

What else might the diner be famous for? Well, says Carl, it is listed in the Library of Congress as a historic landmark. "Artist John Baeder once painted the diner, and some gentleman from Long Island bought the painting for $65,000."

Stuffed Lettuce Salad

3	ounces cream cheese, softened
3	tablespoons sour cream
	Worcestershire sauce to taste
1	teaspoon fresh lemon juice
1/4	teaspoon salt
3	tablespoons minced tomatoes
2	tablespoons grated carrot
1	tablespoon minced green bell pepper
1	tablespoon minced green onion
1	head iceberg lettuce

In a mixing bowl blend together the cream cheese and sour cream. Add Worcestershire sauce to taste, lemon juice, and salt. Mix thoroughly.

Fold in the tomatoes, carrot, green pepper, and onion. Slice the head of lettuce in half. Hollow out the center. Place the filling in the center. Wrap in aluminum foil. Refrigerate for 3 hours.

SERVES 2

Caesar Salad

¼ cup salad oil
¼ cup fresh lemon juice
¼ teaspoon Worcestershire sauce
3 garlic cloves, cut in half
  Endive
  Iceberg lettuce
  Romaine lettuce
  Watercress
2 tablespoons salad oil
2 slices sourdough bread, toasted
¾ cup grated Parmesan cheese
¼ teaspoon dry mustard
½ teaspoon salt
¼ teaspoon pepper

In a large mixing bowl blend together ¼ cup of salad oil, the lemon juice, Worcestershire sauce, and 2 garlic cloves. Refrigerate 1 hour.

Wash the endive, iceberg lettuce, romaine lettuce, and watercress under cold running water. Pat dry with paper towels. Tear into bite-size pieces. Refrigerate 1 hour.

Remove the garlic cloves from the chilled dressing after 1 hour. Set aside. Return the dressing to the refrigerator.

In a large skillet heat the 2 tablespoons of salad oil. Add the garlic from the dressing to the skillet. Trim the crusts from the sourdough bread. Cut the bread slices into cubes. Add to the skillet and cook until all sides are browned.

Rub a large wooden bowl with the remaining garlic clove. Place the salad greens inside the bowl. In a small bowl mix together the Parmesan cheese, dry mustard, salt, and pepper. Sprinkle over the salad greens. Add the toasted bread and dressing. Toss to coat.

SERVES 4

Firehouse Salad

½ cup raisins
¼ cup hot water
½ large head green cabbage, shredded
2 large apples, peeled and chopped
¼ cup roasted peanuts, chopped
½ cup mayonnaise
2 tablespoons vinegar
3 teaspoons sugar
  Salt to taste

In a mixing bowl soak the raisins in the hot water for 30 minutes. Drain. In a large mixing bowl combine the cabbage, apples, raisins, and peanuts. Toss together thoroughly.

In a separate bowl blend together mayonnaise, vinegar, and sugar. Season with salt. Toss the dressing with the cabbage-apple mixture. Chill before serving.

SERVES 4

Spinach Salad with Bacon Dressing

6   slices bacon
1   tablespoon bacon fat
1   tablespoon sugar
2   teaspoons cornstarch
¼   teaspoon salt
     Pepper to taste
¼   cup mayonnaise
½   cup water
¼   cup red wine vinegar
4   to 6 cups fresh spinach, washed
2   tablespoons minced onion

In a skillet fry the bacon until crisp. Drain on paper towels. Cool and crumble. Set aside. Reserve 1 tablespoon of bacon fat.

In the same skillet add to the bacon fat the sugar, cornstarch, salt, and pepper. Blend in the mayonnaise.

In a small bowl combine the water and red wine vinegar.

Slowly pour the mixture into the skillet. Cook over medium for 3 minutes, stirring constantly. In a serving bowl combine the spinach, onion, and bacon. Toss with the dressing until well coated.

SERVES 4

Bean Salad

⅔   cup vinegar
¾   cup sugar
⅔   cup salad oil
1   teaspoon salt
½   teaspoon coarse ground pepper
1   16-ounce can cut green beans
1   16-ounce can black beans
1   16-ounce can garbanzo beans
1   16-ounce can yellow wax beans
1   16-ounce can red kidney beans
½   cup chopped celery
½   cup chopped green bell peppers
½   cup chopped sweet onion
1   16-ounce can pitted black olives

In a mixing bowl combine the vinegar, sugar, oil, salt, and pepper. Refrigerate for 2 hours.

In a large mixing bowl combine the green beans, black beans, garbanzo beans, yellow wax beans, and kidney beans. Toss gently. Add the celery, green pepper, onion, and olives. Pour the chilled dressing over the salad. Toss and coat. Refrigerate overnight.

SERVES 8

Kidney Bean Salad

4   hard-boiled eggs, chopped
2   cups canned kidney beans
¼   cup sweet pickles, chopped
¼   cup finely chopped onion
¼   cup sweet pickle juice
½   cup mayonnaise

Salt and pepper to taste
1   small head iceberg lettuce, shredded

In a mixing bowl toss the chopped eggs with the kidney beans. Add the chopped sweet pickles, onion, and pickle juice, and toss gently. Add the mayonnaise, and toss to coat. Season with salt and pepper. Chill.

To serve, place equal amounts of salad on beds of crisp, shredded lettuce.

SERVES 4

CRESTMONT DINER, COATESVILLE, PENNSYLVANIA

Mega-Bean Salad

1   16-ounce can cut green beans
1   16-ounce can wax beans
1   16-ounce can red kidney beans
1   16-ounce can lima beans
1   16-ounce can peas
1/2 cup chopped cauliflower
1/2 cup chopped celery
1/2 cup chopped onion
1/2 cup chopped green bell pepper
1/4 cup pimientos, chopped
1 1/2 cups sugar
1/2 cup vegetable oil
1/2 teaspoon paprika
1   cup cider vinegar

Drain each can of beans. In a large bowl combine the green beans, wax beans, kidney beans, lima beans, and peas. Toss gently. Add the cauliflower, celery, onion, green peppers, and pimientos.

In a separate bowl blend together the sugar, oil, paprika, and vinegar. Pour over the beans and gently toss to coat. Cover and refrigerate for 12 hours.

SERVES 8

Macaroni Salad

1   pound macaroni shells
1   10-ounce package frozen peas
3/4 cup chopped onion
1   cup chopped dill pickles
1/4 teaspoon pepper
1   cup cubed Cheddar cheese
1/2 teaspoon salt
3/4 cup mayonnaise

Cook the macaroni according to the package directions. Drain well. Rinse the peas under cold running water in a colander. Drain.

In a mixing bowl toss the cooked macaroni with the peas. Add the onion, dill pickles, pepper, cheese, and salt. Blend in the mayonnaise, adding more if needed. Cover and refrigerate for 2 hours.

SERVES 6

Sauerkraut Salad

1¼   cups sugar
⅓   cup vinegar
½   cup salad oil
4   cups sauerkraut, drained
1   cup thinly sliced celery
1   large sweet onion, sliced thin
2   tablespoons chopped pimientos
1   cup finely chopped green bell pepper

In a small saucepan combine the sugar and vinegar. Bring to a boil over medium heat. Let boil for 1 minute. Remove the pan from the heat, and add the salad oil.

In a separate bowl add the vinegar mixture to the sauerkraut. Refrigerate overnight. Before serving toss in the celery, onion, pimentos, and green pepper.

SERVES 6

Sour Cream Salad

1   cup sliced cucumber
1   medium tomato, diced
1   cup chopped onion
1   tablespoon vinegar
1   tablespoon sugar
½   teaspoon salt
   Horseradish to taste
1   cup sour cream
   Pepper to taste

In a mixing bowl toss together the cucumber, tomato, and onion. Set aside.

In a separate bowl blend together the vinegar, sugar, salt, and horseradish. Add the sour cream and blend thoroughly. Add the mixture to the vegetables and toss to coat. Season with pepper. Chill before serving.

SERVES 4

Baked Potato Salad

6   medium potatoes
6   slices bacon
½   cup mayonnaise
1   cup sour cream
½   cup finely chopped chives
½   teaspoon salt
¼   teaspoon pepper
½   teaspoon paprika

Scrub the potatoes and bake. Let cool. Cut into 1-inch cubes. Set aside.

In a skillet fry the bacon until crisp. Drain on paper towels. Cool and crumble. Set aside.

In a mixing bowl blend together the mayonnaise, sour cream, chives, salt, and pepper. Add the potatoes and bacon. Toss gently to coat. Garnish with paprika.

SERVES 4

Sweet Pea Salad

4   slices bacon
2   20-ounce packages frozen peas
½   cup chopped cashews
¼   cup finely chopped sweet onion
2   cups finely chopped celery
½   cup mayonnaise
½   cup sour cream

In a heavy skillet fry the bacon until crisp. Drain on paper towels. Let cool and crumble. Set aside.

In a mixing bowl combine the peas, cashews, onion, and celery. Toss well. Add the crumbled bacon.

In a small mixing bowl blend together the mayonnaise and sour cream. Mix

KENWOOD DINER, SPENCER, MASSACHUSETTS

thoroughly. Pour the dressing into the pea mixture and toss gently just to coat. Refrigerate before serving.

SERVES 4

Sour Cream Potato Salad

7	medium red potatoes, peeled and sliced
1/3	cup Italian dressing
3/4	cup sliced celery
1/3	cup sliced green onions
4	hard-boiled eggs
1	cup mayonnaise
1/2	cup sour cream

1	teaspoon mustard
	Salt and pepper to taste
1/4	cup peeled and diced cucumber

In a large pot cook the potatoes until they are thoroughly done. Drain. Pour the Italian dressing over the potatoes while they are still warm. Add the celery and green onions. Chill for 2 hours.

Chop the egg whites. Mash the egg yolks. In a small bowl combine the mayonnaise, sour cream, egg whites, egg yolks, and mustard. Season with salt and pepper. Pour the dressing over the potatoes and coat thoroughly. Refrigerate for 2 hours. Add the cucumbers just before serving.

SERVES 6

Vegetable Salad

2	tomatoes
1	cucumber, peeled and sliced
6	radishes, chopped
2	celery stalks, chopped
6	large black olives, chopped
1/4	cup chopped walnuts
3	tablespoons vegetable oil
6	tablespoons red wine vinegar
	Salt and pepper to taste

Wash the tomatoes under cold running water. Peel off the skins. Cut the tomatoes into 8 wedges.

In a mixing bowl toss together the tomatoes, cucumber, radishes, celery, olives, and walnuts.

In a small bowl blend together the vegetable oil and red wine vinegar. Pour over the vegetables and toss thoroughly to coat. Season with salt and pepper.

SERVES 4

Potato Salad

2	pounds small red potatoes
1/4	cup mayonnaise
1/2	cup sour cream
1/2	package ranch-style salad dressing mix
3	hard-boiled eggs, peeled and chopped
2	celery stalks, sliced thin
3	tablespoons finely chopped green onions

In a large pot boil the unpeeled potatoes in 2 quarts of salted water until tender.

Do not overcook. Drain and let cool. Cut into 1-inch cubes. Refrigerate.

In a mixing bowl combine the mayonnaise, sour cream, and ranch-style salad dressing mix. Blend thoroughly. Set aside.

In a separate bowl toss the eggs with the celery, green onions, and potatoes. Add the mayonnaise mixture. Toss with the potatoes to coat. Refrigerate for 3 hours.

SERVES 6

Annie's Homeslaw

1	small head cabbage, shredded
1	celery stalk, sliced thin
2	carrots, grated
1	tablespoon grated sweet onion
1/2	cup mayonnaise
3/4	teaspoon celery salt
1/8	teaspoon pepper
1 1/2	tablespoons sugar
1	teaspoon dry mustard
1/2	cup sour cream
2	tablespoons fresh lemon juice

In a large mixing bowl toss together the cabbage, celery, carrots, and sweet onion. Set aside.

In a separate bowl blend together the mayonnaise, celery salt, pepper, sugar, and dry mustard. Add the sour cream and fresh lemon juice. Mix thoroughly. Add to the cabbage mixture. Toss to coat. Refrigerate before serving.

SERVES 4

Home-Style Coleslaw

1	medium head green cabbage
1	small head red cabbage
4	celery stalks, chopped fine
6	green onions, chopped fine
5	carrots, shredded
1	cup mayonnaise
1/4	cup fresh lemon juice
1/4	teaspoon salt
	Pepper to taste

Shred the green and red cabbage. In a large bowl combine the cabbages. Cover with ice water and chill for 1 hour. Drain thoroughly.

In a separate bowl toss the cabbage with the celery, onions, and carrots.

Mix together the mayonnaise, lemon juice, and salt. Pour the dressing over the cabbage and toss to coat. Refrigerate for 1 hour before serving. Season with pepper.

SERVES 4

Tropical Fruit Salad

1	cup shredded coconut
1	cup crushed pineapple
1/2	cup mandarin orange slices
32	miniature marshmallows
1	cup seedless grapes
1	banana, sliced
2	tablespoons fresh lemon juice
1/4	cup pineapple juice
1	cup sour cream

In a large bowl blend together the coconut, pineapple, mandarin orange slices, marshmallows, and grapes.

In a separate bowl sprinkle the sliced banana with the lemon juice. Add the banana to the coconut mixture. Toss together.

Add the pineapple juice to the sour cream. Pour the dressing over the fruit, and toss gently until the fruit is coated. Refrigerate before serving.

SERVES 4

Fruit Salad

2 1/2	cups honeydew melon
1	cup strawberries
1	cup tangerine slices
1/2	cup blueberries
1/2	cup honey
1/2	cup water
1/4	teaspoon cardamom
1	teaspoon fresh mint, crushed
1	tablespoon fresh lemon juice
1/2	cup sherry

Wash the fruit under cold running water. Cut the honeydew melon in half. Remove the seeds and pulp. Scoop out the inside with a melon ball cutter. Remove the stems from the strawberries and cut in half. Remove the seeds from the tangerine slices. Place the melon, berries, and tangerine slices in a bowl and toss.

In a saucepan mix the honey with the water and cardamom. Simmer for 5 minutes. Add the mint and remove the pan from the heat. Strain through a cheesecloth. Add the lemon juice and sherry. Pour over the fruit and toss gently. Refrigerate for 1 hour before serving.

SERVES 6

94

Pineapple Salad

1   cup pineapple juice
2   tablespoons all-purpose flour
½   cup butter
2   tablespoons sugar
    Pinch salt
1   egg, slightly beaten
    Fresh lemon juice
4   slices pineapple, diced
2   oranges, peeled and sectioned
¼   cup chopped walnuts
20 miniature marshmallows
8   maraschino cherries, sliced
2   cups whipped cream

In a large bowl blend together half of the pineapple juice with the flour to make a paste. Slowly add the remaining pineapple juice. Add the butter, sugar, and a pinch of salt.

Place the mixture in the top of a double boiler. Cook over simmering water for 10 minutes. Add the slightly beaten egg, and continue cooking for 2 minutes, stirring constantly. Cool.

Blend in fresh lemon juice. Pour the mixture into a serving bowl. Add the pineapple, oranges, walnuts, marshmallows, and maraschino cherries. Fold in the whipped cream. Chill thoroughly.

SERVES 4

Waldorf Salad

1   small head cabbage, shredded
2   apples, peeled and diced
1   tablespoon fresh lemon juice
½   cup chopped celery
¼   cup raisins
¼   cup chopped walnuts
½   cup mayonnaise

TUMBLE INN DINER, CLAREMONT, NEW HAMPSHIRE

SILVER TOP DINER, PROVIDENCE, RHODE ISLAND

1   tablespoon sugar
1½   tablespoons apple cider vinegar
⅛   teaspoon celery salt

Rinse the cabbage under cold running water. Pat dry with paper towels. Refrigerate.

In a mixing bowl toss the apples with the lemon juice. Add the celery, raisins, and walnuts.

In a separate bowl blend together the mayonnaise, sugar, vinegar, and celery salt. Blend thoroughly. Add the dressing to the apple mixture. Add the shredded cabbage. Refrigerate 2 hours before serving.

SERVES 4

Cranberry Mold

2   envelopes unflavored gelatin
¼   cup cold water
1   cup boiling water

2   cups cranberry sauce
½   cup light corn syrup
¼   cup orange juice
      Salt to taste
¼   cup diced apple
      Mayonnaise
      Lettuce

In a small bowl dissolve the gelatin in the cold water, stirring constantly. Add to the boiling water.

In a separate bowl mix the gelatin with all but ¼ cup of cranberry sauce. Add the corn syrup, orange juice, and salt.

Pour into a mold. Refrigerate until the mixture is somewhat firm.

Add the apples. Refrigerate again until the salad is set. Mix the remaining cranberry sauce with the mayonnaise. Serve on beds of lettuce topped with cranberry sauce.

SERVES 8

Molded Fruit Salad

1	envelope unflavored gelatin
1/4	cup cold water
6	ounces cream cheese, softened
1/4	teaspoon salt
2	tablespoons Fruit Salad Dressing (see recipe at right)
1	tablespoon fresh lemon juice
1/2	cup pineapple chunks
1/2	cup maraschino cherries, sliced
1/2	cup chopped walnuts
2	bananas, sliced
1/2	cup miniature marshmallows, sliced
1/2	cup whipping cream

In a small bowl dissolve the gelatin in the water. Set aside. In a mixing bowl mash the cream cheese with a fork. Add the salt, fruit salad dressing, and fresh lemon juice. Blend thoroughly. Add the gelatin.

Fold in the pineapple chunks, maraschino cherries, walnuts, bananas, and marshmallows. Add the whipping cream.

Pour the mixture into a mold. Refrigerate until set. Serve with Fruit Salad Dressing.

SERVES 6

Fruit Salad Dressing

1/2	cup sugar
1	cup unsweetened pineapple juice
1	cup cold water
1	tablespoon cornstarch
1/8	teaspoon salt
1	tablespoon frozen orange juice concentrate
1	egg yolk
1/3	cup whipping cream

In the top of a double boiler over simmering water combine the sugar, pineapple juice, water, cornstarch, salt, and orange juice concentrate. Cook until thick. Beat the egg yolk with a small amount of the mixture. Return to the dressing.

Cook over low heat until the dressing becomes creamy. Let cool. Blend in the whipping cream. Refrigerate until ready to use.

MAKES ABOUT 2½ CUPS

Avocado Dressing

1	ripe avocado
1	cup mayonnaise
1	teaspoon fresh lemon juice
	Salt and pepper to taste

Peel the avocado. Remove the pit and scoop out the center. In a mixing bowl mash the avocado with a fork. Add the mayonnaise, lemon juice, salt, and pepper. Add more mayonnaise as desired. Blend thoroughly. Refrigerate until ready to use.

MAKES ABOUT 2 CUPS

Blue Cheese Dressing

1	cup mayonnaise
1/2	cup sour cream
1/2	cup blue cheese, crumbled
2	tablespoons vinegar
1	teaspoon Worcestershire sauce
1	tablespoon sugar
1/2	teaspoon salt
	Pepper to taste

In a mixing bowl blend together the mayonnaise, sour cream, and blue cheese. Add the vinegar, Worcestershire sauce, sugar, salt, and pepper. Blend thoroughly. Refrigerate until ready to use.

MAKES ABOUT 2 CUPS

French Dressing

3/4	cup sugar
1/8	teaspoon garlic powder
1/2	teaspoon salt
1/4	teaspoon pepper
1	10-ounce can condensed tomato soup
1/4	cup vinegar
1	tablespoon dry mustard
1	tablespoon celery seed
1	teaspoon paprika
1	cup vegetable oil

In a blender combine the sugar, garlic powder, salt, pepper, tomato soup, vinegar, dry mustard, celery seed, and paprika. Blend well.

In a saucepan heat the vegetable oil to lukewarm. Remove the pan from the heat, and add the tomato mixture. Blend until smooth. Refrigerate until ready to use.

MAKES ABOUT 2 1/2 CUPS

Poppy Seed Dressing

1 1/2	teaspoons sugar
2	teaspoons dry mustard
1/4	teaspoon salt
2/3	cup cider vinegar
3	tablespoons onion juice
2	cups vegetable oil
3	tablespoons poppy seeds

In a mixing bowl combine the sugar, mustard, salt, vinegar, and onion juice. Mix thoroughly. Slowly add the vegetable oil and beat until smooth. Add the poppy seeds. Mix well. Refrigerate until ready to use.

MAKES ABOUT 3 CUPS

Russian Dressing

1/2	cup sugar
1/2	cup ketchup
1/2	teaspoon salt
1	small onion, grated
1	cup salad oil
1/4	cup vinegar

In a mixing bowl blend together the sugar and ketchup. Add the salt, onion, salad oil, and vinegar, and blend thoroughly. Refrigerate until ready to use.

MAKES ABOUT 2 CUPS

CORNER LUNCH, WORCESTER, MASSACHUSETTS

Roquefort Dressing

²/₃ cup evaporated milk
4 ounces Roquefort cheese
¹/₄ teaspoon pepper
2 garlic cloves, minced
¹/₂ teaspoon salt
I teaspoon celery seed
2 cups mayonnaise
I cup buttermilk

In a saucepan add the evaporated milk with the Roquefort cheese, pepper, garlic, salt, and the celery seed.

Cook over low heat until the cheese has melted, stirring constantly. Let cool. Add the mayonnaise and buttermilk. Mix well. Refrigerate until ready to use.

MAKES ABOUT 4½ CUPS

Sour Cream Dressing

¹/₂ teaspoon dry mustard
¹/₂ teaspoon salt
I tablespoon all-purpose flour
I tablespoon sugar
¹/₄ cup vinegar
¹/₄ cup water
I egg yolk
I cup sour cream

In the top of a double boiler over simmering water blend together the mustard, salt, flour, and sugar. Slowly blend in the vinegar and water. Stir constantly until thickened. Add a teaspoon of the mixture to the egg yolk. Mix and return to the double boiler. Cook for 1 minute. Fold in the sour cream and blend thoroughly. Refrigerate until ready to use.

MAKES ABOUT 1½ CUPS

Seafood Dressing

1/2	cup mayonnaise
1/2	cup chili sauce
1	teaspoon Worcestershire sauce
1	teaspoon horseradish
3	sweet pickles, diced
1	celery stalk, diced
2	green onions, minced
	Salt and pepper to taste

In a mixing bowl blend together the mayonnaise and chili sauce. Add the Worcestershire sauce, horseradish, pickles, celery, and onions, and blend thoroughly. Season with salt and pepper. Refrigerate until ready to use.

MAKES ABOUT 2 CUPS

Thousand Island Dressing

1	cup mayonnaise
1/3	cup chili sauce
2	tablespoons minced green bell pepper
1	tablespoon minced onion

In a mixing bowl blend together the mayonnaise and chili sauce. Add the green pepper and onion and blend thoroughly. Refrigerate until ready to use.

MAKES ABOUT 1 1/3 CUPS

Mels

DINER

DEEP DISH PIES MADE WITH
    BOYSENBERRY, PEACH, C

MELS FAMOUS CAKES, PER C

OTHER PIES: APPLE, APRICOT
    COCOANUT, LEMON CRE.

FRESH STRAWBERRY SHORT
    Either kind delicious a la mode

Fruits

TOMATO JUICE . . .

GRAPEFRUIT JUICE . .

FRESH ORANGE JUICE .

SLICED PEACHES OR PINEAP

PRUNES . . . . .

DOUGHNUTS . . . .

COFFEE CAKE, ASSORTED

FULL ORDER TOAST, BUTTER

CINNAMON TOAST, BUTTER

Egg

TWO EGGS — FRIED OR SCR
    TOAST, JELLY, BUTTER

PLAIN OMELETTE, POTATOE

CHEESE OMELETTE, POTATO

HAM OMELETTE, POTATOES,
    (All Eggs Fried

Bakery

RUIT,
PPLE 30
. . . .20
Y, BERRY . . .20
. . .50

v Gold Ice Cream, 10¢ extra

Juices

ALL	.15 — LARGE	.25
ALL	.15 — LARGE	.25
ALL	.15 — LARGE	.25
.	. . .	.30
.	. . .	.25
ONE	.10 — TWO	.20
.	. . .	.20
Y	. . .	.15
Y	. . .	.25

...hes

POTATOES,
. 60

IAM AND TWO EGGS,
OTATOES, TOAST, JELLY
ND BUTTER . . 1.15

ACON WITH TWO EGGS,
OTATOES, TOAST, JELLY
ND BUTTER . . 1.15

ITTLE PIG SAUSAGES
VITH TWO EGGS,
OTATOES, TOAST
ND BUTTER . . 1.15

AND BUTTER . . .75
AND BUTTER . . .85
ND BUTTER . . 1.15
amery Butter)

Fountain Specials

THICK MALTS	.40
THICK MILK SHAKES . .	.35
ICE CREAM SODA . . .	.35
ROOT BEER or COCA-COLA FLOAT	.30
FROSTED ROOT BEER or COCA-COLA	.35
COCA-COLA — Large Glass . .	.15
ROOT BEER — Large Glass . .	.15
LIMEADE, LEMONADE or ORANGEADE — Large . .	.25

Ice Cream & Sundaes

ICE CREAM — TWO SCOOPS 25
DE LUXE HOT FUDGE SUNDAE 60
(With whipped cream and chopped nuts)
PINEAPPLE SUNDAE WITH NUTS AND WHIPPED CREAM . .50
FRESH STRAWBERRY SUNDAE,
WITH NUTS AND WHIPPED CREAM 50
CHOCOLATE SUNDAE, WITH NUTS AND WHIPPED CREAM . .50
MARSHMALLOW SUNDAE,
WITH NUTS AND WHIPPED CREAM 50
STRAWBERRY SHORTCAKE WITH WHIPPED CREAM . . .50
BANANA SPLIT 75
Three scoops ice cream, whole banana, assorted crushed fruits, whipped cream and chopped nuts.
BLACK AND WHITE 50
Chocolate and vanilla ice cream topped with marshmallow, chocolate syrup, whipped cream and nuts.

Beverages

TEA — HOT OR ICED			.15
HOT CHOCOLATE			.20
ORANGE JUICE	SMALL	.15 — LARGE	.25
GRAPEFRUIT JUICE . . .	SMALL	.15 — LARGE	.25
TOMATO JUICE . . .	SMALL	.15 — LARGE	.25
MILK			.15
CHOCOLATE MILK			.20
BUTTERMILK			.15

CALMAR PRINTING 500 SANSOME ST.

Salads

Chef's salad bowl topped with avocado, asparagus tips, diced ham, cheese and choice of dressing 85

AVOCADO SALAD WITH SLICED TOMATOES,
   CHOICE OF DRESSING 90
PINEAPPLE OR PEACH AND COTTAGE CHEESE SALAD,
   CHOICE OF DRESSING 85
POTATO SALAD (LARGE ORDER) WITH SLICED TOMATOES . .50
POTATO SALAD (SIDE ORDER) WITH SLICED TOMATOES . .35
FRUIT SALAD, MIXED FRUIT TOPPED WITH WHIPPED
   CREAM AND NUTS 95
STUFFED TOMATO WITH TUNA OR CHICKEN SALAD . . .95
STUFFED AVOCADO WITH TUNA OR CHICKEN SALAD . . 1.25
COLESLAW (SIDE ORDER) 25

Soups

CLAM CHOWDER, FRIDAY ONLY . . . . . } .15 PER CUP
CHICKEN NOODLE . . . . } .25
GREEN SPLIT PEA . . . . } PER BOWL

Home-made Chili Specials

CHILI WITHOUT BEANS 50
CHILI WITH BEANS 45
CHILI WITH SPAGHETTI 75
CHILI WITH HOT TAMALE 75
CHILI WITH SCRAMBLED EGGS 90
CHILI SIZE (hamburger patty with chili and beans) . .85
ITALIAN SPAGHETTI 75

From Mels Bakery

DEEP DISH PIES MADE WITH FRESH FRUIT,
   BOYSENBERRY, PEACH, CHERRY, APPLE 30
MELS FAMOUS CAKES, PER CUT 20
OTHER PIES: APPLE, PEACH, CHERRY, BERRY
   COCOANUT, PUMPKIN, PER CUT 20
FRESH STRAWBERRY SHORTCAKE 50
   Either kind delicious a la mode with Meadow Gold Ice Cream 10¢ extra

Our F

Specia
CH

HALF FRIED SPRING
CHICKEN . . . 1.6?
(Like mother used to make.) Fried
a golden brown and served unjoint
with giblet gravy. Plenty of shoestri
potatoes, coleslaw, roll and butter.

FRIED JUMBO PRA
Served on toast. Shoestring pe

FISH AND CHIPS
. 95
Served on toast. Filet of Halibut,
shoestring potatoes, coleslaw,
tartar sauce.

GROUND ROUND F
Vegetable, shoestring potatoes

SPECIAL MINUTE S
Grilled onions, salad, shoestrin

BREADED VEAL CU
Country gravy, shoestring pota

CHILD'S PLATE (Ch
Choice of beef, ham or turkey

cy . . .

MELS INDIVIDUAL POT PIE . . .95

e . . . baked in our own kitchen
rved with salad, roll and butter

The Famous Melburger

Made only as we know how . . . large patty of Freshly Ground Steer Beef, served on specially Toasted Bun, with crisp lettuce, tomato, topped with our own delicious mustard barbecue relish.

GRILLED OR RAW ONION .50

WITH CHEESE 60

ST YOUNG TURKEY . . . 1.45

s portions of white and dark meat, sage
giblet gravy, potatoes, cranberry sauce,
e, roll and butter.

. . . . 1.50

w, horseradish and mustard sauce.

. . . . 1.25

r.

. . . . 1.25

and butter.

. . . . 1.25

d, roll and butter.

nder 12 only) . .75

and vegetable.

Sandwiches

BARBECUED BEEF OR HAM SANDWICH 65
Served on a bun with shoestring potatoes

HOT — SERVED ON TOAST (UNLESS OTHERWISE ORDERED) — COLD

HOT		COLD	
STEAK 80		HAM OR BEEF 65	
BACON OR HAM AND EGG .65		CHICKEN SALAD 45	
PORE BOY 75		DEVILED EGG 40	
(With Potato Salad)		LIVERWURST ON RYE . .45	
DENVER 70		TUNA 55	
DUTCH TREAT 70		BACON AND TOMATO .60	
(Ham and melted cheese)		LETTUCE AND TOMATO . .45	
GRILLED CHEESE 40		PEANUT BUTTER 40	
HOT DOG 45		SLICED CHICKEN . . .75	
FRIED EGG 40		(All white meat .85)	
HOT BEEF OR HAM .95		CHEESE 40	
(Vegetable, Potatoes, Gravy)		(Swiss or American)	
HOT TURKEY . . . 1.00		HOT BARBECUED TURKEY .70	
(Vegetable, Potatoes, Gravy)			

HOT CORNED BEEF ON RYE, DILL PICKLE . . .65

LARGE ORDER OF SHOESTRING POTATOES 25

3-Deck Club

No. 1 — SLICED CHICKEN, BACON, TOMATO, LETTUCE
MAYONNAISE 1.00

No. 2 — AVOCADO, BACON
TOMATO, LETTUCE
MAYONNAISE 1.00

No. 3 — HAM, CHEESE, TOMATO,
LETTUCE, MAYONNAISE . . 1.00

No. 4 — SLICED CHICKEN, AVOCADO, TOMATO,
LETTUCE, MAYONNAISE 1.00

No. 5 — PEANUT BUTTER, JELLY, LETTUCE, MAYONNAISE . .65

SANDWICH PLATTERS

Grilled American Cheese Sandwich

Butter, softened
Parmesan cheese, grated
8   slices sourdough bread
8   slices American cheese
8   slices Swiss cheese

Blend grated Parmesan cheese into the butter. Butter the slices of sourdough bread. Top the unbuttered side of the bread with slices of American and Swiss cheese. Place another slice of bread butter side out on top of the cheese.

Melt enough butter to coat the bottom of a skillet. Grill each sandwich until the cheese has melted and the bread becomes lightly browned.

SERVES 4

Grilled Ham & Cheese Shandwich

3   tablespoons mustard
¼   cup mayonnaise
4   slices ham, ½-inch thick
    Butter
8   slices sourdough bread
4   slices sharp Cheddar cheese,
      ¼-inch thick
¼   teaspoon horseradish (optional)

In a small mixing bowl blend together the mustard and mayonnaise. Spread the mixture onto each of the ham slices. Butter one side of each slice of bread. Place 4 slices of bread butter side down on the grill or in a skillet. Place a slice of ham on top of the bread. Top each with a slice of Cheddar cheese. Place another slice of bread butter side out on top of the cheese. Grill until the cheese has melted and the bread becomes lightly browned.

SERVES 4

Denver Sandwich

8   slices sourdough bread

2   tablespoons butter

1/4 cup finely chopped onion

1/4 cup finely chopped green bell pepper

4   eggs

1/2 cup finely chopped cooked ham

1/4 teaspoon salt

    Pepper to taste

Lightly toast the sourdough bread. In a medium skillet melt the butter to coat the bottom of the pan. Sauté the onion with the green pepper until the onion becomes transparent. Remove from the skillet.

In a small bowl beat the eggs. Add the chopped ham and salt. Season with pepper.

Pour the eggs into the skillet and cook over low heat until they are set. Cut into 4 sections. Place on sourdough bread. Top with sautéed onions and green pepper.

SERVES 4

SISSON'S DINER, NEW BEDFORD, MASSACHUSETTS

Monte Cristo #1

3	eggs, well beaten
1	cup milk
1/8	teaspoon salt
8	slices white bread
3	tablespoons butter, melted
4	thick slices Cheddar cheese
4	slices cooked chicken
4	thick slices Monterey Jack cheese
1/4	cup cooking oil

In a flat baking dish combine the beaten eggs, milk, and salt. Spread 4 slices of the bread with butter. Top with Cheddar cheese, cooked chicken, and Monterey Jack cheese. Cover with remaining slices of bread.

Dip the sandwiches carefully into the egg mixture. In a skillet heat the oil. Grill the sandwiches evenly on both sides or until they are light golden brown.

SERVES 4

Monte Cristo #2

12	slices sourdough bread
	Mayonnaise
12	slices Swiss cheese
6	slices cooked ham
6	slices cooked chicken
	Salt and pepper to taste
2	eggs, lightly beaten
1/2	cup milk
1/4	cup butter

Spread one side of each slice of sourdough bread with mayonnaise. Top half the slices of bread with 2 slices of Swiss cheese, 1 slice of cooked ham, and 1 slice of cooked chicken. Season with salt and pepper to taste. Top with the remaining slices of bread.

Cut the sandwiches diagonally. In a flat baking dish combine the eggs with the milk. Season with salt and pepper. Coat the sandwiches in the egg batter.

In a skillet melt the butter so that it coats the bottom of the pan. Grill the sandwiches on both sides until they are light brown. Place them on an ungreased baking sheet. Bake at 400 degrees for 3 minutes or until the cheese begins to melt.

SERVES 6

Patty Melt

1	pound lean ground beef
1/2	teaspoon salt
1/2	teaspoon pepper
2	teaspoons vegetable oil
1	large onion, sliced thin
1	tablespoon butter
8	slices rye bread
4	slices Monterey Jack cheese

In a mixing bowl combine the ground beef with the salt and pepper. Shape into rounded patties.

In a skillet fry the patties for 4 minutes until brown on both sides. Remove from the skillet. Add the oil to the skillet and sauté the onions until lightly browned.

Butter each slice of rye bread. Grill in the skillet. Remove and top with sliced onion, a beef patty, and a slice of cheese. Place under the broiler 5 inches away from the heat. Broil for 2 minutes or until the cheese melts. Top with the remaining grilled bread.

SERVES 4

Johnny's Tuna Melt

1	9-ounce can Albacore tuna, drained
5	tablespoons mayonnaise
3	tablespoons chopped onion
3	tablespoons chopped celery
1	tablespoon chopped black olives
3	teaspoons fresh lemon juice
	Salt and pepper to taste
	Butter
4	slices sourdough bread
	Parmesan cheese
	Cheddar cheese

In a mixing bowl drain and flake the tuna. Add the mayonnaise and blend thoroughly. Add the chopped onion, celery, and black olives, and mix until blended. Add the lemon juice. Season with salt and pepper.

Butter each slice of bread. Sprinkle Parmesan cheese over the top of the butter. Spread together so that they are well blended.

Place a slice of bread butter-side-down in a cold skillet. Top with slices of Cheddar cheese and tuna mixture. Place another slice of bread butter-side-up on top of the tuna. Grill until the cheese has melted and the bread becomes lightly browned.

SERVES 2

BLT Sandwich

12	slices bacon
8	slices sourdough bread
1/4	cup mayonnaise
4	lettuce leaves
2	large tomatoes, sliced
3	tablespoons butter

In a heavy skillet fry the bacon until crisp. Drain on paper towels. Cool and set aside.

Spread one side of 4 slices of bread with the mayonnaise. Arrange one lettuce leaf on each slice of bread. Place slices of tomato on top of the lettuce leaf. Place 3 slices of bacon on top of the tomato. Spread the butter on the remaining bread slices. Top the sandwich with the buttered bread.

SERVES 4

French Dip

1	package au jus mix
4	hard rolls
1	pound cooked roast beef, sliced thin

Prepare the au jus mix according to package directions. Use any available beef drippings off the roast as part of the gravy.

Toast the rolls and split. Place slices of roast beef on the bottom half of each roll. Dip the remaining half in the au jus. Place on top of the sliced roast beef. Serve each sandwich with a bowl of au jus on the side for dipping.

SERVES 4

Philly Cheesesteak

I	pound beef sirloin
2	tablespoons vegetable oil
4	French rolls, 6 inches long
2	large onions, sliced thin
½	teaspoon salt
¼	teaspoon pepper
4	slices American cheese

Partially freeze the sirloin to make it easier to slice across the grain. Slice the meat very thin. In a heavy skillet heat the vegetable oil. Fry the steak quickly. Remove when the meat begins to brown.

Warm the French rolls in a 250° oven for 5 minutes.

Add onions to the skillet and sauté until light brown. Drain. Season the meat and onions with salt and pepper.

Slice the rolls in half lengthwise. Place slices of sirloin in each. Top with onions and cheese. Serve hot.

SERVES 4

Corned Beef Sandwich

I	cup chopped corned beef
½	cup finely chopped celery
I	teaspoon minced onion
I	tablespoon mustard
2	tablespoons mayonnaise
8	slices sourdough bread

In a small mixing bowl combine the corned beef, celery, and onion. Blend in the mustard and mayonnaise.

Toast the sourdough bread until light brown. Spread the corned beef mixture on half of the toasted bread. Top with the remaining bread.

SERVES 4

EMPIRE DINER, NEW YORK, NEW YORK

Grilled Steak Sandwich

1	tablespoon cooking oil
¾	pound beef sirloin, sliced ¼-inch thick
1	yellow bell pepper
½	pound sliced fresh mushrooms
1	onion, sliced
4	round rolls
⅓	cup ketchup
2	tablespoons teriyaki sauce
½	teaspoon light brown sugar
1	tomato, sliced

In a skillet heat the oil. Cook the sliced beef sirloin for 8 minutes or until done. Remove the steak and set aside.

In the same skillet sauté the yellow bell pepper, mushrooms, and onion until tender. Remove the vegetables and set aside.

Split the rolls in half. Place on a baking sheet. Broil for 1 minute or until toasted. Set aside. In the same skillet combine the ketchup, teriyaki sauce, and brown sugar. Blend thoroughly. Return the steak and vegetables to the skillet. Cook until thoroughly heated. Place a slice of tomato on half of each roll. Top with the steak-pepper mixture. Top with the remaining slices of bread.

SERVES 4

Barbecue Beef Sandwich

2	tablespoons vegetable oil
5	pounds beef roast, rolled and tied
2	garlic cloves, chopped fine
2	celery stalks, chopped
2	large onions, chopped
1	cup ketchup
1	16-ounce can whole tomatoes
⅓	cup packed light brown sugar
¼	cup cider vinegar
1	teaspoon chili powder
½	teaspoon cinnamon
½	teaspoon oregano leaves
½	teaspoon basil
½	teaspoon salt
½	teaspoon Liquid Smoke
8	hard rolls

In a large soup pot heat the oil. Brown the roast beef on all sides over medium heat. Remove and set aside.

Add the garlic, celery, and onions to the vegetable oil and sauté until the onions are transparent. Blend in the ketchup, tomatoes, brown sugar, vinegar, and chili powder. Mix thoroughly.

Add the cinnamon, oregano leaves, basil, salt, and Liquid Smoke. Return the cooked roast beef to the pot. Spoon the sauce over the top of the roast. Cover and bake at 325° for 3 hours or until the meat is tender.

Approximately 2 hours before serving remove the fat from the surface of the sauce. Remove the meat and slice thin. Return the meat to the pot. Place the sauce between the layers of meat. Return to a 350° oven and cook for 50 minutes. Serve on rolls.

SERVES 8

Roast Beef Sandwich

1	4-pound chuck roast, oven-baked
½	cup meat drippings
1	medium onion, chopped fine
½	cup ketchup
3	tablespoons sugar
3	tablespoons vinegar
1	tablespoon mustard
1	tablespoon Worcestershire sauce
1	tablespoon celery seed
8	hard rolls
	Mayonnaise
	Lettuce leaves
8	slices Swiss cheese

Slice the cooked roast. Set aside.

In a saucepan combine the meat drippings with the onion, ketchup, sugar, vinegar, mustard, Worcestershire sauce, and celery seed. Simmer for 1 hour. Stir often to keep the sauce well blended.

Cut open the rolls and spread with mayonnaise. Add a crisp lettuce leaf. Place a generous amount of the roast beef into the center. Top with a slice of Swiss cheese. Pour the sauce over the meat.

SERVES 8

Steak Sandwich

3	tablespoons cooking oil
1	pound beef steak
½	teaspoon salt
1	garlic clove, minced
1	tablespoon chopped parsley
½	cup chopped mushrooms
½	cup ketchup
6	hard rolls

In a heavy skillet heat the oil so that it coats the bottom of the pan. Cook the beef steak until tender. Drain off the fat. Shred the meat and return it to the skillet. Add the salt, garlic, parsley, mushrooms, and ketchup. Cover and simmer for 10 minutes. Split the rolls open and spoon the meat mixture into the center.

SERVES 6

Big Beef Sandwich

3	pounds round steak, 2 inches thick
	Meat tenderizer
½	cup butter, softened
2	tablespoons mustard
1	tablespoon horseradish
	Salt and pepper to taste
8	hard rolls
	Lettuce
1	medium tomato, sliced
16	slices Swiss cheese
	Beef drippings

Remove the fat from the round steak. Use the meat tenderizer according to the package directions. Broil the round steak for 20 minutes, making sure the meat is done but not overcooked.

In a small bowl blend together the butter, mustard, and horseradish. Season with salt and pepper.

Split the rolls and toast them. Spread each half with the mustard sauce. Add a crisp lettuce leaf, a slice of tomato, and 2 slices of Swiss cheese. Top with slices of round steak. Sprinkle beef drippings over the meat.

SERVES 8

MAYFAIR DINER

The motto of the Mayfair Diner in Philadelphia, Pennsylvania, is simple: "Quick Service, Quality, and Cleanliness."

Open twenty-four hours a day, the Mayfair has been in business for more than half a century. Ed Mulholland Sr. handed the diner down to his three children: Ed Jr., Jack, and Claire.

The senior Mulholland began working in the diner industry when he and some friends opened a small Philadelphia hot dog stand. With business booming, they were soon looking for something bigger, and in 1928 they purchased a Jerry O'Mahoney Lunch Car.

In 1956 they bought another O'Mahoney Lunch Car to replace the old one. The new car was bigger and had the classic look of a 1950s diner with its mirrored ceilings and Art Deco designs.

The secret of the Mayfair's long run of success is really no secret at all, says Jack Mulholland. "It's the atmosphere and good service. Our customers are the most important thing to us."

Customers agree that it is the food that keeps bringing them back to the Mayfair. The menu is varied, and one can order anything, from a simple omelette to deviled fresh Maryland crab.

"The fish is always fresh," says Jack, "as are the vegetables. Everything is homemade, including all our soups and desserts."

Serving on average 3,000 people daily, the diner sells a lot of food. "We can go through 250 chickens and 80 dozen eggs in one day," says Jack.

In November of 1992, Bill Clinton visited the Mayfair during a stop on his campaign for president. "We got a lot of publicity from that visit," says Jack.

And what did Bill Clinton eat while at the Mayfair? A cheeseburger, perhaps? "He did not," says Jack. "He only had a cup of tea."

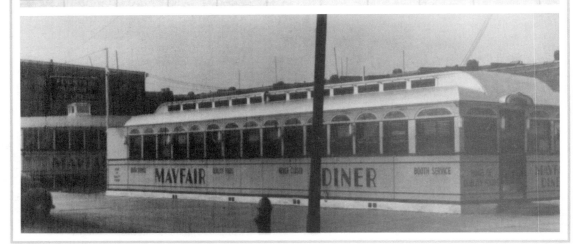

MAYFAIR DINER, PHILADELPHIA, PENNSYLVANIA

Steak & Pepper Sandwich

6	tablespoons butter, softened
3	tablespoons olive oil
½	cup grated Parmesan cheese
¼	teaspoon pepper
1	12-inch loaf French bread
2	tablespoons oil
1	onion, sliced
1	red bell pepper, sliced
½	green bell pepper, sliced
½	yellow bell pepper, sliced
1	pound cooked steak, sliced thin
	Salt and pepper to taste

In a mixing bowl combine the butter, olive oil, and Parmesan cheese. Mix thoroughly. Add the pepper. Spread the butter mixture down the center of the French bread. Place on a baking sheet butter-side-up. Place the bread under the broiler. Cook until the bread is toasted and golden brown.

In a skillet heat the oil over medium-high heat. Add the onions, red pepper, green pepper, and yellow pepper. Sauté until the peppers are tender. Add the steak and season with salt and pepper.

To serve, place the steak and peppers in the middle of the toasted bread.

SERVES 4

THRU-WAY DINER, NEW ROCHELLE, NEW YORK

Spicy Pork Sandwich

1	12-ounce bottle spicy ketchup
1/2	cup finely chopped onion
1/2	cup finely chopped green bell pepper
1	tablespoon packed light brown sugar
1	teaspoon salt
1 1/2	teaspoons dry mustard
	Tabasco to taste
4	cups shredded cooked pork
8	hamburger buns
	Butter

In a medium bowl combine the ketchup, onion, green pepper, brown sugar, salt, and dry mustard. Season with Tabasco. Mix thoroughly.

In a saucepan combine the cooked pork and sauce. Cover and simmer for 10 minutes.

Butter and toast the hamburger buns. Place the pork with sauce in the center.

SERVES 8

Barbecue Pork Sandwich

1	tablespoon oil
1	onion, chopped
1	garlic clove, minced
1	12-ounce bottle spicy chili sauce
2	tablespoons packed brown sugar
1/4	teaspoon pepper
2	tablespoons apple cider vinegar
3	cups chopped cooked pork
4	hard rolls, split
	Mayonnaise
	Lettuce
1	medium tomato, sliced
	Salt

In a saucepan heat the oil over medium heat. Coat the entire bottom of the saucepan.

Sauté the onion and garlic until the onion becomes soft. Remove the saucepan from the heat. Add the chili sauce and brown sugar. Mix thoroughly. Add the pepper and apple cider vinegar. Return the saucepan to the heat. Add the pork. Let simmer for 20 minutes or until thoroughly heated and well blended.

To serve split the hard rolls in half. Spread an even layer of mayonnaise on half of each roll. Add the pork mixture. Top with lettuce and tomato slices. Season with salt to taste. Top with remaining half of the rolls. Serve warm.

SERVES 4

Sloppy Joes

1	tablespoon oil
1	pound lean ground beef
1	cup chopped onion
3/4	cup chopped green bell pepper
2	tablespoons mustard
1	tablespoon brown sugar
1	cup ketchup
1/2	teaspoon salt
6	hamburger buns

In a heavy skillet heat the oil. Brown the ground beef with the onion and green pepper. Drain off the fat.

Add the mustard, sugar, ketchup, and salt. Cover the skillet and simmer for 30 minutes. Spoon the mixture into the hamburger buns.

SERVES 6

Meat Loaf Sandwich

2	pounds ground beef
1/4	cup chopped onion
2	cups soft, seasoned breadcrumbs
1	teaspoon salt
2	eggs, slightly beaten
2	tablespoons horseradish
1	teaspoon dry mustard
1/4	cup chopped green bell pepper
3	tablespoons Worcestershire sauce
3/4	cup ketchup
	Mayonnaise
16	slices sourdough bread
	Dill pickles

In a large mixing bowl blend together the ground beef, onion, breadcrumbs, salt, and eggs. Mash together. Add horseradish, dry mustard, green pepper, Worcestershire sauce, and ketchup. Blend thoroughly.

Shape the meat into a loaf. Place in a greased baking pan. Bake at 350° for 1 hour. Test to make sure the meat is cooked on the inside. Remove and slice when cooled.

Spread mayonnaise on slices of sourdough bread. Top with sliced meat loaf. Add dill pickles.

SERVES 8

Meatball Sandwich

1	pound ground beef
1/2	cup seasoned soft breadcrumbs
2	tablespoons minced onion
1	garlic clove, minced
2	tablespoons grated Parmesan cheese
1/4	teaspoon ground black pepper
1	cup marinara sauce
1	loaf sourdough French bread

In a mixing bowl blend together the ground beef, seasoned breadcrumbs, onion, garlic, and Parmesan cheese. Mix thoroughly. Add the pepper and 1½ tablespoons of marinara sauce. Blend so that all the ingredients are thoroughly mixed together.

Shape the meat into 12 rounded meatballs. Place on a baking sheet. Bake at 350° for 15 to 20 minutes or until the meatballs test done.

In a saucepan heat the remaining marinara sauce. Cut the French bread into fourths. Split each quarter in half. Spoon sauce into the inside of the bread. Add 3 meatballs. Top with remaining slices of bread.

SERVES 4

Chili Dogs

2   pounds ground beef
2   small onions, chopped fine
2   garlic cloves, chopped fine
4   cups cooked pinto beans
2½ cups diced tomatoes
2½ cups diced green chilies
½   teaspoon salt
1   teaspoon black pepper
1   teaspoon ground chili powder
1   cup grated Cheddar cheese
6   hot dogs
6   hot dog buns

In a skillet brown the ground beef with the onions and garlic until the onions turn brown. Add the pinto beans, tomatoes, and green chilies. Mix thoroughly. Season with the salt, pepper, and chili powder. Simmer for 1 hour. Grill the hot dogs until done.

Place a hot dog in the bun. Pour chili over the top. Top with grated Cheddar cheese.

SERVES 6

Liverwurst Sandwich

½   pound liverwurst
2   tablespoons minced green bell pepper
1½ teaspoons minced onion
1½ teaspoons Worcestershire sauce
3   tablespoons mayonnaise
    Butter
8   slices rye bread
    Lettuce leaves

In a mixing bowl mash the liverwurst. Add the green pepper and onion. Blend in the Worcestershire sauce and mayonnaise and mix well.

Butter one side of each slice of the rye bread. Spread 4 slices of bread with the liverwurst mixture. Top with crisp lettuce leaves and the remaining bread.

SERVES 4

Reuben Sandwich

1   cup sauerkraut, well drained
½   teaspoon caraway seed
⅛   teaspoon garlic powder
½   cup Russian dressing
12 slices rye bread
1   pound corned beef, sliced thin
6   thick slices American cheese
3   tablespoons butter, melted

In a medium bowl toss together the sauerkraut, caraway seed, and garlic powder. Set aside.

Spread Russian dressing over one side of each slice of rye bread. Top half the bread with corned beef, sauerkraut, and cheese. Cover with the remaining slices of bread. Brush with melted butter.

In a skillet grill the sandwich butter-side-down. Butter the other side and flip when browned. Continue grilling until the cheese has melted and the bread is lightly browned.

SERVES 6

Clubhouse Sandwich

12	slices lean bacon
9	slices white bread
6	tablespoons mayonnaise
12	slices cooked turkey
2	large tomatoes, sliced
12	lettuce leaves

In a skillet fry the bacon until crisp. Drain on paper towels. Let cool and set aside.

Lightly toast the bread. Spread mayonnaise over one side of each slice. Place 2 slices of turkey over 3 slices of the bread, and top with 1 slice of tomato, 2 slices of bacon, and 2 crisp lettuce leaves. Top each with 1 slice of bread. Again top with 2 slices of turkey, 1 slice of tomato, and 2 slices of bacon. Top with the remaining bread. Cut each sandwich into quarters and secure with toothpicks.

MAKES 3 SANDWICHES

Chicken Sandwich

8	slices sourdough bread
3	tablespoons butter, softened
4	slices cooked chicken
1	large tomato, sliced
1	large ripe avocado, peeled and sliced
4	crisp lettuce leaves
3	tablespoons French salad dressing

Toast the sourdough bread. Butter 4 slices. Layer with a slice of cooked chicken, a slice of tomato, slices of avocado, and a lettuce leaf.

Spread French dressing over the remaining slices of bread. Top the sandwiches. Cut diagonally and serve.

SERVES 4

Chicken Club Sandwich

1	pound cooked boneless chicken breast
	Salt and pepper to taste
3/4	pound bacon
12	slices French bread
1/2	cup mayonnaise
	Lettuce
2	medium tomatoes, sliced
1	red bell pepper, sliced
1	ripe avocado, peeled and sliced

Carve the chicken breast into 4 slices. Season with salt and pepper. In a skillet fry the bacon until crisp. Drain on paper towels. Let cool and set aside.

MIDWAY DINER, RUTLAND, VIRGINIA

Spread the French bread with mayonnaise. Top 4 slices with crisp lettuce, sliced tomatoes, and red bell pepper. Top with slices of French bread. Next layer with a slice of the chicken breast and sliced avocado. Top with the remaining slices of French bread.

SERVES 4

Hot Chicken Sandwich

2	cups cubed cooked chicken
2	hard-boiled eggs, chopped
1/4	cup sliced fresh mushrooms
1/3	cup finely chopped onion
1/4	cup mayonnaise
1/4	cup chopped black olives
	Butter
16	slices white bread
1	cup sour cream
1	10¾-ounce can condensed cream of chicken soup

In a medium bowl combine the cooked chicken, chopped eggs, mushrooms, and onion, and toss thoroughly. Add the mayonnaise and mix well. Add the black olives.

Butter one side of each slice of bread. Spread the chicken mixture evenly on 8 slices of bread. Top with the remaining slices.

In a saucepan combine the sour cream and condensed soup. Heat over low heat until simmering. Before serving pour equal amounts of sauce over each sandwich.

SERVES 8

Chicken Salad Sandwich #1

1	cup chopped cooked chicken
1	hard-boiled egg, chopped fine
1/4	cup mayonnaise
1/2	cup finely chopped celery
1	teaspoon fresh lemon juice
1/4	teaspoon salt
1/8	teaspoon pepper
1/4	cup butter, softened
8	slices white bread
1	medium tomato, sliced thin
4	crisp lettuce leaves

In a medium bowl combine the chicken and hard-boiled eggs. Add the mayonnaise and blend thoroughly. Add the celery and fresh lemon juice. Toss. Season with salt and pepper.

Butter 4 slices of the white bread. Spread equal amounts of the chicken salad over the bread. Top with sliced tomato and lettuce leaves. Top with the remaining bread.

SERVES 4

Chicken Salad Sandwich #2

4	cups diced cooked chicken
1½	cups diced celery
½	cup chopped green olives
1	cup mayonnaise
¼	cup milk
	Tabasco
3	ounces cream cheese, softened
	Salt and pepper to taste
12	slices white bread
	Lettuce leaves
1	medium tomato, sliced

In a medium bowl toss together the chicken, celery, and chopped green olives. Set aside. In a separate bowl blend together the mayonnaise and milk. Add a dash of Tabasco and blend in the softened cream cheese. Season with salt and pepper. Add the mixture to the chicken. Mix thoroughly.

Spread even amounts of chicken salad over 6 slices of white bread. Top with the lettuce, tomato slices, and remaining bread.

SERVES 6

Egg Salad Sandwich #1

4	hard-boiled eggs, chopped fine
3	tablespoons mayonnaise
2	tablespoons minced green bell pepper
2	tablespoons chopped celery
2	tablespoons chopped green olives
2	tablespoons chopped walnuts

1	tablespoon ketchup
	Salt and pepper to taste
	Butter
4	slices white bread
	Lettuce leaves

In a medium bowl mix together the eggs and mayonnaise. Add the green pepper, celery, green olives, chopped walnuts, and ketchup, and mix until thoroughly blended. Season with salt and pepper.

Butter the slices of bread. Spread even amounts of the egg salad over 2 of the bread slices. Top with a crisp lettuce leaf. Top with the remaining slices of bread.

SERVES 2

Egg Salad Sandwich #2

6	hard-boiled eggs, chopped
3	tablespoons mayonnaise
½	cup sweet pickle relish
1	tablespoon mustard
½	teaspoon salt
⅛	teaspoon pepper
	Butter
8	slices white bread
	Lettuce leaves
1	medium tomato, sliced

In a medium bowl blend together the eggs and mayonnaise. Add the sweet pickle relish and mustard. Season with salt and pepper. Blend thoroughly.

Butter each slice of bread. Spread even layers of the egg salad mixture over 4 slices of bread. Place the lettuce and tomato on top. Top with the remaining slices of bread.

SERVES 4

WELLSBORO DINER

For many owner-operators, running a diner is a long-term enterprise. This is certainly true of Ray and Dorothy Cummings, who have run the Wellsboro Diner in Wellsboro, Pennsylvania, for twenty-three years.

A 1939 Sterling Streamliner, the old diner itself can lay claim to a lengthy career. "It's porcelain inside and out," says a proud Dorothy Cummings.

The diner's homemade soup, pies, and daily specials attract both locals and tourists who flock here in the summer to visit Pennsylvania's Grand Canyon— not to be confused with that other, somewhat better known, big ditch out in Arizona.

"We get students, teachers, doctors, and lawyers," says Dorothy. "All kinds of people."

Tuna Salad Sandwich #1

1	7-ounce can Albacore tuna
½	cup mayonnaise
¼	cup sweet pickle relish
3	tablespoons chopped celery
	Salt and pepper to taste
3	tablespoons butter
4	crisp lettuce leaves
8	slices white bread

Drain the tuna. In a medium bowl flake the tuna. Add the mayonnaise and blend well. Add the pickle relish and chopped celery and mix well. Season with salt and pepper.

Butter 4 slices of the white bread. Spread even layers of the tuna mixture over the bread. Top with a lettuce leaf and the remaining bread.

SERVES 4

Turkey Salad Sandwich

2	cups diced cooked turkey
2	green onions, diced
1/2	red bell pepper, sliced
1	celery stalk, diced
1	teaspoon parsley, minced
2/3	cup Russian dressing
	Salt and pepper to taste
	Mayonnaise
8	slices white bread
	Lettuce
1	medium tomato, sliced

In a medium bowl blend together the cooked turkey, onions, red pepper, celery, and parsley. Add the Russian dressing. Mix thoroughly to coat all the ingredients. Season with salt and pepper.

Spread mayonnaise on top of 4 slices of the bread. Spread even layers of the turkey mixture over the bread. Top with crisp lettuce leaves and tomato slices. Top with the remaining bread.

SERVES 4

Tuna Salad Sandwich #2

1	cup Albacore tuna
1/2	cup chopped cucumber
1	tablespoon grated onion
2	teaspoons fresh lemon juice
1/4	cup chopped green bell pepper
1/2	cup chopped celery
	Salt and pepper to taste
1/4	cup mayonnaise
8	lettuce leaves
16	slices white bread

Drain the tuna. In a medium bowl flake the tuna. Add the cucumber, onion, and fresh lemon juice, and toss gently. Add the green pepper and celery. Season with salt and pepper. Blend in the mayonnaise.

Spread the tuna mixture evenly over 8 slices of white bread. Add a crisp lettuce leaf. Top with the remaining slices of bread.

SERVES 8

Crab & Avocado Sandwich

1/4	cup sour cream
2	tablespoons fresh lemon juice
1	teaspoon dill
1/4	teaspoon dry mustard
	Salt and pepper to taste
1/2	pound crab meat
	Butter, softened
4	slices French bread
1	ripe avocado, peeled and sliced

In a medium bowl blend together the sour cream and fresh lemon juice. Add the dill and dry mustard. Season with salt and pepper.

Drain and flake the crab meat. Add it to the sour cream mixture. Butter the slices of French bread. Spread an even layer of crab mixture over the top. Add slices of avocado and top with remaining slices of French bread.

SERVES 2

Hot Crab Sandwich

1¼	cups crab meat
¼	cup finely chopped onion
½	teaspoon finely chopped garlic
1	teaspoon dry mustard
¼	cup mayonnaise
8	slices sourdough bread
½	cup grated Cheddar cheese

In a medium bowl combine the crab meat, onion, and garlic. Add the dry mustard and mayonnaise. Blend thoroughly. Spread the mixture evenly on 4 slices of the sourdough bread. Top with grated Cheddar cheese.

Place the sandwich halves on a baking sheet. Broil for 5 minutes or until the cheese has melted. Top with remaining sourdough bread.

SERVES 4

Crab & Cheese Sandwich

1	7-ounce can crab meat
2	teaspoons fresh lemon juice
½	cup mayonnaise
3	tablespoons milk
	Salt and pepper to taste
8	slices sourdough bread
	Mayonnaise
1	medium tomato, sliced
8	slices American cheese

Drain and flake the crab meat. Place in a medium bowl and add the lemon juice.

In a separate bowl blend together the mayonnaise and milk. Season with salt and pepper. Toss the mixture into the crab meat and blend until thoroughly coated.

Place the bread on a baking sheet. Broil until the bread is lightly toasted. Turn and spread half the slices with mayonnaise. Top with tomato slices and even amounts of the crab mixture. Place a slice of cheese on each sandwich. Broil until cheese has melted. Top with the remaining slices of bread.

SERVES 4

Ham Salad Sandwich

1	cup ground, cooked ham
⅓	cup chopped sweet pickles
⅓	cup sliced black olives
1	tablespoon minced parsley
1	tablespoon minced onion
2	teaspoons light brown sugar
½	teaspoon dry mustard
	Salt and pepper to taste
	Mayonnaise
4	slices white bread
	Lettuce
1	medium tomato, sliced

In a medium bowl blend together the cooked ham, pickles, olives, parsley, and onion. Add the brown sugar and dry mustard. Season with salt and pepper. Spread mayonnaise on slices of bread. Top with crisp lettuce leaves and tomato slices. Spread an even layer of the ham mixture over the bread. Top with the remaining slices of bread.

SERVES 2

Tuna Submarine Sandwich

¾ cup mayonnaise
1 teaspoon mustard
1 tablespoon pickle relish
1 tablespoon minced onion
2 6-ounce cans Albacore tuna
2 12-inch rolls
2 tomatoes, sliced
1 medium red onion, sliced
1 small head iceberg lettuce, shredded
½ pound Swiss cheese, sliced
   Salt and pepper to taste

In a small mixing bowl blend together the mayonnaise, mustard, pickle relish, and onion. Drain and flake the tuna. Add the tuna to the mayonnaise mixture and blend thoroughly.

Slice the rolls in half lengthwise. Spread an even layer of mayonnaise on the inside of the bread. Top one side of each roll with tomato slices, onion, lettuce, and cheese. Spread an even layer of the tuna mixture on the other side of each roll. Season with salt and pepper. Assemble and slice each sandwich in half.

SERVES 4

PORTSIDE DINER, DANVERS, MASSACHUSETTS

Cream Cheese Sandwich

3 ounces cream cheese, softened
1 tablespoon red wine vinegar
1 tablespoon minced onion
1 tablespoon minced green bell pepper
1 tablespoon minced carrot
  Tabasco
4 slices white bread
  Lettuce
1 tomato, sliced
  Pepper to taste

In a small mixing bowl blend together the cream cheese, vinegar, onion, green pepper, and carrot. Add a dash of Tabasco. Mix thoroughly until smooth and well blended.

Spread an even layer of cream cheese mixture over the bread. Top with crisp lettuce leaves and tomato slices. Season with pepper. Top with the remaining slices of bread.

SERVES 2

Poorboy Sandwich

5 oblong hard rolls
  Mayonnaise
2 cups iceberg lettuce, shredded
3 medium tomatoes, sliced
½ pound Swiss cheese, sliced
½ pound Provolone cheese, sliced
½ pound cooked ham, sliced
¼ pound salami, sliced
1 medium onion, sliced
  Dill pickles

Split the hard rolls in half. Spread with mayonnaise. Layer each sandwich with lettuce and a tomato slice. Add a slice of Swiss cheese, Provolone cheese, ham, and salami to each sandwich.

Repeat the process of building the sandwich beginning with the Swiss cheese. After the second layer, add slices of onion. Top with the remaining halves of the hard rolls. Refrigerate about 20 minutes before serving. Serve with dill pickles.

SERVES 5

GLORY JEAN'S DINER

At Glory Jean's Diner, situated in Rumney, New Hampshire, every item served is one of a kind—the chef uses no recipes. Even so, the Glory Jean has the reputation for serving the best meat loaf you are likely to find anywhere. Just ask owner Charlotte Crowell. She'll tell you.

A 1954 O'Mahoney, the diner is very family oriented. Old pictures cover the walls, and sunlight streams through the abundant windows. The diner has plenty of regulars, but it also attracts a lot of tourist traffic.

Glory Jean's Diner, which seats eighty, is open Monday through Saturday, 5:30 A.M. to 8:00 P.M. and Sundays 7:00 A.M. to 8:00 P.M. The diner is closed on Tuesdays.

FROM THE GRILL

All-American Burger

1	pound ground beef
1	tablespoon beef bouillon granules
¼	cup chopped onion
	Salt and pepper to taste
4	slices American cheese
4	hamburger buns
	Butter
	Lettuce
1	medium tomato, sliced

In a mixing bowl combine the ground beef, beef bouillon, and onion. Mix thoroughly. Season with salt and pepper. Shape into 4 equal-size patties.

Prepare a barbecue. Grill each patty for 5 minutes per side or until the meat tests done. Top with slices of American cheese the last few minutes of grilling.

Toast and butter the buns. Add the patties. Top with lettuce and tomato slices.

SERVES 4

Blue Cheese Burgers

2	pounds ground beef
½	cup chopped onion
⅓	cup blue cheese, crumbled
1	tablespoon Worcestershire sauce
1	teaspoon salt
¼	teaspoon pepper
6	teaspoons mayonnaise
6	hamburger buns
	Lettuce
1	tomato, sliced

In a mixing bowl combine the ground beef, onion, blue cheese, Worcestershire sauce, salt, and pepper. Mix thoroughly.

Shape into 6 equal-size patties. Grill over very hot coals or in a heavy skillet until the burgers are smoking. Cook for 3 minutes per side or until done.

Spread the mayonnaise inside the hamburger buns. Top with cooked hamburger patties, crisp lettuce, and tomato slices.

SERVES 6

Baked Burgers

½ cup chopped onion
1 garlic clove, minced
1 tablespoon sugar
1½ teaspoons Tabasco
1 tablespoon chili powder
1 cup water
1 6-ounce can tomato paste
1 tablespoon unsweetened pickle relish
½ teaspoon salt
3 tablespoons fresh lemon juice
¼ cup apple cider vinegar

♦ ♦ ♦

2 pounds ground beef
1 cup milk
¼ teaspoon coarse ground pepper
1 teaspoon salt
1 cup soft seasoned soft breadcrumbs
1 egg
1 garlic clove, peeled and mashed
¼ cup finely chopped onion
¼ cup shortening
6 hamburger buns

In a saucepan combine the onion, garlic, and sugar. Add the Tabasco, chili powder, and water, and bring to a simmer. Add the tomato paste, pickle relish, salt, lemon juice, and vinegar. Bring the mixture to a boil. Reduce the heat and cook for 15 minutes. Set aside.

In a mixing bowl combine the ground beef, milk, pepper, salt, and breadcrumbs. Blend thoroughly. Add the egg, garlic, and onion.

Shape into 6 equal-size patties. Melt the shortening in the bottom of a heavy skillet and brown the patties on both sides. Place them in a deep baking dish. Cover with sauce. Bake at 300° for 1 hour and 30 minutes. Spoon the sauce over the patties every 15 minutes. Serve on hamburger buns and top with the remaining sauce.

SERVES 4

FREEHOLD GRILL, FREEHOLD, NEW JERSEY

Beefque Burgers

1½   pounds ground beef
1   teaspoon salt
½   cup oil
½   cup chili sauce
½   cup vinegar
½   cup water
1   medium onion, diced
1   garlic clove, minced
1   lemon, sliced thin
1   tablespoon Worcestershire sauce
2   tablespoons sugar
1   teaspoon chili powder

In a mixing bowl combine the ground beef with the salt. Shape into 4 equal-size patties.

In a saucepan combine the oil, chili sauce, vinegar, and water. Blend well. Add the onion, garlic, lemon, Worcestershire sauce, sugar, and chili powder. Bring the mixture to a boil. Cook for 10 to 15 minutes, stirring often to blend all of the ingredients. Set aside and let cool.

Place the patties in a deep baking dish. Pour the sauce over the top. Refrigerate for 12 hours.

Remove the patties from the sauce. In a heavy skillet or over hot coals cook the patties. Spoon the remaining sauce over the patties as they are cooking. Cook for 5 to 10 minutes or until done. In a saucepan boil the remaining sauce.

Serve the patties on a hot platter topped with the remaining sauce.

SERVES 4

Chili-Size Burgers

2   pounds ground round
¼   teaspoon garlic salt

♦ ♦ ♦

3   tablespoons cooking oil
3   medium onions, chopped
1   garlic clove, minced
1   green bell pepper, chopped
1½   pounds ground round
1   teaspoon salt
½   teaspoon chili powder
1   large chile pepper, chopped fine
½   pound pork sausage
1   16-oz. can whole tomatoes
1   16-oz. can red kidney beans
4   hamburger buns

In a mixing bowl combine 2 pounds of ground round with the garlic salt. Shape into 4 equal-size patties. In a heavy skillet sear the meat on both sides. Cook on medium heat for 5 to 8 minutes or until the insides are done. Set aside and keep warm.

In a heavy skillet heat the oil and sauté the onions, garlic, and green pepper. Cook until the vegetables are tender. Remove the mixture from the pan.

In the same skillet brown the 1½ pounds ground round. Drain the fat. Add the salt, chili powder, chile pepper, sausage, tomatoes, and kidney beans. Simmer over low heat for 30 minutes. Add the onion, garlic, and green pepper.

Place a cooked patty on each hamburger bun. Top with chili sauce.

SERVES 4

Deluxe Burgers

1½	pounds ground round
½	teaspoon salt
½	teaspoon coarse ground pepper
1½	teaspoons Worcestershire sauce
1	teaspoon fresh lemon juice
¾	teaspoon garlic salt
4	teaspoons mayonnaise
2	teaspoons mustard
4	hamburger buns
	Lettuce
1	medium tomato, sliced

In a mixing bowl blend together the ground round, salt, pepper, Worcestershire sauce, and lemon juice. Mix thoroughly.

Shape into 4 equal-size patties. Heat a skillet until very hot. Sprinkle garlic salt in the center. Place the patties in the hot skillet. Reduce the heat to medium and sear both sides. Reduce the heat once more and cook for 3 minutes or until done.

Spread mayonnaise and mustard on each bun. Add a cooked patty. Top with lettuce and tomato.

SERVES 4

Giant Burgers

2	pounds ground round
1	teaspoon salt
⅛	teaspoon coarse ground pepper
1	tablespoon oil
3	tablespoons minced onion
½	cup sliced fresh mushrooms
3	tablespoons fresh lemon juice
¼	cup butter, melted
2	tablespoons finely chopped parsley
4	hamburger buns
¼	cup grated Cheddar cheese

In a mixing bowl break up the ground round. Sprinkle with salt and pepper.

In a heavy skillet heat the oil and sauté the onion and mushrooms. Drain. Add the onion and mushrooms to the ground round. Shape into 4 equal-size patties. Broil or barbecue for 5 to 8 minutes per side.

In a mixing bowl combine the lemon juice, melted butter, and parsley. Baste the patties before serving. Place in hamburger buns. Top with Cheddar cheese.

SERVES 4

TOWN DINER, WATERTOWN, MASSACHUSETTS

Grilled Burgers

1½ pounds ground beef
2 tablespoons minced onion
1 teaspoon salt
½ teaspoon pepper
1 cup ketchup
2 teaspoons Worcestershire sauce
½ teaspoon celery salt
   Tabasco to taste
   Butter
6 hamburger buns, toasted

In a mixing bowl blend together the ground beef, onion, salt, and pepper. Shape into 6 equal-size patties. Broil for 6 minutes. Turn and broil for 4 minutes more or until done.

In a small bowl combine the ketchup, Worcestershire sauce, celery salt, and Tabasco to taste. Blend thoroughly.

When the burgers are done, spread the sauce over the tops. Butter the toasted hamburger buns. Place a patty inside each bun. Serve the remaining sauce on the side.

SERVES 6

Mexicali Burgers

1 pound ground beef
1 tablespoon beef bouillon granules
¼ cup chopped onion
1 4-ounce can chopped green chilies, drained
   Salt and pepper to taste
   Butter
4 hamburger buns
1 medium tomato, sliced
½ cup chopped black olives
1 ripe avocado, peeled and sliced
   Spicy salsa
   Sour cream

In a mixing bowl combine the ground beef, beef bouillon, and onion. Mix thoroughly. Add the green chilies and season with salt and pepper. Shape into 4 equal-size patties.

Prepare a barbecue. Grill each patty for 5 minutes per side or until done.

Toast and butter the hamburger buns. Add the patties. Top with tomato, black olives, and avocado slices. Garnish with salsa and sour cream.

SERVES 4

Hawaiian Burgers

1½	pounds ground beef
1½	cups crushed pineapple, drained
1	teaspoon salt
¼	teaspoon pepper
¼	cup oil
14	cups soy sauce
2	tablespoons ketchup
1½	teaspoons vinegar
6	slices bacon
6	hamburger buns

In a mixing bowl combine the ground beef, crushed pineapple, salt, and pepper. Shape into 6 equal-size patties. Set aside.

In a separate mixing bowl combine the oil, soy sauce, ketchup, and vinegar. Place the patties into a deep baking dish. Pour the sauce over the top of the patties. Cover and marinate for 30 minutes, turning after 15 minutes.

Remove the patties from the marinade. Wrap a slice of bacon around each hamburger patty. Secure with a toothpick. Barbecue for 8 to 10 minutes per side or broil for 12 minutes per side or until done.

To serve place each patty on a hamburger bun. Top with marinade.

SERVES 6

♦ ♦ ♦

Note: After raw meat sits in marinade, the marinade should be boiled to kill harmful bacteria! Serve the remaining marinade on the side.

CAPITOL DINER, LYNN, MASSACHUSETTS

TED'S DINER, MILFORD, MASSACHUSETTS

Mountain Burgers

1	pound ground beef
1/4	cup quick-cooking oats
2	tablespoons ketchup
2	tablespoons milk
1	tablespoon mustard
1	egg
1/2	teaspoon salt
1/4	teaspoon pepper
1/4	teaspoon Liquid Smoke
1	small onion, sliced
4	hamburger buns
1/4	cup sweet pickle relish

In a mixing bowl combine the ground beef with the oats, ketchup, milk, mustard, and egg. Blend thoroughly. Add the salt, pepper, and Liquid Smoke. Mix well.

Shape the mixture into 4 equal-size patties. Barbecue over hot coals for 6 minutes on each side or until the meat tests done.

Top with a slice of onion and continue cooking another 4 minutes. Place on toasted hamburger buns and serve with pickle relish.

SERVES 4

Mushroom Burgers

- 1½ pounds ground sirloin
- ¼ cup sherry
- ¼ teaspoon garlic salt
- ¼ teaspoon coarse ground pepper
- ½ cup sliced fresh mushrooms
- 1 large onion, sliced
- 4 sesame seed rolls
- 1 large ripe avocado, peeled and sliced
- 1 large tomato, sliced
- ¼ pound Monterey Jack cheese, sliced

In a mixing bowl blend together the ground sirloin, sherry, garlic salt, and coarse pepper. Shape into 4 equal-size patties. Fry in a heavy skillet. Remove the patties from the skillet. Reduce the heat and add the mushrooms and onions. Sauté until the onions become transparent but not brown.

Lightly toast the sesame seed rolls until golden. Place the toasted buns on a platter. Add a cooked patty to each. Top with avocado and tomato slices, onions, mushrooms, and cheese.

SERVES 4

Outdoor Burgers

- 1 pound lean ground beef
- 2 tablespoons chopped green bell pepper
- 1½ teaspoons horseradish
- 2 teaspoons mustard
- ¼ teaspoon pepper
- ¼ cup chopped sweet onion
- ¼ cup ketchup
- ½ teaspoon salt
- ½ teaspoon garlic powder
- 4 slices Monterey Jack cheese
- 4 hamburger buns
  Lettuce
- 1 medium tomato, sliced

In a mixing bowl blend together the ground beef, green pepper, horseradish, and mustard. Add the pepper, onion, ketchup, salt, and garlic powder.

Shape into 4 equal-size patties. Broil over very hot coals about 3 minutes per side. Top with cheese the last minute of cooking.

Lightly toast the hamburger buns until golden. Place a burger on each bun. Top with lettuce and tomato slices.

SERVES 4

Roadside Burgers

- 1½ pounds ground steak
- ¼ cup finely chopped green bell pepper
- ¼ cup finely chopped onion
- 1 medium tomato, peeled and chopped
- 1 teaspoon paprika
- 1 teaspoon Worcestershire sauce
- ¼ teaspoon salt
- ¼ teaspoon pepper
- 2 tablespoons oil
- 4 hamburger buns
- 1 medium tomato, sliced
  Lettuce
  Sliced sweet onion
- ¼ pound Cheddar cheese, sliced

In a mixing bowl blend together the ground steak with the green pepper, onion, and chopped tomato. Add the paprika, Worcestershire sauce, salt, and pepper. Shape into 4 equal-size patties.

In a heavy skillet heat the oil. Sear the patties on both sides. Reduce heat and cook for 3 to 5 minutes or until done.

Place a burger on each bun. Top with tomato slices, lettuce, sweet onion, and Cheddar cheese.

SERVES 4

Southwest Burgers

1½	pounds ground round
½	teaspoon salt
½	teaspoon coarse ground pepper
¾	teaspoon garlic salt

♦ ♦ ♦

¼	cup butter
⅓	cup water
2	tablespoons fresh lemon juice
½	teaspoon salt
¼	teaspoon pepper
⅔	cup ketchup
2	tablespoons mustard
¼	cup packed light brown sugar
1	tablespoon Worcestershire sauce
½	cup vinegar
2	tablespoons soy sauce
2	tablespoons Liquid Smoke
⅛	teaspoon cayenne pepper
4	hamburger buns, toasted

In a mixing bowl blend together the ground round, salt, and pepper. Mix thoroughly. Shape into 4 equal-size patties.

Heat a skillet until very hot. Sprinkle garlic salt in the center. Place the patties in the hot skillet and reduce the heat. Sear both sides. Reduce the heat once more and cook for 3 minutes or until done.

In a medium saucepan melt the butter. Add the remaining ingredients. Simmer over low heat for 30 minutes, stirring occasionally.

Place the cooked patties on toasted hamburger buns. Spread the sauce over the top. Serve the remaining sauce on the side.

SERVES 4

Spicy Burgers

1¼	pounds ground beef
1	cup finely chopped onion
1	garlic clove, minced
½	cup soy sauce
½	teaspoon ginger
1	tablespoon fresh lemon juice
¼	cup unsweetened pineapple juice
8	hamburger buns

In a mixing bowl combine the ground beef and onion. Shape into 8 equal-size patties.

In a separate bowl combine the garlic, soy sauce, ginger, lemon juice, and pineapple juice.

Place the patties in the bottom of a baking dish. Pour the sauce over the top. Let stand for 30 minutes.

Broil the patties for 5 to 8 minutes per side or until the meat tests done. Baste with the remaining sauce while broiling. Serve on hamburger buns.

SERVES 8

Stuffed Burgers

2 pounds ground round
1½ teaspoons salt
¼ teaspoon pepper
¼ cup minced onion
1¼ cups grated sharp Cheddar cheese
1 cup mild chili sauce
¼ teaspoon garlic salt
6 hamburger buns
12 onion rings (see recipe on pg. 49)

In a mixing bowl combine the ground round, salt, pepper, and onion. Mix thoroughly. Shape into 12 equal-size patties.

Top 6 of the patties with the grated Cheddar cheese. Place the remaining patties over the cheese. Press the edges of the meat together. Broil for 6 to 8 minutes or until the meat tests done.

In a saucepan heat the chili sauce with the garlic salt. Place cooked burgers inside the buns. Top with chili sauce and onion rings.

SERVES 6

Topeka Burgers

1 pound ground beef
1 tablespoon beef bouillon granules
¼ cup chopped onion
2 tablespoons spicy barbecue sauce
½ cup diced cooked potatoes
  Salt and pepper to taste
4 slices American cheese
4 hamburger buns
  Butter
  Lettuce
1 medium tomato, sliced

In a mixing bowl combine the ground beef, beef bouillon, and onion. Mix thoroughly. Add the barbecue sauce and potatoes. Season with salt and pepper. Shape into 4 equal-size patties.

Prepare a barbecue. Grill each patty for 5 minutes per side or until done. Top with slices of American cheese the last few minutes of grilling.

Toast and butter the hamburger buns. Add the patties. Top with lettuce and tomato slices.

SERVES 4

NITE OWL DINER, FALL RIVER, MASSACHUSETTS

Western Burgers

4 strips bacon
¾ cup chopped sweet onion
½ cup chopped green bell pepper
2 pounds ground beef
1 8-ounce can tomato sauce
½ teaspoon salt
¼ teaspoon pepper
1 tablespoon chili powder
1 1-pound can red kidney beans, drained
6 hamburger buns
1 cup grated Parmesan cheese

In a heavy skillet fry the bacon until crisp. Drain on paper towels. Set aside. In the same skillet sauté the onion and green pepper until soft. Drain on paper towels and set aside.

Shape the ground beef into 6 equal-size patties. Cook in the same skillet until the meat is almost done.

In a mixing bowl blend together the bacon, tomato sauce, salt, pepper, chili powder, and kidney beans. Add the sautéed onions and green peppers. Pour the mixture over the patties. Reduce the heat and simmer for 5 minutes.

Lightly toast the hamburger buns until golden. Place the patties on buns. Garnish with grated Parmesan cheese.

SERVES 6

Zip Burgers

1½ pounds ground beef
1 medium onion, chopped
¼ cup soy sauce
1 teaspoon dry mustard
1 16-ounce can tomato sauce
1 garlic clove, minced
2 tablespoons sugar
⅛ teaspoon cayenne pepper
3 teaspoons oil
4 hamburger buns

Shape the ground beef into 4 equal-size patties.

In a saucepan combine the onion, soy sauce, dry mustard, tomato sauce, garlic, sugar, and cayenne pepper. Mix thoroughly.

Heat the oil in a heavy skillet. Sear the patties on both sides. Reduce the heat and continue cooking for 5 minutes or until the patties are done. During the last minute of cooking baste the patties with the sauce. Place the patties on the hamburger buns. Top with sauce. Serve the remaining sauce on the side.

SERVES 4

Hamburger Buns

8 cups all-purpose flour
2 envelopes active dry yeast
2 cups warm water
¾ cup vegetable oil
½ cup sugar
I tablespoon salt
3 eggs

In a large mixing bowl combine 4 cups of flour with the yeast. In a separate bowl combine the water, oil, sugar, and salt. Mix well. Add the liquid mixture to the dry ingredients. Beat the eggs with an electric mixer on low for 30 seconds. Beat 3 minutes more on high. Add by hand the remaining 4 cups of flour and eggs. Turn out on a floured board and knead until smooth. Place the dough in a large greased bowl, turning once to coat the surface. Cover. Let rise in a warm place until the dough has doubled in size.

Punch down and divide into 3 sections. Cover and let rise for 5 minutes.

Divide each portion into 8 balls. Turn each ball in your hands and fold the edges under to make even circles. Press flat. Place on a greased baking sheet. Let rise until the dough has doubled in size. Bake at 375° for 10 minutes or until golden brown.

MAKES 2 DOZEN

Diner Steak

2 pounds cube steak
2 tablespoons oil
½ teaspoon salt
½ teaspoon pepper
¼ cup butter

Remove the fat from the steak. In a heavy skillet heat the oil until it is near smoking. Sear the steaks quickly on both sides.

Reduce the heat to medium and cook for 2 to 3 minutes longer or until the steaks are done.

Remove the steaks from the skillet. Place on a warm platter. Season with the salt and pepper. Spread even layers of butter over each steak.

SERVES 4

Green Pepper Steak

1½ pounds round steak
 Salt and pepper to taste
2 tablespoons soy sauce
¼ cup all-purpose flour
3 tablespoons oil
I cup diced green bell pepper
I cup water

Remove the fat from the steak. Cut into 1-inch strips that are approximately 2 inches long. Pound the strips to tenderize them. Season with salt and pepper.

Brush the soy sauce on each of the strips. Then dredge the meat in the flour.

In a skillet heat the oil. Brown the strips over medium heat. Add the green peppers and sauté for 2 minutes. Add the water. Cover and simmer for 40 minutes or until the meat is tender.

SERVES 6

Grilled Pepper Steak

⅓ cup fresh lemon juice
2 tablespoons oil
2 garlic cloves, minced
1 teaspoon chili powder
1 teaspoon salt
½ teaspoon coarse black pepper
4 beef steaks, 1 inch thick

In a shallow mixing bowl combine the lemon juice, oil, garlic, chili powder, salt, and pepper.

Add the beef steaks and marinate for 4 hours. Remove the steaks and reserve the marinade.

Prepare a barbecue. Grill the steaks over medium-hot coals until brown or until the meat is done. Brush all sides of the steaks with sauce. In a saucepan heat the remaining sauce and serve on the side.

SERVES 4

Grilled Steak

1 3-pound Porterhouse steak
1 cup chopped onion
2 garlic cloves, minced
⅛ teaspoon salt
⅛ teaspoon pepper
⅛ teaspoon celery salt
¼ cup soy sauce
¼ cup butter
¼ cup sliced fresh mushrooms

Remove the fat from the Porterhouse steak. Cut small pockets into the sides.

In a mixing bowl combine the onion, garlic, salt, pepper, and celery salt. Toss to mix thoroughly. Fill the pockets with the seasoning mixture.

Brush the steak with the soy sauce. Place over a prepared barbecue. Grill for 25 minutes or until the meat is done. Turn once during the cooking process. Brush with soy sauce.

In a skillet melt the butter and sauté the mushrooms. Serve over the cooked steak.

SERVES 4

Steak & Onions

4 cube steaks
¼ cup oil
4 small onions, sliced
Salt and pepper to taste
2 teaspoons all-purpose flour
½ cup water

Remove the fat from the steaks. In a skillet heat the oil and sauté the onions until golden brown. Remove and set aside.

Increase the heat and fry the steaks. Season with salt and pepper. Remove the steaks from the skillet. Set aside and keep warm.

Add the flour to the pan drippings, blending well. Slowly add the water, stirring constantly so that the flour does not scorch. Let the mixture come to a boil.

Top the steaks with the onions and gravy.

SERVES 4

MAX'S GRILLE, HARRISON, NEW JERSEY

Grilled Spareribs

¼ cup dried herb salad dressing mix
½ cup corn syrup
¼ cup vinegar
2 tablespoons packed dark brown sugar
4 pounds spareribs

In a mixing bowl blend together the dried salad dressing mix, corn syrup, vinegar, and dark brown sugar. Set aside.

Place the spareribs on a grill over slow-cooking coals bone-side-down. Cook for 20 minutes, basting occasionally, and turn. Cook until the meat has browned, basting occasionally. Turn once again and continue cooking 20 minutes more or until the meat is done. Baste with the sauce as needed.

SERVES 4

Classic Spareribs

4 pounds spareribs
Salt
3 tablespoons butter
2 garlic cloves, minced
2 tablespoons mustard
¼ cup packed light brown sugar
1 cup ketchup
¾ cup mild chili sauce
1 tablespoon celery seed
⅛ teaspoon Tabasco
½ teaspoon salt
1½ cups water
1 lemon, sliced thin
1 large onion, sliced thin

Rub the spareribs thoroughly with salt. Place in a shallow roasting pan, meat-side-down. Bake at 450° for 30 minutes.

In a heavy skillet melt the butter. Add the garlic and sauté for 5 minutes. Blend in the mustard, brown sugar, ketchup, chili sauce, and celery seed. Add the Tabasco, salt, and water. Bring the mixture to a boil. Reduce the heat and simmer for 5 minutes.

Remove the ribs from the oven. Drain off any fat. Turn the ribs and cover with sauce. Add the lemon and onion slices. Turn once again. Reduce the oven to 350°. Bake for 1 hour and 30 minutes, basting occasionally with the remaining sauce.

SERVES 4

Prepare a barbecue. Remove the ribs from the sauce. Grill the ribs over hot coals. Grill each side evenly until brown or until the meat tests done. Brush all sides of the ribs with the remaining sauce.

SERVES 4

Oven Spareribs

4	pounds beef ribs
2	tablespoons cooking oil
½	cup chopped onion
⅓	cup vinegar
2	tablespoons packed dark brown sugar
½	cup mild chili sauce
2	tablespoons horseradish
3	tablespoons Worcestershire sauce
	Salt and pepper to taste

Cut the beef ribs into serving-size portions. Place in a covered casserole dish. Bake at 350° for 30 minutes.

Coat the bottom of a skillet with the oil and sauté the onions until brown. Drain. Add the vinegar, brown sugar, chili sauce, horseradish, and Worcestershire sauce. Season with salt and pepper. Blend thoroughly.

Uncover the casserole dish. Spread the sauce over the ribs. Return the dish to the oven and bake uncovered for 1 hour.

SERVES 6

Country Spareribs

4	pounds pork ribs
	Salt and pepper to taste
2½	cups crushed pineapple, drained
1	cup ketchup
½	cup packed brown sugar
⅓	cup vinegar
¼	cup soy sauce
½	teaspoon ginger
½	teaspoon dry mustard
¼	teaspoon garlic powder

Cut the pork ribs into serving-size portions. Place in a deep baking dish. Season with salt and pepper. Cover and bake at 350° for 1 hour.

Remove the pork ribs and drain. Set aside. In a mixing bowl combine the crushed pineapple, ketchup, brown sugar, vinegar, soy sauce, ginger, dry mustard, and garlic powder. Blend thoroughly. Spoon generous amounts of sauce over the pork ribs.

Glazed Spareribs

1	cup butter
1	small onion, chopped
4	garlic cloves, minced
¼	cup mustard
¼	cup honey
½	teaspoon Liquid Smoke
1	teaspoon pepper
½	teaspoon salt
1	teaspoon light brown sugar
5	pounds beef ribs

In a saucepan melt the butter and sauté the onion and garlic over low heat until the onions are tender but not brown. Remove the pan from the heat. Blend in the mustard, honey, Liquid Smoke, pepper, salt, and brown sugar. Blend thoroughly.

Cut the beef ribs into serving-size portions. Place in a deep baking dish. Pour the sauce over the top.

Prepare a barbecue. Remove the ribs from the sauce. Grill each side evenly until brown or until the meat tests done. Brush all sides of the ribs with remaining sauce.

SERVES 4

Maple Barbecue Spareribs

4	pounds beef ribs
	Salt and pepper to taste
¾	cup maple syrup
¼	cup mild chili sauce
¼	cup chopped onion
1	tablespoon vinegar
1½	teaspoons Worcestershire sauce
1	teaspoon dry mustard
1	garlic clove, minced

Cut the beef ribs into serving-size portions. Place in a deep baking dish. Season

JOE'S DINER, TAUNTON, MASSACHUSETTS

with salt and pepper. Cover and bake at 350° for 1 hour.

Remove the beef ribs and drain. Set aside. In a mixing bowl combine the maple syrup, chili sauce, onion, vinegar, Worcestershire sauce, mustard, and garlic. Blend thoroughly. Spoon generous amounts of sauce over the beef ribs. Refrigerate 6 hours.

Prepare a barbecue. Remove the ribs from the sauce. Grill the ribs over hot coals. Grill each side evenly until brown or until the meat is done. Brush all sides of the ribs with the remaining sauce.

SERVES 4

Spicy Spareribs

2	tablespoons paprika
1	teaspoon salt
1	teaspoon garlic powder
½	teaspoon onion powder
½	teaspoon celery salt
¼	teaspoon hot pepper
5	pounds pork ribs

♦ ♦ ♦

1	6-ounce can tomato paste
¼	cup molasses
¼	cup packed brown sugar
2	tablespoons soy sauce
2	tablespoons Worcestershire sauce
	Tabasco to taste
1	onion, chopped

In a mixing bowl combine the paprika, salt, garlic powder, onion powder, celery salt, and hot pepper. Toss until the ingredients are well blended. Rub the seasoning mixture over the pork ribs. Set aside.

In a saucepan combine the tomato paste, molasses, brown sugar, soy sauce,

Worcestershire sauce, Tabasco, and onions. Cook over medium heat for 15 minutes, stirring occasionally, until thickened.

Place the ribs on a rack in the broiler. Bake at 325° for 45 to 60 minutes or until the meat is done. Baste the ribs with the sauce during the cooking process.

To serve place the ribs on a warm platter. Top with the remaining sauce.

SERVES 6

Southwestern Spareribs

4	pounds pork ribs
	Salt
1	16-ounce jar unsweetened applesauce
¼	cup dark corn syrup
2	tablespoons vinegar
½	teaspoon grated lemon rind
¼	teaspoon ginger
¼	teaspoon cloves

Cut the pork ribs into serving-size portions. Rub with salt. Place in a deep baking dish meat-side-up. Bake at 450° for 30 minutes. Reduce heat to 350° and continue cooking for 30 minutes more.

In a saucepan combine the applesauce with the corn syrup, vinegar, grated lemon rind, ginger, and cloves. Blend thoroughly. Simmer on low for 5 minutes.

Remove the baking dish from the oven. Drain off any fat. Top the ribs with the applesauce mixture. Continue baking for 1 hour, spooning the sauce over the ribs during the cooking process.

SERVES 4

Stick-to-Your-Ribs Spareribs

4	pounds pork ribs
	Salt and pepper to taste
1	cup French salad dressing
1	small onion, chopped
½	cup mild chili sauce
2	tablespoons packed brown sugar
2	tablespoons fresh lemon juice
2	tablespoons Worcestershire sauce

Rub the pork ribs thoroughly with salt and pepper. Place in a deep baking dish. Set aside.

In a mixing bowl combine the French salad dressing, onion, chili sauce, brown sugar, lemon juice, and Worcestershire sauce. Mix thoroughly.

Pour the sauce over the ribs. Refrigerate overnight. Drain and reserve any remaining sauce. Place the ribs on a barbecue grill over hot coals. Cook for 45 minutes to 1 hour or until the meat is done. Brush the sauce over the ribs during the cooking process.

SERVES 4

Texas-Style Spareribs

¼	cup oil
½	cup Worcestershire sauce
¼	cup apple cider vinegar
2	cups beef stock
¾	teaspoon chili powder
¾	teaspoon Tabasco
2	garlic cloves, minced
1	teaspoon dry mustard

♦ ♦ ♦

1¼	teaspoons coarse ground pepper
3	tablespoons salt
1½	teaspoons paprika
3	tablespoons sugar

♦ ♦ ♦

10	pounds spareribs
¼	cup fresh lemon juice

In a small mixing bowl combine the oil, Worcestershire sauce, and cider vinegar. Slowly add the beef stock. Mix thoroughly. Add the chili powder, Tabasco, garlic, and dry mustard. Refrigerate for 24 hours before using.

In a small mixing bowl blend together the pepper, salt, paprika, and sugar.

Sprinkle the ribs with the fresh lemon juice. Rub with the seasoning mixture. Place on a warm section of the grill. Cook slowly for 1 hour per slab of ribs. Brush the Tabasco mixture on the ribs as they are cooking. Serve the remaining sauce on the side.

SERVES 6

Barbecue Lemon Chicken

2	3-pound broiling chickens, halved
1	cup oil
½	cup fresh lemon juice
1	teaspoon salt
2	teaspoons onion powder
1	teaspoon paprika
1	teaspoon sweet basil, crushed

INGLESIDE DINER, THORNSDALE, PENNSYLVANIA

½   teaspoon thyme, crushed
I   teaspoon garlic powder
⅛   teaspoon coarse black pepper

Clean and cut the chicken into serving pieces. Place the chicken in the bottom of a shallow baking dish.

In a mixing bowl blend together the oil and lemon juice. Add the salt, onion powder, and paprika. Mix well. Add the crushed basil, thyme, garlic powder, and pepper. Blend thoroughly, making sure the oil does not separate from the rest of the mixture. Pour the mixture over the chicken pieces. Refrigerate for 6 hours.

Prepare a barbecue. Place the chicken on the grill skin-side-up. Grill for 20 minutes. Turn and baste with sauce. Grill for another 20 minutes or until the chicken is golden and done, basting often.

SERVES 4

Batter Fried Chicken

I   4-pound frying chicken
I¾ cups all-purpose flour
3   teaspoons baking powder
½   teaspoon salt
I   egg, beaten
I   cup milk
I   tablespoon oil
    Cooking oil

Clean and cut the chicken into serving pieces. In a mixing bowl sift together the flour with the baking powder and salt. Add the egg, milk, and 1 tablespoon of oil. Dip the chicken pieces in the batter, coating thoroughly.

Coat the bottom of a heavy skillet with oil. Heat to 350°. Fry the chicken for 10 to 15 minutes or until golden brown, turning occasionally to avoid scorching. Drain on paper towels.

SERVES 4

146

Diner Fried Chicken

1	3-pound frying chicken
3	cups cooking oil
½	cup all-purpose flour
2½	cups milk
½	teaspoon salt
¼	teaspoon pepper

Clean and cut the chicken into serving pieces. Remove the excess skin and fat.

In a large, heavy skillet heat the oil. Brown the chicken on all sides. Drain on paper towels.

Remove all but ¼ cup of the oil. Return all the chicken pieces to the skillet. Cover the pan and cook over low heat for 15 minutes. Uncover and continue to cook for 10 minutes.

Remove the chicken when done. Remove all but 4 tablespoons of fat from the skillet. In a mixing bowl blend together ¼ cup of flour with ½ cup of milk. Add the mixture to the skillet. As the gravy thickens add more milk and flour to create an even blend. Season with salt and pepper. Pour the gravy over the chicken before serving.

SERVES 6

Santa Fe Chicken

1	3-pound frying chicken
	Salt
1	tablespoon cooking oil
1	onion, chopped
1	garlic clove, minced
1	16-ounce can whole tomatoes
¼	teaspoon salt
¼	cup finely chopped cilantro
1	teaspoon lime juice
	Tabasco to taste
	Pepper to taste

Clean and cut the chicken into serving pieces. Rub with salt. Set aside.

In a saucepan heat the oil and sauté the onion and garlic until tender. Add the entire can of whole tomatoes and salt. Simmer for 15 minutes.

In a mixing bowl blend the chopped cilantro with the lime juice. Season with Tabasco and pepper. Add the seasonings to the tomato mixture.

Prepare a barbecue. Grill the chicken for 20 minutes or until done, turning often and basting with sauce. Serve the remaining sauce on the side.

SERVES 6

UNIVERSITY DINER, NEW ROCHELLE, NEW YORK

Dixie Chicken

1	3-pound frying chicken
	Salt
1	8-ounce can tomato sauce
¼	cup ketchup
¼	cup vinegar
2	tablespoons packed brown sugar
1	tablespoon mustard
1	tablespoon Worcestershire sauce
	Salt and pepper to taste

Clean and cut the chicken into serving pieces. Rub with salt. Set aside.

In a saucepan combine the tomato sauce, ketchup, vinegar, brown sugar, mustard, and Worcestershire sauce. Season with salt and pepper. Simmer for 15 minutes.

Prepare a barbecue. Grill the chicken for 20 minutes or until done, turning often and basting with sauce. Serve the remaining sauce on the side.

SERVES 6

Grilled Ham

2	slices cooked ham, ½-inch thick
⅔	cup ketchup
3	tablespoons packed light brown sugar
1½	tablespoons spicy mustard
2	tablespoons Worcestershire sauce
2	tablespoons fresh lemon juice
2	teaspoons chili powder

Remove fat from the slices of ham. Set aside.

In a mixing bowl blend together the ketchup, brown sugar, mustard, Worcestershire sauce, lemon juice, and chili powder. Brush the ham slices liberally with the glaze. Set aside for 1 hour.

Prepare a barbecue. Grill the ham for 5 minutes per side. Turn once during the cooking process and brush with the remaining glaze. Serve on a warm platter with the remaining glaze on the side.

SERVES 4

O'ROURKE'S DINER

Brian O'Rourke, the owner of O'Rourke's Diner in Middletown, Connecticut, says it flatly: "Owning a diner is not my occupation. It is my life."

O'Rourke's, a 1945 Mountain View diner seating forty-four, has been in the family for fifty-three years. Brian has run it for the past eighteen years. "We are a national landmark," says the proud owner. "My uncle started the business back in 1941, so it's in my blood, in the genes."

Everything at O'Rourke's is made fresh daily. "I start working at 2:00 A.M., making my breads, soups, tomato sauces, potato chips—you name it," says Brian.

O'Rourke's, which has eleven booths and an L-shaped counter that seats fifteen, opens every day at 4:30 A.M., and there are usually customers already waiting to come inside. The customers, Brian says, come in all types. "In the diner trade you get the best of the best and the worst of the worst. We get street people, housewives, mayors, college students—all kinds. Our diner is a community within a community."

He recalls that one of his busiest days coincided with the opening of fishing season. "That Saturday I know I went through ninety

dozen eggs, at least. We served orders for 450 people, and that does not include those just having coffee."

Grilled Hot Dogs

2 onions, sliced
⅓ cup mild chili sauce
1 tablespoon water
1 tablespoon vinegar
¾ teaspoon sugar
8 hot dogs
8 hot dog buns
Mustard

In a casserole dish combine the onions, chili sauce, water, vinegar, and sugar. Bake at 450° for 30 minutes.

Prepare a barbecue. Place the hot dogs over warm coals. Grill for 6 minutes, turning once, or until the hot dogs are done.

To serve spread mustard inside the hot dog buns. Add the grilled hot dogs. Pour chili sauce over the top.

SERVES 8

Grilled Fish

2 pounds whitefish
½ cup butter
1 teaspoon salt
Pepper to taste
2 tablespoons fresh lemon juice
1 cup plain yogurt
Dill

Clean and debone the whitefish. In a saucepan melt the butter. Add the salt and pepper. Blend in the lemon juice and yogurt. Coat the fish with the sauce.

Prepare a barbecue. Place the fish on the grill over hot coals. Grill until the fish is browned on both sides. The fish is done when it flakes easily with a fork. Baste with the remaining sauce while grilling. Garnish with dill.

SERVES 4

Grilled Vegetables

3 ears corn, with husks
½ cup salad oil
1 tablespoon oregano
1 teaspoon salt
2 zucchini
3 yellow squash
1 green bell pepper
1 red bell pepper
8 large mushrooms

Remove the silk from the corn, but leave the husks. Soak the corn for 12 minutes in cold water. Remove and dry.

In a mixing bowl blend the salad oil, oregano, and salt. Set aside.

Cut the zucchini, yellow squash, green bell pepper, and red bell pepper in half lengthwise. Remove the seeds. Brush all vegetables with the oil mixture.

Prepare the barbecue. Place the vegetables on the grill over medium-hot coals. Grill for 15 minutes. Baste the vegetables as they cook with the remaining oil.

SERVES 4

AN AMERICAN TRADITION

An all-American institution, the roadside diner has roots reaching as far back as 1872. That was the year Walter Scott started traveling around Providence, Rhode Island, late at night in a small horse-drawn cart offering food and drink to factory workers who were getting off shift. Scott did his business after the city's restaurants had closed.

Scott converted his cart into a lunch wagon by adding a tarpaulin with holes cut out to simulate windows. Known as the Providence Lunch Counter, Scott's rolling diner served up sandwiches, pies, and hot coffee.

In 1877 another New Englander named Samuel Jones introduced a newer and much bigger lunch wagon with a working kitchen and an entryway where customers could stand while placing orders. This model proved so successful that it was soon widely copied.

Within two years, Jones had sold his business to Charles Palmer of Worcester, Massachusetts, who later built an even larger wagon with counters separating the kitchen from the dining area. It could accommodate up to twenty customers at a time.

Entrepreneur Thomas Buckley took the lunch wagon idea and began to manufacture standardized versions. Buckley's popular Owl model lunch counter, which first appeared in 1892, earned him recognition as the "Lunch Wagon King." The Owl featured not only a counter, but all the necessary items needed to set up for business. Built-in cooking stoves allowed owners to offer expanded menus that included soups, stews, breakfasts, and other simple, hot meals.

Buckley's Owl and other similar lunch wagons proved so successful that they were soon popping up in cities across the United States. Although business was booming, residents soon complained that the wagons were becoming eyesores and causing traffic congestion. With that in mind, Patrick Tierney of

HICKEY'S DINER, TAUNTON, MASSACHUSETTS

New Rochelle, New York, designed a new, improved, and much better looking lunch wagon. Tierney gave his prefabricated structures a sleek, narrow appearance similar to that of a railroad dining car. Each contained separate booths for at-table service, working toilet facilities, and other amenities. Tierney's design became the basic blueprint for the diners we recognize today.

BLUE PLATE SPECIALS

Baked Meat Loaf

2   eggs
⅓   cup ketchup
1   tablespoon Worcestershire sauce
1   teaspoon basil
     Salt and pepper to taste
1   potato, peeled and grated
1   onion, grated
1   red bell pepper, chopped fine
2   pounds ground beef

In a large mixing bowl blend together the
eggs, ketchup, Worcestershire sauce, and
basil. Season with salt and pepper.

Add the grated potato, onion, and red
bell pepper. Blend in the ground beef and
mix thoroughly. Shape the meat into a
loaf and place in a 9x5-inch pan. Bake at
350° for 1 hour or until the meat loaf is
done.

SERVES 6

Just-Like-Mom's Meat Loaf

2   pounds ground round
2   eggs, beaten
1½   cups cracker crumbs
¾   cup ketchup
1   package onion soup mix
½   cup warm water
1   8-ounce can tomato sauce

In a mixing bowl blend together the
ground round, beaten eggs, cracker
crumbs, ketchup, onion soup mix, and
warm water. Mix thoroughly.

Shape the meat into a loaf and place in
a 9x5-inch pan. Pour the tomato sauce
over the top. Bake at 350° for 1 hour or
until the meat loaf is done.

SERVES 6

Incredible Meat Loaf

1	pound ground beef
½	pound ground pork
½	pound ground turkey
¾	cup chopped onion
2	eggs, beaten
1	tablespoon Worcestershire sauce
1½	teaspoons dry mustard
½	teaspoon salt
¼	teaspoon pepper
1½	cups dry breadcrumbs
¼	teaspoon garlic powder
¾	cup tomato juice
1	8-ounce can tomato sauce

In a large mixing bowl combine the ground beef, ground pork, ground turkey, onion, eggs, and Worcestershire sauce. Mix thoroughly. Add the dry mustard, salt, pepper, dry breadcrumbs, garlic powder, and tomato juice. Mix thoroughly.

Shape the meat into a loaf and place in a 9x5-inch pan. Pour the tomato sauce over the top. Bake at 350° for 1 hour and 15 minutes or until the meat loaf is done.

SERVES 6

PARKWAY DINER, SOUTH BURLINGTON, VERMONT

Mushroom Meat Loaf

¼ cup butter
1 pound mushrooms, sliced
1 teaspoon fresh lemon juice
1 onion, diced
4 cups seasoned breadcrumbs
½ teaspoon salt
  Pepper to taste
¼ teaspoon thyme
2 eggs
3 pounds ground beef
1 tablespoon salt
¼ cup milk
⅓ cup ketchup
1½ teaspoons dry mustard
6 large whole mushrooms

In a skillet melt the butter. Sauté the sliced mushrooms, lemon juice, and onion. Add the breadcrumbs, salt, pepper, and thyme.

In a mixing bowl beat the eggs. Blend in the ground beef. Add the salt, milk, ketchup, and dry mustard, and mix thoroughly.

Place half the meat mixture in the bottom of a loaf pan. Pour the sautéed mushroom mixture over the meat. Top with the remaining ground beef. Press the whole mushrooms into the top of the meat loaf. Bake at 375° for 90 minutes or until the meat loaf is done.

SERVES 6

Pretty Much Meat Loaf

1½ pounds ground chuck
½ pound ground pork
2 tablespoons horseradish
2 onions, chopped
½ teaspoon salt
1 teaspoon dry mustard
½ teaspoon thyme
3 tablespoons chopped parsley
2 large eggs
¼ cup milk
2 cups breadcrumbs
4 slices bacon
¼ cup ketchup

In a mixing bowl blend together the ground chuck, ground pork, horseradish, onions, salt, mustard, thyme, and parsley, and mix thoroughly.

In a separate mixing bowl blend together the eggs and milk. Add the mixture to the meat with the breadcrumbs. Shape the meat into a loaf and place in a 9x5-inch pan. Top with bacon slices. Pour ketchup over the bacon slices. Bake at 350° for 50 minutes or until the meat loaf is done.

SERVES 6

Quick & Easy Meat Loaf

1	pound ground beef
1	pound ground pork
1	cup cottage cheese
2	cups seasoned breadcrumbs
1	cup sliced stuffed olives
1	egg, beaten
	Salt and pepper to taste

In a mixing bowl blend together the ground beef, ground pork, cottage cheese, and seasoned breadcrumbs. Mix thoroughly.

Add the sliced olives to the egg and season with salt and pepper. Add the mixture to the meat and mix thoroughly. Shape the meat into a loaf and place in a 9x5-inch pan. Bake at 350° for 1 hour or until the meat loaf is done.

SERVES 6

Salisbury Steak

1	pound ground beef
¼	cup seasoned breadcrumbs
¼	cup water
1	egg, slightly beaten
	Salt and pepper to taste
¼	cup dry white wine
2	cups thinly sliced onions
2	cups thinly sliced mushrooms
1	8-ounce can tomato sauce
½	teaspoon basil

In a mixing bowl combine the ground beef, breadcrumbs, water, egg, salt, and pepper. Mix well. Shape the meat into 4 oval-shaped patties. Place in the bottom of a 1½-quart baking dish. Set aside.

PARKWAY DINER, SOUTH BURLINGTON, VERMONT

In a skillet heat the white wine and sauté the onions and mushrooms until tender. Add the tomato sauce and basil, and blend thoroughly.

Spoon the tomato mixture over the hamburger patties. Bake at 350° for 30 minutes or until the meat is done.

SERVES 4

Behind-the-Counter Swiss Steak

2	pounds round steak
1/4	cup all-purpose flour
1	teaspoon salt
1/4	teaspoon pepper
2	tablespoons oil
2	cups cooked tomatoes
2	cups diced onion
1	cup diced celery
1	cup sliced mushrooms
1	garlic clove, minced
1	teaspoon salt
2	tablespoons all-purpose flour
1/4	cup water

Clean the round steak and trim off any fat. In a mixing bowl combine 1/4 cup of flour with the salt and pepper. Dredge the meat in the flour mixture, pressing it into all sides of the meat.

In a skillet heat the oil. Brown the meat quickly. Add the tomatoes, onion, celery, mushrooms, garlic, and salt. Cover and simmer for 1 hour and 30 minutes or until the meat is tender.

Remove the meat and vegetables from the skillet. Set aside. Add 2 tablespoons of flour to the water and mix with the drippings from the skillet. Cook for 5 minutes or until the gravy thickens, stirring constantly. Pour over the round steak. Serve with vegetables.

SERVES 6

Delicious Swiss Steak

1/4	cup all-purpose flour
1 1/2	teaspoons salt
	Pepper to taste
2	pounds round steak
1/4	cup cooking oil
2	onions, chopped
1	cup water
1	8-ounce can tomato sauce

In a large mixing bowl blend together the flour, salt, and pepper. Dredge the round steak in the flour mixture, pressing it into all sides of the meat.

In a skillet heat the oil and brown the meat on both sides. Remove. In the same skillet sauté the onion until tender. Add the water and tomato sauce. Bring the mixture to a boil, stirring constantly until the sauce thickens.

Return the round steak to the skillet. Cover and simmer for 1 hour and 30 minutes or until the meat is tender and tests done.

SERVES 6

AVOCA DINER, AVOCA, NEW YORK

Just Swiss Steak

3	tablespoons cooking oil
2	pounds flank steak
½	cup all-purpose flour
1	cup water
1	16-ounce can whole tomatoes with liquid
½	teaspoon basil
1	medium onion, chopped
1	garlic clove, minced
1	teaspoon salt
¼	teaspoon pepper

In a skillet heat the oil. Dredge the flank steak in the flour, pressing it into all sides of the meat. Place the flank steak in the skillet and brown thoroughly.

Remove the meat and place it in a covered baking dish. Add the water to the skillet and scrape the sides of the skillet. Pour the water into the baking dish with the steak. Add the whole tomatoes with juice, basil, onion, garlic, salt, and pepper. Bake at 300° for 2 hours or until the meat is done.

SERVES 6

Dreamy Beef Stroganoff

1	pound round steak
1	8-ounce package egg noodles
6	tablespoons all-purpose flour
½	teaspoon salt
	Pepper to taste
¼	cup butter
½	cup chopped onion
1	8-ounce jar sliced mushrooms, drained
½	cup chopped celery
¼	cup chopped green bell pepper
1	tablespoon Worcestershire sauce
1	10-ounce can beef broth
1	cup sour cream
¼	cup dry sherry

Cut the round steak into ¼-inch strips. Prepare the egg noodles according to package directions. Drain and set aside. In a mixing bowl blend together 4 tablespoons of flour with the salt and pepper. Dredge the beef strips in the flour mixture.

In a heavy skillet heat 2 tablespoons of butter and brown the meat on all sides. Add the onion, mushrooms, celery, and green pepper, and sauté until the onions are tender. Remove the meat and vegetables from the skillet. Set aside.

Add the remaining butter and remaining flour to the skillet. Add the Worcestershire sauce. Slowly add the beef broth. Simmer until the mixture thickens, stirring constantly. Add the meat and vegetable mixture. Blend in the sour cream and sherry. Serve over egg noodles.

SERVES 4

Fill-'Er-Up Beef Stroganoff

1½	pounds beef sirloin
½	teaspoon salt
½	teaspoon paprika
	Garlic salt to taste
	Pepper to taste
¼	cup butter
1	onion, chopped
⅓	cup sliced mushrooms
1	cup water
1	beef bouillon cube
1	teaspoon Worcestershire sauce
2	cups sour cream
6	cups cooked white rice

Cut the beef sirloin into thin strips. Season with the salt, paprika, garlic salt, and pepper.

In a skillet melt the butter. Brown the sirloin strips, onion, and mushrooms until tender. Add the water and beef bouillon cube. Mix thoroughly. Add the Worcestershire sauce and simmer for 15 minutes.

Remove the pan from the heat. Blend in the sour cream. Serve over cooked rice.

SERVES 6

Patrolman Beef Stroganoff

1½ pounds beef sirloin
1 8-ounce package egg noodles
3 tablespoons cooking oil
1 onion, chopped
½ teaspoon salt
   Pepper to taste
½ pound sliced mushrooms
1 cup sour cream

Cut the beef sirloin into thin strips. Prepare the egg noodles according to package directions. Drain and set aside.

In a skillet heat the oil and brown the sirloin strips thoroughly. Remove and set aside. Add the onion to the skillet and sauté until tender. Season with salt and pepper. Return the sirloin strips to the skillet. Cover and simmer for 30 minutes or until the beef is tender. Add the mushrooms. Increase the heat to medium and cook for 3 minutes or until the mushrooms are tender, adding water if necessary. Remove the skillet from the heat. Blend in the sour cream, blending well. Serve over egg noodles.

SERVES 6

Hungarian Goulash

4 slices bacon
1½ cups chopped onion
1 small green bell pepper, chopped
1½ pounds boneless beef chuck
1½ teaspoons paprika
½ teaspoon salt
¼ teaspoon coarse black pepper
⅛ teaspoon marjoram
2 cups beef broth
¾ cup dry white wine
4 cups cooked white rice

In a heavy pot fry the bacon until light brown. Remove and drain on paper towels. Add the onion and green pepper, and sauté until the onion becomes transparent. Remove and set aside.

Add the boneless beef chuck and brown on all sides. Sprinkle the paprika, salt, pepper, and marjoram over the top. Add the bacon and vegetables. Slowly pour in the beef broth and white wine.

Bring to a boil. Reduce the heat, cover, and let simmer for 2 to 2½ hours or until the meat is tender. Remove the meat with a slotted spoon. Serve with gravy from the pot over cooked white rice.

SERVES 4

Maryland Pot Roast

1 teaspoon salt
½ teaspoon peppercorns
1 teaspoon allspice
2 medium onions, chopped
1 garlic clove, minced
1 cinnamon stick
1½ tablespoons parsley
1 4-pound bottom round
2 cups apple cider

In a small bowl crush together the salt, peppercorns, and allspice.

In a large pot combine the onions, garlic, cinnamon stick, parsley, and crushed spices. Place the beef in the pot and cover

with apple cider. Bring the cider to a boil.
Reduce the heat and simmer for 4 hours
or until tender. Turn once while cooking.

SERVES 6

Pot Roast

1	4-pound beef pot roast
½	cup all-purpose flour
	Cooking oil
	Salt and pepper to taste
2	medium onions, diced
½	cup water
¼	cup ketchup
⅓	cup cooking sherry
1	garlic clove, minced
¼	teaspoon dry mustard
¼	teaspoon thyme
1	bay leaf
1	tablespoon all-purpose flour
¼	cup water

Dredge the pot roast in ½ cup of flour.
Heat the oil and brown the meat on all
sides. Season with salt and pepper.

Place the meat in a large pot. Add the
onions, ½ cup water, ketchup, sherry,
garlic, dry mustard, thyme, and bay leaf.
Cover and cook for 2 hours and 30 minutes or until the meat is done.

Remove the meat and bay leaf. Skim
the fat from the broth. Add 1 tablespoon
of flour and the ¼ cup of water. Blend
until the sauce thickens. Serve over the
pot roast.

SERVES 6

Highway Beef Stew

4	pounds boneless beef chuck
¼	cup cooking oil
1½	teaspoons salt
	Pepper to taste
3	cups dry red wine
2	cups water
2	tablespoons tomato paste
1	garlic clove, minced
½	teaspoon crushed thyme
12	small boiling onions, chopped
4	carrots, quartered
4	stalks celery, diced
3	turnips, quartered
¼	pound sliced mushrooms
1	cup all-purpose flour
2	teaspoons baking powder
½	teaspoon sugar
1	egg, beaten
½	cup milk
2	tablespoons cooking oil

Cut the beef chuck into 2-inch cubes. In
a skillet heat the oil and brown the beef
on all sides. Season with salt and pepper.
Add the wine, water, tomato paste, garlic,
and thyme. Bring to a boil. Cover and
simmer for 1 hour.

Add the onions, carrots, celery,
turnips, and mushrooms. Cover and simmer for 2 hours more or until the vegetables are tender. Add flour, if necessary, to
thicken.

In a mixing bowl combine 1 cup of
flour with the baking powder, sugar, egg,
milk, and oil. Blend. Drop by tablespoonfuls into the stew. Cook uncovered for 10
minutes.

SERVES 6

On-the-Road Beef Stew

4   pounds boneless beef chuck
½   cup plus 1½ tablespoons all-purpose flour
1½   cups dry red wine
1   garlic clove, peeled and chopped
¼   cup shallots
1   bay leaf
¼   cup cubed salt pork
¼   cup cooking oil
1   teaspoon salt
½   teaspoon paprika
2   medium onions, chopped
¼   cup chopped parsley
¾   pound mushrooms
2   tablespoons butter
2   medium carrots
2   cups water
2   cups beef stock

Cut the boneless chuck into 2-inch cubes. Dredge in the flour. In a skillet heat the red wine and brown the meat evenly on all sides. Add the garlic and shallots and sauté until tender.

In a large soup pot combine the browned meat, garlic, and shallots. Add the bay leaf. Cut the cubed salt pork into ¼-inch pieces.

In the skillet heat the oil and sauté the cubed pork. Transfer the pork to the soup pot. Blend in the salt and paprika. Add the onions, parsley, mushrooms, butter, carrots, water, and beef stock. Cover and simmer for 1 hour and 30 minutes or until the vegetables are tender. Remove the bay leaf before serving.

SERVES 6

Countertop Beef Stew

¼   cup all-purpose flour
1½   teaspoons salt
      Pepper to taste
1   pound beef chuck, cut in 1-inch cubes
¼   cup cooking oil
1   onion, chopped fine
1   carrot, chopped fine
¼   cup finely chopped celery
      Thyme
3   cups water
2   medium potatoes, diced
2   carrots, diced
1   onion, diced
1   10-ounce package frozen peas

In a mixing bowl blend together the flour, salt, and pepper. Coat the beef in the flour mixture.

In a large skillet heat the oil. Brown the beef with the chopped onion. Add the chopped carrot, celery, thyme, and water. Cover and cook on low for 1 hour and 30 minutes, stirring often.

Add the diced potatoes, diced carrots, and onion. Cook for 30 minutes more. Add the peas and continue cooking for 15 minutes.

SERVES 6

7-Card Beef Stew

2 tablespoons shortening
2 pounds chuck, cut in 1-inch cubes
1 medium onion, chopped
1 garlic clove, minced
2 cups boiling water
½ teaspoon salt
1 teaspoon sugar
1 teaspoon Worcestershire sauce
¼ teaspoon pepper
½ teaspoon paprika
1 bay leaf
6 carrots
1 pound small boiling onions
6 medium potatoes, cubed

¼ cup cold water
2 tablespoons all-purpose flour

In a Dutch oven melt the shortening. Coat pieces of chuck in the flour. Cook for 20 minutes, browning evenly on all sides. Add the onion and garlic, and brown for 2 minutes more.

Add the boiling water, salt, sugar, Worcestershire sauce, pepper, paprika, and bay leaf. Simmer for 1 hour and 30 minutes. Remove the bay leaf. Chop all the vegetables into 1-inch pieces. Add to the meat. Cover and simmer for 30 minutes.

In a small bowl blend the cold water and flour until smooth. Pour into the pot. Cook until the flour mixture thickens.

SERVES 6

ROSIE'S DINER, GROTON, CONNECTICUT

Diner Chicken Fried Steak

1½ pounds beef round steak
1   egg, beaten
2   tablespoons milk
2   tablespoons all-purpose flour
¾   cups seasoned breadcrumbs
¼   cup cooking oil
1   teaspoon salt
    Pepper to taste
♦ ♦ ♦
2   tablespoons cooking oil
2   tablespoons all-purpose flour
½   teaspoon salt
    Pepper to taste
1   cup milk

Pound the round steak very thin and cut into serving portions. In a small bowl mix together the egg and the milk. Have the flour and the breadcrumbs ready in shallow bowls. Coat the round steak in the flour. Dip into the egg and then the breadcrumbs.

In a skillet heat ¼ cup of oil. Cook the round steak on all sides until brown. Season with salt and pepper.

In a saucepan blend together 2 tablespoons of oil and the flour. Add the salt and pepper. Gradually pour in the milk. Cook over medium heat for 1 minute, stirring constantly until the gravy thickens. Pour over the round steak.

SERVES 6

Stuffed Beef Rolls

1   tablespoon cooking oil
1   green bell pepper, cubed
1   onion, sliced
1   garlic clove, minced
♦ ♦ ♦
1½ cups seasoned breadcrumbs
¼   cup grated Parmesan cheese
4   beef cube steaks
3   tablespoons cooking oil
1   cup water
¾   cup chili sauce
1   beef bouillon cube

In a large skillet heat 1 tablespoon of oil and sauté the green pepper, onion, and garlic until tender. Remove and set aside.

In a mixing bowl blend together the seasoned breadcrumbs and the Parmesan cheese. Pour even amounts of the mixture over each steak. Roll and secure with toothpicks.

In the same skillet heat the 3 tablespoons of oil and brown the steaks on all sides. Combine the water, chili sauce, and bouillon cube. Add the vegetables. Pour over the beef rolls.

Cover and simmer for 30 minutes. Baste the rolls while simmering. Remove the toothpicks and serve the beef rolls with the sauce.

SERVES 4

Stuffed Green Peppers

4 green bell peppers
½ cup uncooked long-grain rice
1 pound ground beef
¼ cup finely chopped onion
2 tablespoons finely chopped celery
¼ teaspoon dry mustard
½ teaspoon garlic salt
¼ teaspoon coarse black pepper
½ cup grated Cheddar cheese
1½ cups tomato sauce

Cut the tops from the green peppers. Remove the insides. Place in a saucepan of boiling water. Simmer for 5 minutes. Remove and drain upside-down on paper towels.

Cook the rice until fluffy. In a skillet brown the ground beef. Drain the beef on paper towels. In the same skillet sauté the onion and celery until tender. Drain the fat. Return the beef to the skillet. Add the mustard, garlic salt, pepper, and rice.

Fill the peppers with the beef mixture. Place the peppers in a baking dish. Top with grated Cheddar cheese. Pour tomato sauce around the peppers. Bake at 350° for 20 minutes. Increase the heat to 400° and continue baking for 10 minutes more or until the cheese is brown. Spoon tomato sauce over the peppers before serving.

SERVES 4

Cabbage Rolls

3 quarts water
1 teaspoon salt
1 large head cabbage
1 pound ground beef
½ cup uncooked rice
¾ cup finely chopped onion
2 eggs, beaten
½ teaspoon salt
⅛ teaspoon pepper
½ teaspoon garlic powder
½ cup finely chopped celery
2 tablespoons cooking oil
1 12-ounce can stewed tomatoes

In a large soup pot bring 3 quarts of water to a boil. Add 1 teaspoon of salt. Remove 12 of the largest outer leaves from the head of cabbage. Drop, a few at a time, into the boiling water. Cook for 5 minutes. Drain on paper towels. Remove the center veins. Set aside.

In a mixing bowl blend together the ground beef, rice, ¼ cup of onion, eggs, ½ teaspoon of salt, pepper, garlic powder, and celery. Mix thoroughly.

Place a heaping teaspoon of the beef mixture on each of the cabbage leaves. Roll up, folding in the sides. Fasten with a toothpick.

In a skillet heat the oil. Brown the cabbage rolls, turning at least once. Place the cabbage rolls in an uncovered baking dish. Pour the tomatoes with juice over the top. Add the remaining chopped onion. Bake 325° for 1 hour and 15 minutes.

SERVES 6

Corned Beef & Cabbage

4   pounds corned beef
½   pound salt pork
3   quarts boiling water
¼   cup sugar
3   bay leaves
2   garlic cloves
10   small red potatoes
4   small turnips, peeled
5   carrots, scraped
8   boiling onions, peeled
4   parsnips, scraped
1   head cabbage

Soak the corned beef in cold water for 30 minutes. In a large soup pot place the beef with the salt pork, and cover with the boiling water. Add the sugar, bay leaves, and garlic, and simmer for 3 hours. Remove the bay leaves.

Add the potatoes, turnips, carrots, onions, and parsnips. Continue cooking for 30 minutes more, or until all of the vegetables are tender.

Cut the cabbage into 6 equal-size wedges. Place the cabbage over the meat in the soup pot the last 15 minutes of cooking. Cover and simmer until the cabbage is cooked. Remove the vegetables from the pot. Serve the meat with the cabbage and the vegetables on the side.

SERVES 6

WILSON'S DINER, WALTHAM, MASSACHUSETTS

WESSON'S DINER, SOUTH BURLINGTON, VERMONT

Beef Brisket

1	cup hot water
1	beef bouillon cube
1	package onion soup mix
1	2-pound beef brisket
1½	pounds carrots
1½	pounds red potatoes

In a small mixing bowl add the hot water to the beef bouillon cube. Stir until the cube has dissolved.

In a large casserole dish combine the beef bouillon and onion soup mix. Add the beef brisket. Coat the beef on all sides. Cover and bake at 350° for 2 hours.

Clean the vegetables. Chop the carrots into 2-inch chunks. Place the potatoes and carrots into the dish. Bake for 1 additional hour or more, until the meat and vegetables are tender. Serve with the gravy from the casserole dish.

SERVES 6

Sauerbraten

1	4-pound beef pot roast
1	large onion, sliced
1	cup sliced carrots
2	bay leaves
2	cups buttermilk
1/4	cup butter
1	8-ounce package egg noodles
12	gingersnap cookies, crushed
2	tablespoons packed light brown sugar

Place the pot roast in a baking dish. Add the onions, carrots, and bay leaves. Pour in the buttermilk. Cover with foil. Refrigerate for 36 hours, turning the meat 2 times. Remove the meat. Drain and reserve the marinade.

In a heavy skillet melt the butter. Brown the meat on all sides. Add the reserved marinade. Reduce the heat and simmer for 2 hours and 30 minutes or until the meat is done.

Prepare the noodles according to package directions.

Remove the meat. Add the gingersnaps and brown sugar to the sauce remaining in the skillet. Simmer for 2 minutes. Serve the meat with the gravy over egg noodles

SERVES 6

Lasagna

6	ounces pork sausage
1	tablespoon cooking oil
1/4	cup chopped onion
2	garlic cloves, minced
2	28-ounce cans tomatoes
1/2	teaspoon salt
12	lasagna noodles
2¾	cups Ricotta cheese
1/4	cup chopped parsley
	Salt to taste
3	tablespoons grated Parmesan cheese
2½	cups grated Mozzarella cheese

Remove the skins from the sausage. In a skillet heat the oil and brown the sausage. Drain on paper towels. In the same skillet sauté the onion and garlic until tender.

In a large saucepan blend together the onion, garlic, and tomatoes. Add the cooked sausage and 1/2 teaspoon of salt, and simmer for 20 minutes.

Prepare the lasagna noodles according to package directions. In a small bowl blend together the Ricotta cheese, parsley, and salt.

In the bottom of a 13x9-inch baking pan spread 1 cup of sauce. Place 4 noodles over the sauce. Top with 1 cup of the Ricotta cheese mixture. Sprinkle with Parmesan cheese and Mozzarella. Continue layering with the remaining ingredients. Cover with aluminum foil. Bake at 375° for 1 hour. Uncover and continue baking for 10 minutes more.

SERVES 6

Liver & Onions

2	pounds liver, ¾-inch thick
8	slices bacon
½	cup all-purpose flour
½	teaspoon salt
⅛	teaspoon coarse black pepper
½	teaspoon garlic powder
¼	cup butter
1	pound sweet onions, sliced

♦ ♦ ♦

2	tablespoons butter
2	tablespoons all-purpose flour
¼	cup water
1	cup milk
¼	teaspoon salt
⅛	teaspoon coarse black pepper

Wash the liver under cold running water. Cut into 4 servings. In a large skillet fry the bacon until crisp. Drain on paper towels. Set aside.

In a mixing bowl blend together ½ cup of flour, salt, pepper, and garlic powder. Dredge the liver in the flour mixture. In a skillet melt ¼ cup of butter and brown the liver on all sides.

Butter a 1½-quart casserole dish. Place the browned liver in the bottom. In the same skillet sauté the onions until transparent. Pour over the liver.

In a saucepan melt 2 tablespoons of butter for the sauce. In a cup mix together 2 tablespoons of flour and the water. Add the mixture to the melted butter. Cook until the mixture bubbles and begins to thicken. Gradually pour in the milk.

Continue cooking for 1 minute more. Add the salt and pepper. Pour the gravy over the liver. Cover and bake at 350° for 30 minutes.

SERVES 4

Shepherd's Pie

1	egg
2	tablespoons grated Parmesan cheese
1	tablespoon cooking oil
1	onion, diced
1	pound ground beef
1	cup stewed tomatoes
2	tablespoons cornstarch
1	tablespoon chicken bouillon granules
¼	teaspoon basil
1	teaspoon salt
¼	teaspoon pepper
3	carrots, sliced
¼	pound sliced mushrooms
½	cup peas
¾	cup water
1¾	cups mashed potatoes

In a small mixing bowl combine the egg and the Parmesan cheese. Set aside. In a skillet heat the oil and sauté the onion with the ground beef until the beef is thoroughly cooked. Drain the fat.

In a separate mixing bowl combine the tomatoes, cornstarch, chicken bouillon granules, basil, salt, and pepper. Blend until smooth. Add to the beef with the carrots, mushrooms, peas, and water. Mix in the egg and Parmesan cheese mixture. Cover and simmer for 5 minutes. Top with mashed potatoes. Cover and simmer for 3 minutes longer.

SERVES 4

Spaghetti with Meatballs

MEATBALLS

1	pound ground beef
½	pound ground pork
1	egg, beaten
½	teaspoon salt
	Pepper to taste
¼	cup seasoned breadcrumbs
	Cooking oil

♦ ♦ ♦

1½	cups chopped onion
½	cup chopped green bell pepper
1	16-ounce can tomatoes
1	6-ounce can tomato paste
1	garlic clove, minced
3	cups water
1	teaspoon oregano
¼	teaspoon basil

♦ ♦ ♦

1	pound spaghetti, uncooked
½	cup grated Parmesan cheese

In a mixing bowl blend together the ground beef and pork. Add the egg, salt, pepper, and seasoned breadcrumbs. Mix thoroughly.

Shape the meat into 12 even-size balls. In a skillet heat the oil and brown the meatballs on all sides. Remove and drain on paper towels.

In the same skillet sauté the onion and green pepper until tender. Add the tomatoes, tomato paste, garlic, water, oregano, and basil. Bring to a boil. Add the meatballs and simmer for 2 hours or until the sauce becomes thick.

Bring a saucepan of water to a boil. Cook the spaghetti for 10 minutes or until tender. Drain. Serve with sauce. Top with Parmesan cheese.

SERVES 6

Swedish Meatballs

1½	cups of soft breadcrumbs
¾	cup milk
3	tablespoons cooking oil
3	tablespoons chopped onion
1	pound ground beef
¼	teaspoon nutmeg
1½	teaspoons salt
	Pepper to taste
1	egg, beaten
1	cup beef stock
1	tablespoon all-purpose flour
1	tablespoon water

In a small bowl soak the breadcrumbs in the milk. In a skillet heat the oil and sauté the onion until tender.

In a large mixing bowl blend together the onion and ground beef. Add the nutmeg, salt, pepper, egg, and soaked breadcrumbs. Shape the meat into 1-inch balls.

Brown the meatballs in the same skillet used to sauté the onion, adding more oil if necessary. Add the beef stock, cover and simmer for 5 minutes. Add the flour and water to the skillet and blend until thick and smooth. Serve the gravy over the meatballs.

SERVES 6

Stuffed Veal

1	3-ounce package cream cheese, softened
2	tablespoons grated Parmesan cheese
1	teaspoon mustard
½	teaspoon dried parsley
⅛	teaspoon garlic powder
½	cup all-purpose flour
	Salt and pepper to taste
1	cup seasoned breadcrumbs
2	eggs, beaten
8	slices cooked ham
8	veal cutlets
8	slices Swiss cheese
	Cooking oil

In a mixing bowl blend together the cream cheese, Parmesan cheese, mustard, parsley, and garlic powder.

In a separate bowl mix the flour with salt and pepper. Have ready the breadcrumbs and eggs in separate shallow dishes.

Place a ham slice on each veal cutlet. Spread an even layer of the cream cheese mixture over the top. Top with Swiss cheese. Brush the tops with egg. Fold in half and pound with a meat mallet. Coat both sides with the flour mixture. Dip into the eggs and then the breadcrumbs. Cover and refrigerate for 1 hour.

In a skillet heat the oil. Fry one cutlet at a time. Cook for 2 to 3 minutes on both sides or until golden brown. Drain on paper towels.

SERVES 4

ANGELO'S ORCHID DINER, NEW BEDFORD, MASSACHUSETTS

Veal Cutlets

½	teaspoon salt
	Pepper to taste
2	tablespoons all-purpose flour
4	veal chops
l	egg, beaten
½	cup seasoned breadcrumbs
¼	cup cooking oil
l	cup half-and-half
2	tablespoons minced parsley
¼	cup chopped green onions

In a mixing bowl combine the salt, pepper, and flour. Dredge the veal in the flour. Dip the veal into the egg, then the breadcrumbs. In a skillet heat the oil and fry the veal until golden brown on both sides. Remove and keep warm.

To the same skillet add the half-and-half, parsley, and green onions. Simmer for 2 minutes or until thoroughly heated. Serve over the veal.

SERVES 4

Veal Parmesan

2	tablespoons cooking oil
l	onion, sliced and separated into rings
½	cup chopped green bell pepper
l	garlic clove, minced
2	cups tomato sauce
½	teaspoon dried basil
½	teaspoon sugar
	Salt and pepper to taste
	♦ ♦ ♦
l	cup seasoned breadcrumbs
¾	cup grated Parmesan cheese
2	eggs, beaten
3	tablespoons cooking oil
l	pound veal cutlets, ¼-inch thick

In a skillet heat 2 tablespoons of oil and sauté the onion, green pepper, and garlic until tender. Add the tomato sauce, basil, sugar, salt, and pepper. Bring to a boil. Reduce the heat and simmer for 30 minutes or until thick.

In a shallow mixing bowl toss the breadcrumbs with ¼ cup of the Parmesan cheese. Dip the veal cutlets into the beaten eggs and then the breadcrumbs.

In a separate skillet heat the 3 tablespoons of oil. Fry the veal for 3 minutes or until golden, turning once. Drain on paper towels.

Place the cutlets in a baking dish. Pour the sauce over the top. Sprinkle the remaining cheese over the sauce. Bake at 350° for 15 minutes or until the cheese has melted.

SERVES 4

Pork Tenderloins

l	2-pound pork tenderloin
	Whole cloves
½	cup packed light brown sugar
2	tablespoons mustard
	Salt
	Pepper to taste
½	cup water

In a skillet add enough water to cover the pork tenderloin. Place cloves in the upper pockets of the meat. Simmer for 45 minutes. Remove the cloves.

In a mixing bowl blend together the brown sugar and mustard. Place the pork

BARBARA'S PLACE, WHITINSVILLE, MASSACHUSETTS

tenderloin in a square baking dish. Pour mustard sauce over the meat. Season with salt and pepper.

Pour ½ cup water into the baking dish. Bake at 400° for 30 minutes or until the meat is done. Slice while warm and serve.

SERVES 6

Ham & Sweet Potatoes

2	cups milk
1	tablespoon chopped onion
¼	teaspoon ground cloves
1	tablespoon finely chopped celery
¼	cup butter

6	tablespoons all-purpose flour
2	cups milk
2	cups chopped ham
2	cups cooked sweet potatoes, mashed
3	tablespoons chopped walnuts

In a saucepan heat the milk. Add the onion, cloves, and celery, and cook for 1 minute. Strain and set aside.

In a heavy skillet melt the butter. Add the flour, stirring constantly. Gradually add the milk and continue stirring until the mixture has thickened. Add the ham.

Pour the mixture into a casserole dish. Top with cooked sweet potatoes and walnuts. Bake at 375° for 30 minutes.

SERVES 6

Baked Ham

| | 12-ounce can apricot nectar
| | cup packed light brown sugar
| | cinnamon stick
6 | whole cloves
| | 6-pound ham

In a saucepan combine the apricot nectar and brown sugar. Cook over low heat until all of the sugar has dissolved. Add the cinnamon stick and cloves. Bring to a gentle boil for 10 minutes or until the sauce begins to thicken. Remove the cinnamon stick and cloves.

Place the ham in a shallow baking dish. Brush glaze over the tops and sides of the ham. Bake at 325° for 1 hour or until the meat is done, glazing the tops and sides of ham periodically.

SERVES 8

Southern Pork Chops

| | Cooking oil
6 | pork chops
| | Salt and pepper to taste
3 | cups seasoned bread stuffing
| | 14-ounce can sliced tomatoes
| | 12-ounce can whole kernel corn
| | 4-ounce jar sliced mushrooms
| | 10½-ounce can condensed chicken gumbo soup

In a skillet heat enough oil just to cover the bottom of the pan. Brown the pork chops on both sides. Season with salt and pepper.

In a mixing bowl blend together the seasoned bread stuffing, sliced tomatoes, whole corn, sliced mushrooms, and chicken gumbo soup.

Place 2 pork chops into the bottom of a loaf pan. Spread an even layer of stuffing mixture over the pork chops. Continue layering with pork chops and stuffing. Place any remaining stuffing mixture inside the loaf pan.

Cover and bake at 350° for 30 minutes. Uncover and bake for 30 minutes more or until the meat is done.

SERVES 6

Stuffed Pork Chops

2 | tablespoons cooking oil
| | onion, chopped
½ | cup chopped celery
| | cup water
| | beef bouillon cube
3 | cups breadcrumbs
¼ | cup minced parsley
6 | double pork chops, halved
2 | tablespoons cooking oil
| | 6-ounce can tomato sauce
½ | cup water

In a skillet heat the oil and sauté the onion and celery until tender. To the cup of water add the beef bouillon cube. Pour the liquid into the skillet. Simmer for 10 minutes.

Add the breadcrumbs and parsley to the skillet. Stuff the pork chops with the onion-breadcrumb mixture. Secure the meat with string and toothpicks.

In a separate skillet heat the oil. Brown the pork chops on both sides. Add the tomato sauce and water. Cover and let simmer for 1 hour or until the meat is tender.

SERVES 6

Pork Chops with Peppers

1	cup red wine
1/4	cup fresh orange juice
1	garlic clove, minced
1	teaspoon marjoram
1/2	teaspoon salt
1/2	teaspoon Tabasco
4	pork chops
2	tablespoons cooking oil
2	red bell peppers, sliced

In a mixing bowl combine the red wine, orange juice, garlic, marjoram, salt, and Tabasco. Blend thoroughly. Place the pork chops in the marinade. Cover and chill for 1 hour.

Remove the pork chops from the marinade and pat dry on paper towels. Set aside any remaining marinade.

In a skillet heat the oil and brown the pork chops on both sides. Set aside. Sauté the red peppers until tender. Return the pork chops to the skillet. Add the marinade and bring to a boil. Cover and simmer for 20 minutes or until the meat is done. Serve with the remaining marinade.

SERVES 4

Baked Chicken

2	4-pound fryer chickens, halved
1/4	cup butter, melted
1/2	teaspoon salt
1/4	teaspoon pepper
1	cup hot water
	Giblets from chicken
1	small onion, chopped
3	tablespoons all-purpose flour

In a large baking pan place the chickens skin-side-down. Drizzle melted butter over the top. Season with salt and pepper. Pour the hot water into the pan. Bake at 400° for 30 minutes. Turn once and baste with juice. Lower heat to 350° and continue baking for 20 minutes more or until the chicken is brown and tender. Remove the chicken to a warm platter.

In a saucepan cook the giblets with the onion in boiling water until tender.

In a separate saucepan blend the juice from the baking pan with the flour. Add water if necessary to create a smooth gravy. Chop up the giblets and add to the gravy. Pour the gravy over the chicken.

SERVES 4

Chicken Cacciatore

I	3-pound fryer chicken
½	cup all-purpose flour
I	teaspoon salt
	Pepper to taste
½	cup cooking oil
2	onions, chopped
I	16-ounce can whole tomatoes
I	8-ounce can tomato sauce
2	garlic cloves, minced
I	teaspoon oregano
I	teaspoon celery seed
I	teaspoon salt
¼	teaspoon pepper

Clean and dry the chicken with paper towels. Cut the chicken into serving pieces. In a mixing bowl blend together the flour with the salt and pepper. Coat the chicken in the flour mixture.

In a skillet heat the oil and brown the chicken on all sides. Remove. Add the onions and sauté until tender. Add the tomatoes, garlic, tomato sauce, oregano, celery seed, salt, and pepper. Cover and simmer for 30 minutes. Return the chicken to the skillet. Simmer for 30 minutes more or until the chicken is tender.

SERVES 6

Chicken à la King

¼	cup butter
2	chicken breasts
4	chicken legs
4	chicken thighs
I	cup finely chopped onion
3	garlic cloves, minced
¾	cup chopped green bell pepper
2	cups whole tomatoes
I	8-ounce can tomato sauce
½	teaspoon salt
¼	teaspoon pepper
½	teaspoon thyme, crushed
I	bay leaf
⅛	teaspoon cayenne

In a skillet melt the butter and brown the chicken pieces on all sides. Remove the chicken from the skillet. Add the onions, garlic, and green pepper, and sauté for 5 minutes.

Return the chicken to the skillet. Spoon the vegetables over the chicken.

In a mixing bowl blend together the whole tomatoes, tomato sauce, salt, pepper, thyme, bay leaf, and cayenne.

Pour over the chicken. Bring to a boil. Reduce heat and simmer for 30 minutes or until the chicken is tender. Remove bay leaf. Skim off fat from the sauce. Serve chicken with sauce poured over the top.

SERVES 6

PAL'S DINER, MAHWAH, NEW JERSEY

Chicken & Dumplings

1	5-pound stewing hen
	Hot water
1	teaspoon salt
1/8	teaspoon pepper
1/8	teaspoon garlic powder
1	cup chopped celery
1	medium onion, chopped
3	tablespoons all-purpose flour
3	cups chicken broth
3/4	cup evaporated milk

◆ ◆ ◆

2	cups all-purpose flour
3/4	teaspoon salt
3	teaspoons baking powder
1	teaspoon sugar
1/4	cup shortening
3/4	cup plus 3 tablespoons milk

Place the chicken in a large pot and cover with hot water. Add the salt, pepper, garlic powder, celery, and onion, and simmer for 1 hour or until tender.

Strain and reserve the broth. Remove one-fourth of the broth, and set aside. Skim the fat from the remaining broth, and return to the pot. Bring to a simmer.

Debone the chicken and cut into serving portions. Set aside. In a small jar shake together the 3 tablespoons of flour with 1/4 cup of the cooled broth. Slowly add the mixture to the pot. Stir until thick. Add the evaporated milk. Set the gravy aside.

In a mixing bowl sift together 2 cups of flour, salt, baking powder, and sugar. Cut in the shortening until it has the consistency of coarse meal. Add the milk. Do not overblend.

In a saucepan over medium heat warm the gravy. When simmering, drop in the dumpling mixture by teaspoonfuls. Cover and simmer for 10 minutes. Serve with the chicken.

SERVES 6

MISS ADAMS DINER

Rescued from obscurity and, perhaps, the junkyard at a foreclosure auction during the late 1980s, the Miss Adams Diner continues to serve hungry people in Adams, Massachusetts. A 1949 model Worcester Lunch Car, the diner offered breakfasts, sandwiches, and filling meals to customers for almost forty years before falling on hard times.

The current owner, Barry Garton, who runs the Miss Adams along with his wife, stepson, and daughter, has done much to return the diner to its original, sparkling condition. The kitchen was completely renovated, broken fixtures were replaced, and everything received several fresh coats of paint. "We really tried to make it shine like new," says Barry.

He also built on an addition, increasing the available seating from thirty-four to fifty-five. The extra space proved necessary, because the diner's business has blossomed. "We get a lot of tourists who make the diner one of their destinations," says Barry. "And, of course, we get our regular customers. Some of them show up two or three times a day for a meal. One old farmer comes in every day at 8:30 for his oatmeal."

The Miss Adams is a typical diner with some very atypical dishes. "We offer vegetarian plates," says Barry. "Because there are a lot of Polish people in this area, we offer a kielbasa and cabbage dish for breakfast along with the usual eggs, home fries, and toast."

Ingredients for omelettes are sautéed before cooking. The western omelette comes in casserole form, and the diner serves up a multigrain waffle.

Not surprisingly, the Miss Adams attracts a clientele as varied as its menu. "We get all types of people," says Barry. "They come from all over."

Barry believes the history and unique atmosphere of diners give them a marketing advantage, but notes that this can be a mixed blessing. It takes a lot of money to keep a diner in pristine condition. "Unfortunately, commercial lending institutions always seem to put them at the bottom of the list," he says. Even so, he is convinced that owners should do all they can to take advantage of their diners' historic appeal.

Chicken & Potatoes

1	3-pound fryer chicken
1½	teaspoons salt
¼	teaspoon pepper
¼	cup butter
16	boiling onions
12	small red potatoes
10	baby carrots, scraped
1	chicken bouillon cube
½	cup boiling water
1	teaspoon basil
1½	tablespoons finely chopped parsley

Sprinkle the inside of the chicken with ½ teaspoon of salt and the pepper.

In a deep skillet melt the butter. Add the chicken and brown on all sides. Place the chicken, onions, potatoes, and carrots in a large casserole dish.

Add the chicken bouillon cube to the boiling water and stir until the cube has dissolved completely. Pour over the chicken and the vegetables.

Sprinkle the basil and remaining salt over the top. Bake, covered, at 325° for 1 hour and 30 minutes. Top with parsley before serving.

SERVES 4

MISS ADAMS DINER, ADAMS, MASSACHUSETTS

Chicken Divan

¾	pound boneless chicken breast
2	teaspoons cooking oil
1	cup water
1	10-ounce package frozen broccoli
1	10¾-ounce can condensed cream of chicken soup
	Salt and pepper to taste
1½	cups white rice
½	cup grated Cheddar cheese

Clean and dry the chicken with paper towels. Cut into strips. In a skillet heat the oil and cook the chicken until light brown. Add water, broccoli, and condensed cream of chicken soup. Season with salt and pepper. Bring to a boil. Add the rice.

Cover and simmer until the rice is done. Remove from the heat and let stand. Fluff the rice with a fork. Top with grated Cheddar cheese.

SERVES 4

Chicken Fricassee

1½	teaspoons dried parsley
½	teaspoon dried rosemary
½	teaspoon dried thyme
1	bay leaf
1	6-pound roasting chicken
½	teaspoon salt
¼	teaspoon pepper
¼	cup all-purpose flour
¼	cup olive oil
2	cups chicken stock
1	cup white wine
1	cup water
1	cup boiling mushrooms
1	cup boiling onions
2	tablespoons olive oil
3	medium carrots, sliced thin
3	ribs celery, chopped
½	cup heavy cream
2	egg yolks
⅛	teaspoon nutmeg

Tie the parsley, rosemary, thyme, and bay leaf in a piece of cheesecloth or metal tea-leaf strainer.

Cut the roasting chicken into 8 or 10 pieces. Sprinkle each piece with salt and pepper. Dredge the chicken in the flour so that it is lightly coated. Shake off any excess flour.

In a large pot heat ¼ cup of olive oil and brown the chicken pieces a few at a time. When all the chicken is browned, return it to the pot. Add the chicken stock, white wine, water, and the bundle of herbs. Bring to a simmer. Reduce the heat, cover, and cook for 20 minutes. Remove the breast meat. Continue cooking the dark meat for 10 minutes more.

Place the chicken on a serving platter. Cover and keep warm.

Strain the broth. Return it to the pot. Let the broth boil until it is reduced to 2 cups. Add the mushrooms. Cook for 1 minute and remove. Add the boiling onions, cook for 3 minutes, and remove. Rinse under cold water.

In a separate pot heat 2 tablespoons of olive oil and sauté the carrots for 1 minute. Add the mushrooms, onions, and celery. Add the reduced chicken broth and simmer until the vegetables are tender.

In a mixing bowl blend together the heavy cream, egg yolks, and nutmeg. Remove ½ cup of the chicken broth from the pot. Slowly add the broth to the cream mixture. Return the cream mixture to the broth and bring back to a simmer. Add the chicken pieces and cook until the chicken is thoroughly heated. Remove the bundle of herbs before serving.

SERVES 6

Chicken Croquettes

3	tablespoons cooking oil
½	cup all-purpose flour
½	teaspoon salt
	Pepper to taste
1	cup milk

♦ ♦ ♦

2	cups finely chopped cooked chicken
¾	teaspoon salt
½	teaspoon celery salt
	Pepper to taste
1	teaspoon grated onion

1   tablespoon chopped parsley
1   cup breadcrumbs
1   egg, beaten
2   tablespoons water
     Cooking oil

In a saucepan heat the oil and blend in the flour. Add the salt and pepper. Gradually blend in the milk. Cook over medium heat for 1 minute or until the sauce thickens. Set aside.

In a mixing bowl blend together the cooked chicken, salt, celery salt, pepper, grated onion, and parsley. Add the sauce and chill.

Shape the mixture into 10 balls. Roll in the breadcrumbs, then the egg, and then the water. In a skillet heat the oil to 375°. Fry each croquette for 1 to 2 minutes or until golden brown. Drain on paper towels.

SERVES 4

Chicken Loaf

4   cups finely chopped cooked chicken
2   cups chicken broth
3   eggs
1½   cups soft breadcrumbs
1   teaspoon salt
¼   teaspoon paprika
1   teaspoon Worcestershire sauce
½   cup finely chopped celery
¼   teaspoon curry powder
1   medium onion, chopped fine
1½   tablespoons fresh lemon juice

In a large mixing bowl combine the chicken, broth, eggs, breadcrumbs, salt, paprika, Worcestershire sauce, celery, curry powder, onion, and lemon juice. Mix thoroughly.

Shape the mixture into a loaf. Press into a 9x5-inch pan. Place the pan in a larger pan filled with hot water. Bake at 350° for 1 hour and 30 minutes or until the loaf is done. Let stand for 10 minutes before serving.

SERVES 6

Brunswick County Stew

2   cups peeled tomatoes
2   cups lima beans
1   2-pound frying chicken, cut into pieces
1   13-ounce can chicken broth
2   6-ounce cans tomato paste
2   tablespoons vinegar
2   tablespoons Worcestershire sauce
¼   teaspoon pepper
     Salt to taste
2   cups cooked cubed pork

Drain and reserve the liquid from the tomatoes and lima beans. Chop the tomatoes. In a large soup pot combine the chicken, broth, tomato paste, reserved tomato and lima bean juices, vinegar, Worcestershire sauce, pepper, and salt. Bring to a boil.

Cover and simmer for 20 minutes. Add the tomatoes, lima beans, and cooked pork. Cover and simmer for 20 minutes more or until the chicken is done.

SERVES 6

Chicken Pot Pie

1	pound boneless white chicken meat
1¾	cups chicken broth
2¾	cups all-purpose flour
¾	teaspoon salt
½	cup butter, chilled
7	tablespoons water
4	carrots, cut in ½-inch slices
¼	cup butter, chilled
1	cup sliced mushrooms
½	cup diced sweet onion
¼	teaspoon salt
½	teaspoon pepper
½	teaspoon thyme
1	cup half-and-half
2	cups frozen peas

Place the chicken in a large soup pot with half of the chicken broth. Cover and simmer for 5 minutes. Remove the chicken and cut into 1-inch chunks.

In a mixing bowl combine 2½ cups of flour with ¾ teaspoon of salt and ½ cup of butter. Blend until it resembles a coarse meal. Add the water one tablespoon at a time. Form the dough into a ball. Wrap in waxed paper. Refrigerate.

Place the carrots into a saucepan of boiling water and cook for 5 minutes. Drain. In a skillet melt ¼ cup of butter and sauté the mushrooms, onion, ¼ teaspoon of salt, pepper, and thyme for 5 minutes.

In a cup blend together the remaining flour with the remaining chicken broth. Pour over the sautéed vegetables and stir for 1 minute or until thick. Add the half-and-half and stir for 1 minute. Add the chicken, carrots, and peas.

Roll out the dough into 12 equal-size circles. Pat half into the bottom of 5-inch pie pans. Fill with the chicken mixture. Top with the remaining dough. Pinch the edges together. Cut slits into the top. Place the pans on a cookie sheet. Bake at 425° for 35 minutes or until the crusts are golden brown.

SERVES 6

Spicy Chicken

6	boneless chicken breasts
¼	cup all-purpose flour
¼	teaspoon paprika
	Pepper to taste
3	tablespoons butter
2	cups sliced mushrooms
¾	cup water
2	chicken bouillon cubes
1	teaspoon chopped parsley
⅛	teaspoon thyme

Clean and dry the chicken with paper towels. Cut in half. In a mixing bowl combine the flour, paprika, and pepper. Toss to combine all of the ingredients. Dredge the chicken with the flour mixture, coating thoroughly.

In a skillet melt the butter. Brown the chicken on all sides. Remove. In the same skillet sauté the mushrooms. Add the water, bouillon cubes, parsley, and thyme. Simmer for 2 minutes. Add the chicken. Cover and let simmer for 15 minutes more or until the chicken is tender.

SERVES 6

Stuffed Chicken Breasts

4	boneless chicken breasts
1/2	teaspoon pepper
	Salt to taste
1	cup cooked white rice
1/4	cup diced tomato
1/4	cup grated Mozzarella cheese
1	tablespoon basil
	Cooking oil

Cut the chicken breasts in half. Pound each one with a mallet until 1/4 inch thick. Season the chicken with the pepper and salt.

In a mixing bowl combine the white rice, tomatoes, Mozzarella cheese, and basil. Toss all of the ingredients until well blended.

Spoon an even amount of the rice mixture on top of each chicken breast. Fold and secure with string and toothpicks.

In a skillet heat enough oil to coat the bottom of the pan. Brown the chicken on both sides for 1 minute or until golden.

Remove from the skillet and place in the bottom of a baking dish. Bake at 350° for 10 minutes.

SERVES 4

Chicken Tetrazzini

2	chicken bouillon cubes
2	cups hot water
1/2	pound thin spaghetti
2	tablespoons butter
2	tablespoons all-purpose flour
1/2	teaspoon salt
1/4	teaspoon pepper
	Cayenne pepper to taste
1	cup milk
1	cup sour cream
1	cup cottage cheese
2	cups diced cooked chicken
1	4-ounce jar sliced mushrooms
2	tablespoons minced parsley
1/2	cup grated Cheddar cheese

In a saucepan combine the chicken bouillon cubes and hot water. Cook over low heat until the bouillon has dissolved. Boil the spaghetti in the chicken bouillon until done. Set aside.

In a separate saucepan melt the butter. Add the flour, salt, pepper, and cayenne pepper. Blend thoroughly. Pour in the milk. Add the sour cream, cottage cheese, cooked chicken, sliced mushrooms, and parsley. Mix thoroughly. Bring to a boil. Add the spaghetti.

Pour the mixture into a large baking dish. Top with grated Cheddar cheese. Bake at 350° for 40 minutes or until the top is golden brown.

SERVES 6

Roast Turkey

1	12-pound turkey
	Salt and pepper to taste
2	tablespoons butter
2	tablespoons cooking oil
1	cup chopped onion
1	cup chopped celery
1	cup diced carrots
1	cup sour cream
2¼	cups bread cubes
2	teaspoons sage
1	teaspoon poultry seasoning
	Salt and pepper to taste
1	cup chicken broth

Clean the turkey thoroughly. Season the cavity with salt and pepper. Place on a rack in a roasting pan breast-side-up. Top with aluminum foil. Pierce with a fork.

In a large skillet melt the butter with the oil and sauté the onion, celery, and carrots until tender. Remove the pan from the heat and add the sour cream.

In a mixing bowl blend the vegetables with the bread cubes, sage, poultry seasoning, salt, and pepper. Add the chicken broth. Toss so that all of the ingredients are well coated. Stuff into the cavity of the turkey or spoon into a baking dish. Cover and bake at 350° for 35 minutes.

Add water to the roasting pan. Roast the turkey, uncovered, at 400° for 15 minutes. Reduce to 325°. Cover and roast for 2 hours and 30 minutes. Uncover and roast for 45 minutes more or until a meat thermometer inserted into the turkey's thigh registers 185°. Make sure the turkey is thoroughly cooked before carving.

SERVES 12

Turkey Croquettes

2	tablespoons butter
3	tablespoons all-purpose flour
½	cup milk
½	cup chicken broth
2	cups diced cooked turkey
1	tablespoon chopped parsley
	Salt and pepper to taste
1	egg, beaten
1	cup dry breadcrumbs
1	tablespoon butter, melted

In a saucepan melt the butter. Blend in the flour. Slowly add the milk and chicken broth and cook until thick. Remove the pan from the heat and let cool. Add the cooked turkey, parsley, salt, and pepper. Blend well. Cover and refrigerate for 2 hours.

Shape the mixture into 8 even-size balls. Dip into the egg and then the breadcrumbs. Place onto a greased baking sheet. Brush with melted butter. Bake at 350° for 25 minutes.

SERVES 4

Creamy Mac & Cheese

1	8-ounce package elbow macaroni
¼	cup butter
¼	cup all-purpose flour
½	teaspoon salt
2	tablespoons mustard
2	cups milk
¼	cup grated Cheddar cheese
2	tablespoons sliced black olives

NEWARK DINER, NEWARK, NEW YORK

Cook the macaroni in a large pot of boiling salted water until done. Drain and set aside.

In a large saucepan melt the butter. Add the flour and salt. Blend thoroughly. Add the mustard and milk. Cook over low heat until the mixture has thickened, stirring constantly. Add the cheese and cook until the cheese has melted. Add the cooked macaroni and sliced olives. Mix thoroughly. Pour the mixture into a baking dish. Bake at 375° for 15 minutes or until golden brown.

SERVES 6

Sunday Macaroni & Cheese

1	pound elbow macaroni
1	tablespoon all-purpose flour
3	cups milk
½	cup chopped onion
1	garlic clove, minced
¾	teaspoon dry mustard
¼	teaspoon salt
	Pepper to taste
3	cups grated Cheddar cheese
⅓	cup grated Parmesan cheese
1	teaspoon fresh lemon juice
	Tabasco sauce to taste

Grease a large baking dish. Set aside. Cook the macaroni according to package directions.

In a saucepan blend the flour with 1 cup of milk. Cook until smooth. Add the remaining milk, onion, garlic, mustard, salt, and pepper. Bring to a boil. Simmer until thick. Blend in the cheeses. Add the lemon juice and Tabasco.

In a large mixing bowl combine the macaroni and the cheese mixture. Pour into the prepared baking dish. Bake at 375° for 25 minutes or until golden brown.

SERVES 6

Clam Fritters

4   eggs, separated
2   cups toasted breadcrumbs
4   cups minced clams
1   teaspoon salt
½   teaspoon pepper
1   tablespoon chopped chives
1½   teaspoons chopped parsley
⅔   cup milk
¼   cup cooking oil

In a mixing bowl beat the egg whites until stiff.

In another mixing bowl lightly beat the egg yolks. Add the breadcrumbs, clams, salt, pepper, chives, and parsley. Blend thoroughly. Add the milk and beaten egg whites and mix well.

In a heavy skillet heat the oil. Drop the batter by heaping tablespoonfuls into the oil. Cook, turning once, until all sides are golden brown.

SERVES 8

Codfish Hash

2   cups salted codfish, flaked
1   medium onion, chopped fine
1   garlic clove, minced
3   cups cooked and chopped potatoes
¼   cup butter
⅛   teaspoon pepper
½   cup water

♦ ♦ ♦

¼   pound mushrooms
1   tablespoon butter
1   slice bacon
1   tablespoon all-purpose flour
1   teaspoon sugar
¼   teaspoon celery salt
1   cup tomato juice

In a mixing bowl blend together the codfish, onion, garlic, and potatoes. In a heavy skillet melt ¼ cup of butter. Pour

VILLAGE DINER, MILFORD, PENNSYLVANIA

the codfish mixture into the skillet. Add pepper and water. Cook until the bottom browns. Fold over and continue cooking for 2 minutes more.

Remove the stems from the mushrooms. Chop fine. In a separate skillet melt 1 tablespoon of butter and sauté the mushrooms until tender and lightly browned. Remove and set aside. Fry the bacon until crisp. Drain on paper towels. Let cool and chop.

Return the bacon to the skillet. Add the flour, sugar, and salt. Cook over low heat until the mixture begins to bubble. Remove the pan from the heat. Add the tomato juice and return to the heat. Bring to a boil and cook for 1 minute. Add the mushrooms. Continue cooking for 1 minute more. Serve over codfish hash.

SERVES 6.

Crab Cakes

2	eggs
½	cup breadcrumbs
¼	cup fresh lemon juice
¼	cup diced green onions
½	teaspoon dry mustard
	Salt and pepper to taste
½	pound crab meat
	Cooking oil

In a mixing bowl beat the eggs. Add ¼ cup of the breadcrumbs, lemon juice, green onions, dry mustard, and pepper. Blend thoroughly.

Separate and flake the crab. Add to the breadcrumb mixture. Shape into 8 equal-size cakes. Coat with the remaining breadcrumbs.

In a deep skillet heat the oil. Fry the crab cakes until golden brown.

SERVES 4

Fish & Chips

4	large Russet potatoes
	Lard for frying
1	teaspoon salt
2	pounds cod fillets
1½	cups pancake mix
1¼	cups milk
½	teaspoon salt

Peel the potatoes. Cut into oversize strips and place in a bowl of ice water. Let stand for 30 minutes. Drain and dry with paper towels.

In a deep skillet heat the lard to 375°. Fry the potatoes a few at a time for 3 to 5 minutes or until golden brown. Drain on paper towels. Season with salt while still warm.

Cut the cod fillets into serving portions. In a mixing bowl add the pancake mix to the milk and salt. Add the fillets and soak for 1 minute. In the same deep skillet used to fry the potatoes cook the fillets for 4 minutes or until golden brown.

SERVES 4

Fried Oysters

1	garlic clove, minced
5	sweet gherkin pickles, chopped fine
1/4	teaspoon white pepper
1	teaspoon capers, chopped fine
1/2	teaspoon tarragon vinegar
1	teaspoon finely chopped parsley
1 1/2	cups mayonnaise

◆ ◆ ◆

24	large oysters
2	eggs
1/2	teaspoon salt
1/4	teaspoon cayenne pepper
1/4	teaspoon white pepper
1	cup milk
2	cups soft breadcrumbs
	Lard for frying

In a mixing bowl blend together the garlic and pickles. Add the white pepper, capers, tarragon vinegar, and parsley. Slowly blend in the mayonnaise. Chill the sauce for 1 hour.

Drain the oysters. In a mixing bowl beat the eggs. Add the salt, cayenne pepper, white pepper, and milk. Blend thoroughly. Dip the oysters into the egg mixture and then into the soft breadcrumbs. Let stand for 5 minutes.

In a deep skillet heat the lard to 350°. Fry the oysters a few at a time for 1 to 2 minutes or until golden brown. Serve with the sauce.

SERVES 4

Scalloped Halibut

2	pounds halibut
	Salt and pepper to taste
6	tablespoons butter
6	tablespoons all-purpose flour
2	cups milk
1	cup stock
2	tablespoons Worcestershire sauce
1	tablespoon chopped parsley
1/2	cup seasoned breadcrumbs

Grease a baking dish. Set aside. Wipe the halibut with paper towels. Season with salt and pepper. Wrap in a cheesecloth. Cook for 15 minutes in a large pot of boiling salted water. Drain, reserving 1 cup of stock. Let the halibut cool. Remove the bones and skin. Break the fish apart.

In a saucepan melt the butter and blend in the flour. Gradually add the milk and reserved stock, stirring constantly. Cook until smooth. Add the Worcestershire sauce and parsley.

Place the halibut in the bottom of the prepared baking dish. Pour the sauce over the halibut. Top with seasoned breadcrumbs. Bake at 350° for 30 minutes.

SERVES 6

Salmon Pie

1	9-inch pastry shell, unbaked
1	cup shredded American cheese
1	16-ounce can salmon
5	tablespoons all-purpose flour
2	tablespoons butter
5	green onions, chopped
1	10½ -ounce can mushroom soup
¾	cup sour cream
1	teaspoon dill
⅛	teaspoon coarse ground pepper
1	4-ounce jar button mushrooms
⅛	teaspoon oregano
2	eggs, slightly beaten

Bake the pastry shell at 350° for 15 minutes or until golden brown. Let cool. Sprinkle ½ cup of American cheese into the bottom.

In a mixing bowl flake the salmon. Add the flour and toss. Place on top of the cheese in the pastry shell.

In a skillet melt the butter and sauté the onions until tender. Add the soup, sour cream, dill, pepper, mushrooms, and oregano, stirring often. Bring to a gentle boil. Remove the skillet from heat. Blend in the beaten eggs and pour over the salmon. Top with the remaining cheese. Bake at 325° for 30 minutes or until set. Let stand for 10 minutes before serving.

SERVES 6

Scallops in Cream Sauce

1	pound scallops
2	tablespoons butter
1	red bell pepper, sliced
1	cup uncooked rice
1	package onion soup mix
2¼	cups water
1	tablespoon fresh lemon juice
¼	cup half-and-half
2	green onions, sliced
	Salt and pepper to taste

Wash the scallops under cold water. Pat dry with paper towels. Set aside.

In a skillet melt the butter so that it coats the bottom of the pan. Sauté the red pepper until crisp. Add the rice.

In a small bowl blend together the onion soup mix, water, and lemon juice. Add to the rice mixture and blend thoroughly. Bring the mixture to a boil, cover, and simmer for 30 minutes or until the rice is tender. Add the half-and-half, scallops, and green onions, and cook for 5 minutes or until the scallops are tender. Season with salt and pepper.

SERVES 4

Fried Eastern Scallops

3   cups fresh scallops
2   eggs
1   tablespoon water
1   cup dry breadcrumbs
½   teaspoon salt
¼   teaspoon pepper
1   cup cooking oil

♦ ♦ ♦

1½   cups stewed tomatoes
¼   cup finely chopped onion
1   teaspoon parsley
1   teaspoon sugar
½   teaspoon salt
½   teaspoon coarse black pepper
¼   teaspoon ground cloves
2   tablespoons butter
2   tablespoons all-purpose flour

Wash the scallops. Drain on paper towels. In a mixing bowl beat the eggs with the water. In a separate bowl blend together the breadcrumbs, salt, and pepper.

In a deep skillet heat the oil to 375°. Dip the scallops in the egg batter and then in the breadcrumbs. Fry the scallops until they are golden brown.

In a medium saucepan combine the tomatoes, onion, parsley, sugar, salt, pepper, and cloves. Bring to a boil. Reduce the heat and simmer for 15 minutes.

In a skillet melt the butter. Add the flour and blend until smooth. Purée the tomato mixture in a blender. Add to the flour and cook until thick and smooth. Serve with fried scallops.

SERVES 6

Southern-Style Shrimp

2   tablespoons butter
2   green bell peppers, chopped
½   cup chopped onion
½   cup chopped celery
2   cups whole tomatoes, chopped, with juice
½   cup dry white wine
½   teaspoon salt
½   teaspoon pepper
½   teaspoon garlic powder
¼   teaspoon crushed thyme
1   pound shrimp
6   cups cooked white rice

In a skillet melt the butter and sauté the green pepper, onion, and celery. Add the tomatoes with juice, white wine, salt, pepper, garlic powder, and thyme. Blend thoroughly. Bring to a boil and simmer for 20 minutes. Add the shrimp and cook for 12 minutes or until the shrimp turns pink. Serve over cooked rice.

SERVES 6

Seaside Stew

¼   cup cooking oil
1   medium onion, chopped
1   garlic clove, minced
⅛   teaspoon oregano
⅛   teaspoon sage
½   teaspoon salt
¼   teaspoon pepper
1   bay leaf
2   20-ounce cans whole tomatoes
1   4-ounce can tomato paste

SUMMIT DINER

What should you order at the Summit Diner in Sommerset, Pennsylvania? "Whatever you like," says co-owner Don Bailey. "Everything on the menu is good."

The cooks at the Summit start from scratch on every order. "We grind our own hamburger, make our own sausage, and bake our own pies," says Don. "Our philosophy is home cooking."

The diner is especially well known for its pancakes. "We use our own formula for hotcakes," he says. "Each order is mixed on the spot. We weigh out the batter, add milk, and cook them over the grill immediately. That way they don't go flat. We have used that same system for thirty-five years."

And it works. The original seating capacity of thirty-six has been boosted to sixty-four with the addition of a second dining room, and the customers keep on coming.

The atmosphere at the Summit Diner is strictly down home. "Somebody said the other day that so-and-so was coming in from the parking lot," says Don. "So we got something going on the grill for him."

½ cup water
5 large oysters, quartered
8 scallops
1 pound boneless cod
8 prawns
1½ pounds cooked crab meat

In a skillet heat the oil and sauté the onion and garlic until transparent. Add the oregano, sage, salt, pepper, and bay leaf. Simmer for 5 minutes.

Add the whole tomatoes, tomato paste, and water. Simmer for 1 hour. Remove the bay leaf. Strain the mixture through a sieve. Pour into a large saucepan. Add the oysters, scallops, cod, and prawns. Simmer for 5 minutes. Add the crab meat and simmer for 5 minutes more or until the fish is tender.

SERVES 4

FOUR SISTERS OWL DINER

The Four Sisters Owl Diner in Lowell, Massachusetts, was originally called the Monarch Diner and was part of a chain of diners operating in the Boston area. In 1951 the Monarch was relocated to Lowell and renamed the Owl Diner. The current owner, Tom Shanahan, purchased it in 1982 and gave it yet another new identity by adding "Four Sisters" to the name.

The customers who pour through the door every morning of the week are far less interested in the diner's name than its food. For breakfast, they can choose any one of thirty omelettes, each of them named for a street in Lowell. To accompany the omelettes, the menu also features a boneless ham cut one-inch thick, like a steak.

The grill is still out front where customers can sit and watch as their food is prepared fresh, an arrangement that still appeals to just about everybody. Doctors, lawyers, truckers, and factory workers eat side by side here, and together they make for a very congenial and hungry crowd.

FOUNTAIN ALLEY

Hot Chocolate

6	tablespoons cocoa powder
4	tablespoons sugar
	Salt
½	cup water
5	cups milk
	Whipped Cream

In a saucepan blend the cocoa powder with the sugar. Add a pinch of salt with the water. Place over low heat. Boil for 3 minutes. Stir until the sugar has dissolved. Add the milk. Bring the cocoa just to the boiling point. Serve with whipped cream.

SERVES 4

Caboose Chaser

¾	cup pineapple juice
	Ice cubes
	Ginger ale
	Lemon, sliced

In a tall glass pour the pineapple juice over ice cubes. Fill to the top with ginger ale. Stir well to blend. Add lemon slices.

SERVES I

Diner Delight

¾	cup pineapple juice
⅓	cup orange juice
	Ice cubes
I	tablespoon grenadine syrup

Fill a tall glass with the pineapple juice and orange juice. Add ice cubes to about halfway full. Slowly add the grenadine syrup. Stir well to blend thoroughly.

SERVES I

PALACE DINER, BIDDLEFORD, MAINE

Lemonade

½ cup sugar
½ cup lemon juice concentrate
3½ cups water
    Ice
1   teaspoon grenadine syrup (optional)

In a large pitcher add the sugar to the
lemon juice concentrate. Stir until the
sugar has dissolved. Add the water.
Refrigerate until chilled. To serve pour in
tall glasses over ice. For pink lemonade
add 1 teaspoon of grenadine syrup.

MAKES 1 QUART

Fountain Smoothie

1½ cups strawberries
2   ripe bananas, diced
    Crushed ice
4   cups apple cider

Purée the strawberries in a blender. Add
the bananas and blend until smooth.
Place 1½ cups of the puréed fruit into
the bottom of 4 10-ounce glasses. Add 2
tablespoons of crushed ice to each glass.
Fill to the top with cider. Stir until well
blended.

SERVES 4

Orange Pick-Me-Up

⅓ cup orange juice
½ cup milk
½ cup water
¼ cup sugar
1 egg
½ teaspoon almond extract
½ cup crushed ice

Place the orange juice, milk, water, and sugar in a blender. Blend for 20 seconds. Add the egg, almond extract, and crushed ice. Blend until frothy and smooth.

SERVES 2

Sunrise Icy

3 large scoops lemon sherbet
⅔ cup 7-Up
3 tablespoons raspberry syrup

Place the lemon sherbet in a blender. Cut into the scoops with a knife to loosen the sherbet. Add half the 7-Up. Blend until smooth. Add the remaining 7-Up and stir by hand. Pour into a tall glass. Float raspberry syrup on top. Stir gently.

SERVES 1

AMERICAN DINER, PHILADELPHIA, PENNSYLVANIA

194

Chocolate Cola

Ice cubes
3 tablespoons chocolate syrup
1 12-ounce can cola
¼ teaspoon vanilla extract

Fill a tall glass half full with ice cubes. Add the chocolate syrup with a small amount of the cola. Add the vanilla and stir gently. Slowly add the remaining cola. Stir to blend.

SERVES 1

Cherry Cola

Ice cubes
3 tablespoons maraschino cherry juice
1 12-ounce can cola
4 maraschino cherries

Fill a tall glass half full with ice cubes. Add the maraschino cherry juice with a small amount of the cola. Stir to blend. Add the rest of the cola. Stir once more. Top with maraschino cherries.

SERVES 1

Chocolate Malted Milk

3 large scoops chocolate ice cream
½ cup milk
1 tablespoon chocolate syrup
1½ teaspoons malted milk powder

Place the chocolate ice cream in a blender. Cut into the scoops with a knife to loosen the ice cream. Add the milk, chocolate syrup, and malted milk powder. Blend until smooth.

SERVES 1

Black Cow

3 large scoops chocolate ice cream
½ cup milk
1 tablespoon chocolate syrup
¼ teaspoon vanilla extract

Place the chocolate ice cream in a blender. Cut into the scoops with a knife to loosen the ice cream. Add the milk, chocolate syrup, and vanilla. Blend until smooth.

SERVES 1

White Cow

3 large scoops vanilla ice cream
½ cup milk
½ teaspoon sugar
¾ teaspoon vanilla extract

Place the vanilla ice cream in a blender. Cut into the scoops with a knife to loosen the ice cream. Add the milk, sugar, and vanilla. Blend until smooth.

SERVES 1

Black Jack

3 tablespoons chocolate syrup
2 tablespoons vanilla ice cream
1 12-ounce can root beer soda

In a tall glass add the chocolate syrup to the vanilla ice cream. Stir until smooth.

Add a small portion of the root beer soda. Stir again. Slowly add the remaining root beer. Skim off the foam, leaving enough to produce a good head as it reaches the top of the glass.

SERVES 1

Banana Milk Shake

1   large ripe banana
3   large scoops vanilla ice cream
⅔   cup milk

Knead the banana gently inside the peel so that the inside begins to feel like a paste. Cut the end of the banana, and squeeze out the contents into a blender.

Add the vanilla ice cream to the banana paste. Cut into the scoops with a knife to loosen the ice cream. Add the milk. Blend until smooth.

SERVES 1

Chocolate Milk Shake

3   large scoops vanilla ice cream
⅔   cup milk
¼   cup chocolate syrup

Place the vanilla ice cream in a blender. Cut into the scoops with a knife to loosen the ice cream. Add the milk and chocolate syrup. Blend until smooth.

SERVES 1

Thick Chocolate Milk Shake

3   large scoops vanilla ice cream
⅔   cup milk
3   tablespoons chocolate syrup
¼   cup heavy cream
    Whipped cream
    Chocolate sprinkles

Place the vanilla ice cream in a blender. Cut into the scoops with a knife to loosen the ice cream. Add the milk, chocolate syrup, and heavy cream. Blend until smooth. Pour into a tall glass. Top with whipped cream and chocolate sprinkles.

SERVES 1

Chocolate—Peanut Butter Milk Shake

3   large scoops vanilla ice cream
⅔   cup milk
3   tablespoons chocolate syrup
1   tablespoon peanut butter

Place the vanilla ice cream in a blender. Cut into the scoops with a knife to loosen the ice cream. Add the milk, chocolate syrup, and peanut butter. Blend until smooth.

SERVES 1

Coffee Milk Shake

3   large scoops coffee ice cream
⅓   cup milk
¼   cup strong brewed coffee, cooled
2   teaspoons finely ground coffee

Place the coffee ice cream in a blender.
Cut into the scoops with a knife to loosen
the ice cream. Add the milk and brewed
coffee. Blend for 20 seconds. Add the
ground coffee. Blend until smooth.

SERVES I

Orange Cream Milk Shake

3   large scoops vanilla ice cream
⅔   cup milk
2   tablespoons orange syrup
⅔   cup heavy cream
     Whipped cream

Place the vanilla ice cream in a blender.
Cut into the scoops with a knife to loosen
the ice cream. Add the milk, orange
syrup, and heavy cream. Blend until
smooth. Pour into a tall glass. Top with
whipped cream.

SERVES I

English Toffee Milk Shake

3   scoops praline ice cream
¼   cup caramel topping
⅔   cup milk
     Whipped cream

Place the praline ice cream in a blender.
Cut the scoops with a knife to loosen the
ice cream. Add half the caramel topping.
Blend. Add milk. Blend until smooth.

Holding a tall glass at a 45 degree
angle, drizzle the remaining caramel topping inside of the glass. Add shake. Top
with whipped cream.

SERVES I

Vanilla Milk Shake

3   large scoops vanilla ice cream
⅔   cup milk

Place the vanilla ice cream in a blender.
Cut into the scoops with a knife to loosen
the ice cream. Add the milk. Blend until
smooth.

SERVES I

HIGHLAND PARK DINER, ROCHESTER, NEW YORK

Banana Syrup

1	cup sugar
½	cup water
1½	teaspoons banana extract
2	drops yellow food coloring

In a saucepan add the sugar to the water. Cook until the syrup is thick and about to reach a full boil. Add the banana extract and food coloring. Remove the pan from the heat. Let cool. Pour into a container with an airtight lid. Label the flavor of syrup. Refrigerate any unused portion.

MAKES ABOUT ½ CUP

Cherry Syrup

1	cup sugar
½	cup water
1½	teaspoons cherry extract
2	drops red food coloring

In a saucepan add the sugar to the water. Cook until the syrup is thick and about to reach a full boil. Add the cherry extract and food coloring. Remove the pan from the heat. Let cool. Pour into a container with an airtight lid. Label the flavor of syrup. Refrigerate any unused portion.

MAKES ABOUT ½ CUP

Orange Syrup

1	cup sugar
½	cup water
1½	teaspoons orange extract
2	drops orange food coloring

In a saucepan add the sugar to the water. Cook until the syrup is thick and about to reach a full boil. Add the orange extract and food coloring. Remove the pan from the heat. Let cool. Pour into a container with an airtight lid. Label the flavor of syrup. Refrigerate any unused portion.

MAKES ABOUT ½ CUP

Raspberry Syrup

1	cup sugar
½	cup water
1½	teaspoons raspberry extract
2	drops red food coloring

In a saucepan add the sugar to the water. Cook until the syrup is thick and about to reach a full boil. Add the raspberry extract and food coloring. Remove the pan from the heat. Let cool. Pour into a container with an airtight lid. Label the flavor of syrup. Refrigerate any unused portion.

MAKES ABOUT ½ CUP

Peppermint Syrup

1	cup sugar
½	cup water
1½	teaspoons peppermint extract
2	drops green food coloring

In a saucepan add the sugar to the water. Cook until the syrup is thick and about to reach a full boil. Add the peppermint extract and food coloring. Remove the pan from the heat. Let cool. Pour into a container with an airtight lid. Label the flavor of syrup. Refrigerate any unused portion.

MAKES ABOUT ½ CUP

Root Beer Syrup

1	cup sugar
½	cup water
1½	teaspoons root beer extract
1	drop red food coloring
1	drop blue food coloring

In a saucepan add the sugar to the water. Cook until the syrup is thick and about to reach a full boil. Add the root beer extract and food coloring. Remove the pan from the heat. Let cool. Pour into a container with an airtight lid. Label the flavor of syrup. Refrigerate any unused portion.

MAKES ABOUT ½ CUP

Vanilla Syrup

1   cup sugar
½   cup water
1½   teaspoons vanilla extract

In a saucepan add the sugar to the water. Cook until the syrup is thick and about to reach a full boil. Add the vanilla extract and food coloring. Remove the pan from the heat. Let cool. Pour into a container with an airtight lid. Label the flavor of syrup. Refrigerate any unused portion.

MAKES ABOUT ½ CUP

Strawberry Syrup

1   cup sugar
½   cup water
1½   teaspoons strawberry extract
2   drops red food coloring

In a saucepan add the sugar to the water. Cook until the syrup is thick and about to reach a full boil. Add the strawberry extract and food coloring. Remove the pan from the heat. Let cool. Pour into a container with an airtight lid. Label the flavor of syrup. Refrigerate any unused portion.

MAKES ABOUT ½ CUP

Banana Soda

⅓   cup vanilla ice cream
3   tablespoons banana syrup
1   cup seltzer water

Place the vanilla ice cream in the bottom of a tall glass. Add the banana syrup and stir to make a smooth paste. Slowly pour the seltzer water over a spoon inside the glass so that the seltzer water cascades over the spoon. Scoop off foam to make room for all of the water. Stir until well blended.

SERVES 1

Cherry Soda

⅓   cup vanilla ice cream
3   tablespoons cherry syrup
1   cup seltzer water

Place the vanilla ice cream in the bottom of a tall glass. Add the cherry syrup and stir to make a smooth paste. Slowly pour the seltzer water over a spoon inside the glass so that the seltzer water cascades over the spoon. Scoop off foam to make room for all of the water. Stir until well blended.

SERVES 1

MORE DINER HISTORY

Diners during the 1930s and 1940s took on a streamlined appearance much like that of the airplanes, railroad cars, and automobiles of the period. With its bullet shape and rounded edges, the Sterling Streamliner diner perhaps captured this look the best, giving patrons the illusion of speed, as if they were eating on a moving train.

Nearly every diner manufacturer paid homage to the new "modernist" styling. This was, after all, the high point of the Art Deco movement, and diner designs were deeply influenced by its futuristic styling and colorful geometric shapes. Diner window frames, mirrors, and even coffeepots and salt and pepper shakers took on the distinctive Art Deco look. Since this was also the golden age of the diner, we tend nowadays to associate them with the Art Deco style.

At the same time, newer materials, such as stainless steel and glass blocks, were being employed in walls and interiors. Formica, first used by the Paramount Diner Company, made counters and tabletops much cheaper and more durable. The now-ubiquitous Naugahyde began to be used for booths.

The post–World War II era marked another period of dramatic change for the diner industry. Smaller diners became the rage as returning GIs looked for ways to set themselves up in business. For instance, the Kullman Company produced a small diner known as the Kullman Jr.; and the Valentine Diner Company of Wichita, Kansas, designed an even smaller unit called the Portable Steel Sandwich Shop.

Homemade diners were also popping up in cities across America. Usually, homemade diners looked like the real thing, except that they were built on-site and not in a factory.

By the late 1950s, there were more than 6,000 diners of all types open for business in towns and cities all across America and

BURLINGTON DINER, BURLINGTON, NEW JERSEY

twenty manufacturing companies producing new models every day. This was a growth industry, and there seemed little likelihood it would ever slow down. But times changed, and by the early 1960s, the grip that fast-food chains held on the diner industry was extremely tight and would continue for the next fifteen years.

Chocolate Soda

⅓ cup vanilla ice cream
3 tablespoons chocolate syrup
1 cup seltzer water

Place the vanilla ice cream in the bottom of a tall glass. Add the chocolate syrup and stir to make a smooth paste. Slowly pour the seltzer water over a spoon inside the glass so that the seltzer water cascades over the spoon. Scoop off foam to make room for all of the water. Stir until well blended.

SERVES 1

Maple Soda

⅓ cup vanilla ice cream
3 tablespoons maple syrup
1 cup seltzer water

Place the vanilla ice cream in the bottom of a tall glass. Add the maple syrup and stir to make a smooth paste. Slowly pour the seltzer water over a spoon inside the glass so that the seltzer water cascades over the spoon. Scoop off foam to make room for all of the water. Stir until well blended.

SERVES 1

SKEE'S DINER, TORRINGTON, CONNECTICUT

Orange Soda

⅓ cup vanilla ice cream
3 tablespoons orange syrup
1 cup seltzer water

Place the vanilla ice cream in the bottom of a tall glass. Add the orange syrup and stir to make a smooth paste. Slowly pour the seltzer water over a spoon inside the glass so that the seltzer cascades over the spoon. Scoop off foam to make room for all of the water. Stir until well blended.

SERVES 1

Raspberry Soda

⅓ cup vanilla ice cream
3 tablespoons raspberry syrup
1 cup seltzer water

Place the vanilla ice cream in the bottom of a tall glass. Add the raspberry syrup and stir to make a smooth paste. Slowly pour the seltzer water over a spoon inside the glass so that the seltzer water cascades over the spoon. Scoop off foam to make room for all of the water. Stir until well blended.

SERVES 1

Peppermint Soda

⅓ cup vanilla ice cream
3 tablespoons peppermint syrup
1 cup seltzer water

Place the vanilla ice cream in the bottom of a tall glass. Add the peppermint syrup and stir to make a smooth paste. Slowly pour the seltzer water over a spoon inside the glass so that the seltzer water cascades over the spoon. Scoop off foam to make room for all of the water. Stir until well blended.

SERVES 1

Root Beer Soda

⅓ cup vanilla ice cream
3 tablespoons root beer syrup
1 cup seltzer water

Place the vanilla ice cream in the bottom of a tall glass. Add the root beer syrup and stir to make a smooth paste. Slowly pour the seltzer water over a spoon inside the glass so that the seltzer water cascades over the spoon. Scoop off foam to make room for all of the water. Stir until well blended.

SERVES 1

Strawberry Soda

⅓ cup vanilla ice cream
3   tablespoons strawberry syrup
I   cup seltzer water

Place the vanilla ice cream in the bottom
of a tall glass. Add the strawberry syrup
and stir to make a smooth paste. Slowly
pour the seltzer water over a spoon inside
the glass so that the seltzer water cascades
over the spoon. Scoop off foam to make
room for all of the water. Stir until well
blended.

SERVES I

Vanilla Soda

⅓ cup vanilla ice cream
3   tablespoons vanilla syrup
I   cup seltzer water

Place the vanilla ice cream in the bottom
of a tall glass. Add the vanilla syrup and
stir to make a smooth paste. Slowly pour
the seltzer water over a spoon inside the
glass so that the seltzer water cascades
over the spoon. Scoop off foam to make
room for all of the water. Stir until well
blended.

SERVES I

New York Egg Cream

3   tablespoons chocolate syrup
¼ cup half-and-half
¼ teaspoon vanilla extract
2   cups seltzer water

In a tall glass blend the chocolate syrup
with the half-and-half and vanilla. Add ¼
cup of seltzer water. Stir to blend. Add
the remaining seltzer water. Stir gently.

SERVES I

Ice Cream Float

⅓ cup vanilla ice cream
3   tablespoons any flavor syrup
I   cup seltzer water
I   large scoop vanilla ice cream

Follow the exact recipe for making a
soda. Float the large scoop of vanilla ice
cream on the top of the soda.

SERVES I

Sidecar

⅓ cup vanilla ice cream
3 tablespoons any flavor syrup
I cup seltzer water
I large scoop vanilla ice cream

Follow the exact recipe for making a
soda. Press the scoop of vanilla ice cream
a third of the way directly down to the lip
of the glass.

SERVES I

Butterscotch Sauce

I cup light brown sugar
⅓ cup butter, melted
⅓ cup heavy cream

In a saucepan blend the brown sugar and
melted butter. Add the heavy cream and
bring to a boil. Boil for 5 minutes without
stirring. Remove. Beat the mixture for 30
seconds or until foamy. Serve warm.

MAKES ABOUT I CUP

Caramel Sauce

I pound dark brown sugar
¼ cup butter
I cup heavy cream

In the top of a double boiler over hot
water combine the brown sugar and butter. Blend in the heavy cream. Heat the
sauce to the boiling point. Let cool.
Refrigerate any unused portion.

MAKES ABOUT 2 CUPS

Chocolate Fudge Sauce

1½ squares unsweetened chocolate
I tablespoon butter
2 tablespoons corn syrup
½ cup boiling water
I cup sugar
⅛ teaspoon salt
½ teaspoon vanilla extract

In the top of a double boiler over simmering water melt the unsweetened chocolate. Add the butter, corn syrup, boiling
water, sugar, and salt. Stir constantly.
Place over direct heat and bring to a boil.
Let boil for 3 minutes. Add the vanilla
and blend until smooth. Let cool.
Refrigerate any unused portion.

MAKES ABOUT ¾ CUP

Chocolate-Peppermint Sauce

12   chocolate-covered peppermint patties
1   cup heavy cream
1   tablespoon peppermint schnapps

In the top of a double boiler over hot water melt the chocolate-covered peppermint patties. Blend in the heavy cream. Heat the sauce to the boiling point. Add the peppermint schnapps. Let cool. Refrigerate any unused portion.

MAKES ABOUT 1½ CUPS

English Toffee Sauce

1   cup sugar
1   cup cream
⅛   teaspoon salt
⅓   cup butter
½   teaspoon vanilla extract
4   drops almond extract

In the top of a double boiler over simmering water combine the sugar, cream, salt, and butter. Heat until the mixture begins to boil. Stir frequently. Remove from the heat. Before serving add the vanilla and almond extracts. Let cool. Refrigerate any unused portion.

MAKES ABOUT 1½ CUPS

Milk Chocolate Sauce

1   cup confectioners' sugar
½   cup cocoa powder
¼   teaspoon salt
½   cup water
½   cup milk
      Vanilla extract

In a mixing bowl sift together the sugar, cocoa powder, and salt. Add the water and milk. Blend until the mixture becomes a smooth paste.

Place in the top of a double boiler over hot water. Cook for 25 minutes, stirring frequently. Flavor to taste with vanilla. Let cool. Refrigerate any unused portion.

MAKES ABOUT 1 CUP

Chocolate Sundae

2   large scoops chocolate ice cream
¼   cup chocolate syrup
2   tablespoons marshmallow creme
¼   cup chopped walnuts
      Whipped Cream
      Maraschino cherry

Place the chocolate ice cream in the bottom of a large sundae dish. Drizzle the chocolate syrup and marshmallow creme over the top. Sprinkle with chopped walnuts. Cover with whipped cream. Garnish with maraschino cherry.

SERVES 1

Caramel-Nut Sundae

1	large scoop vanilla ice cream
1	large scoop chocolate ice cream
½	cup caramel sauce
	Whipped cream
2	tablespoons chopped walnuts
2	tablespoons chopped pecans
2	tablespoons chopped almonds

Place the vanilla ice cream and the chocolate ice cream side by side in the bottom of a large sundae dish. Top with caramel sauce. Cover with whipped cream. Sprinkle the chopped walnuts, pecans, and almonds over the whipped cream.

SERVES 1

Maple-Pecan Sundae

1	large scoop vanilla ice cream
1	large scoop maple ice cream
2	tablespoons maple syrup
2	tablespoons chopped pecans
	Cinnamon to taste
	Whipped cream

Place the vanilla and maple ice cream into a large sundae dish. Pour maple syrup over the top. Sprinkle pecans over the syrup. Sprinkle with cinnamon to taste. Cover with whipped cream.

SERVES 1

Marshmallow Sundae

⅔	cup marshmallow creme
⅓	cup heavy cream
2	large scoops vanilla ice cream
6	large marshmallows, halved
¼	cup chocolate syrup
2	tablespoons chopped walnuts

In a mixing bowl blend the marshmallow creme with the heavy cream. Blend so that the mixture is smooth and creamy. Set aside.

Place the vanilla ice cream in the bottom of a large sundae dish. Place halved marshmallows around the scoops of ice cream. Drizzle the chocolate syrup and marshmallow-cream mixture over the top. Sprinkle with chopped walnuts.

SERVES 1

Peaches & Cream Sundae

2	large scoops vanilla ice cream
½	cup sliced peaches
¼	cup chopped walnuts
	Whipped cream
1	maraschino cherry, halved

Place the vanilla ice cream in a large sundae dish. Place sliced peaches over the top. Sprinkle the chopped walnuts over the peaches. Cover with whipped cream. Garnish with maraschino cherry halves.

SERVES 1

Pistachio Sundae

2 large scoops pistachio ice cream
¼ cup crushed pineapple, drained
4 maraschino cherries, chopped
2 tablespoons pistachio nuts, chopped
Whipped cream

Place the pistachio ice cream in the bottom of a large sundae dish. Place crushed pineapple over the ice cream. Sprinkle the maraschino cherries and pistachio nuts over the pineapple. Cover with whipped cream.

SERVES 1

Strawberry Sundae

2 large scoops strawberry ice cream
½ cup strawberries, puréed
Whipped cream
¼ cup walnuts, chopped
2 large strawberries, sliced

Place the scoops of strawberry ice cream side by side in the bottom of a large sundae dish. Top with puréed strawberries. Cover with whipped cream. Sprinkle chopped walnuts over the whipped cream. Garnish with sliced strawberries.

SERVES 1

VILLAGE DINER, MILLERTON, NEW YORK

Tin Pan Alley Sundae

2   large scoops vanilla ice cream
½   cup sliced peaches
½   cup crushed pineapple
    Whipped cream
¼   cup chopped walnuts

Place the vanilla ice cream in the bottom
of a large sundae dish. Top one scoop
with the sliced peaches and the other
scoop with the crushed pineapple. Cover
with whipped cream over all. Sprinkle
chopped walnuts over the whipped
cream.

SERVES 1

Vanilla-Mint Sundae

2   large scoops vanilla ice cream
2   tablespoons peppermint extract
¼   cup chopped walnuts
    Whipped cream
    Maraschino cherry

Place the scoops of vanilla ice cream side
by side in the bottom of a large sundae
dish. Pour the peppermint extract over
the ice cream. Sprinkle the chopped walnuts over the extract. Cover with
whipped cream. Garnish with a
maraschino cherry.

SERVES 1

Black & White

4   vanilla wafers
1   large scoop vanilla ice cream
1   large scoop chocolate ice cream
    Whipped cream
2   tablespoons chocolate sauce
2   tablespoons chopped walnuts
2   tablespoons chopped pecans

Place the vanilla wafers in the bottom of a
large sundae dish. Place the vanilla ice
cream over half of the wafers and the
chocolate ice cream over the other half.
Top the chocolate ice cream with the
whipped cream. Top the vanilla ice cream
with the chocolate sauce. Sprinkle
chopped walnuts and pecans over all.

SERVES 1

The Skyscraper

2   large scoops vanilla ice cream
2   vanilla wafers
1   large scoop strawberry ice cream
¼   cup chocolate sauce
1   tablespoon marshmallow creme
    Whipped cream

Place the vanilla ice cream side by side in
the bottom of a large sundae dish. Attach
the vanilla wafers to the vanilla ice cream
so that they form a bridge between the
two scoops. Gently place the scoop of
strawberry ice cream on top of the vanilla
wafers. Top with chocolate sauce and
marshmallow creme. Cover with whipped
cream.

SERVES 1

Roadside Flip

1	tablespoon vanilla syrup
1½	tablespoons pineapple syrup
1	tablespoon raspberry syrup
1	egg
	Crushed ice
1	scoop vanilla ice cream
	Seltzer water

Place in a shaker the vanilla syrup, pineapple syrup, and raspberry syrup. Add the egg and a little bit of crushed ice. Shake so that all of the ingredients are well blended. Add the scoop of vanilla ice cream. Fill the shaker to the top with seltzer water. Pour into a serving glass.

SERVES 1

Sunrise Flip

2	tablespoons raspberry syrup
1	tablespoon orange syrup
1	egg
	Lime juice
	Crushed ice
	Seltzer water
1	orange, sliced
1	maraschino cherry, halved

Place in a shaker the raspberry and orange syrups. Add the egg with 3 to 4 drops of lime juice and a little bit of crushed ice. Shake so that all of the ingredients are well blended. Fill the shaker to the top with seltzer water. Pour into a serving glass. Garnish with orange slices and maraschino cherry halves.

SERVES 1

Banana Split

1	large banana
1	large scoop vanilla ice cream
1	large scoop chocolate ice cream
1	large scoop strawberry ice cream
¼	cup chocolate sauce
¼	cup marshmallow creme
¼	cup strawberries, puréed
¼	cup chopped walnuts
	Whipped cream
2	maraschino cherries, chopped

Split the banana in half, lengthwise. Place the banana halves cut-side-up in the bottom of a banana split dish. Place the scoop of vanilla ice cream at one end of the dish. At the other end place the scoop of chocolate ice cream. Place the strawberry ice cream in the center.

Pour the chocolate sauce over the scoop of vanilla ice cream. Pour the marshmallow creme over the chocolate ice cream. Pour the puréed strawberries over the strawberry ice cream. Sprinkle the chopped walnuts evenly over all the scoops of ice cream. Cover with whipped cream. Garnish with chopped maraschino cherries.

SERVES 1

Orange Fizz

Ice cubes
3   tablespoons orange syrup
1   tablespoon lemon syrup
¼   cup fresh orange juice
    Seltzer water
½   teaspoon confectioners' sugar
1   orange, sliced

Fill a tall glass one-fourth full with ice cubes. Pour the orange and lemon syrups into the glass. Add the fresh orange juice. Stir to blend. Add seltzer water to the top of the glass. Add sugar. Stir to blend well. Garnish with sliced orange.

SERVES 1

Chocolate Eggnog

3   tablespoons chocolate syrup
1   egg
    Crushed ice
    Milk
    Cinnamon

Place in a shaker the chocolate syrup and egg. Add a little bit of crushed ice. Fill the shaker about two-thirds full with cold milk. Shake so that all ingredients are well blended. Strain the mixture into a tall glass. Top with cinnamon.

SERVES 1

Mississippi Eggnog

3   tablespoons molasses
1   tablespoon heavy cream
1   egg
    Cinnamon
1   scoop vanilla ice cream
    Crushed ice
    Milk

Place in a shaker the molasses and heavy cream. Add the egg. Add a dash of cinnamon, the scoop of vanilla ice cream, and a little bit of crushed ice. Fill the shaker about two-thirds full with cold milk. Shake so that all of the ingredients are well blended. Strain the mixture into a tall glass.

SERVES 1

Malted Milk Eggnog

3   tablespoons chocolate syrup
1   egg
2   teaspoons malted milk powder
    Crushed ice
    Milk

Place in a shaker the chocolate syrup, egg, and malted milk powder. Add a little bit of crushed ice. Fill the shaker about two-thirds full with cold milk. Shake so that all ingredients are well blended. Strain the mixture into a tall glass.

SERVES 1

BIGGER ⅜ BETTER

Most early diners were situated near factories, retail outlets, and business districts. But as the popularity of the family automobile increased, they began popping up along highways.

In 1928 HiWay Diners of New England set up a chain of roadside diners with soda fountains, a feature sure to appeal to anyone traveling with children. To enhance their family image, signs and advertisements touted them as "The Cleanest Place To Eat."

The increase in traffic and business on highways led some optimistic manufacturers to build new diners at the previously unheard of rate of one a day. Even the infamous stock market crash of 1929 did little to slow the growth of the diner industry. In fact, with the onset of the Great Depression, diners became one of the few places people could afford to eat. Even hotels began to convert their fancy in-house restaurants into lunch counters.

With business on the rise, owners soon outgrew their original diners, and manufacturers readily agreed to take them back as trade-ins on larger, upgraded models. The old diners were then reconditioned and resold, much like used cars.

First-time diner owners were also thinking big. In 1931 the Bixler Manufacturing Company of Norwalk, Ohio, jumped into the business with a diner much larger than those sold by its competitors. After early successes, Bixler was finally overwhelmed by the depression and closed its doors in 1937.

However, a few diner manufacturers managed to survive. Established in 1927, the Silk City Diner Company advertised the lowest priced diners available and, in this

HI-WAY DINER, NEW HAVEN, CONNECTICUT

way, managed to march through the hard economic times. Silk City remained in business until 1964. The Paramount Diner Company, which sold its first models in 1931, remains in business to this day. Paramount made famous the stainless steel Art Deco-style diner.

212

Strawberry Eggnog

3 tablespoons strawberry syrup
1 tablespoon raspberry syrup
¼ cup heavy cream
1 egg
   Milk
   Whipped cream
   Cinnamon

Place in a shaker the strawberry and raspberry syrups. Add the heavy cream. Add
the egg. Fill the shaker with cold milk.
Shake so that all ingredients are well
blended. Strain the mixture into a tall
glass. Top with whipped cream and a
dash of cinnamon.

SERVES 1

Caramel Parfait

   Caramel sauce
1 scoop vanilla ice cram
¼ cup chopped pecans
   Whipped cream

Cover the inside of a parfait glass with the
caramel sauce. Place the vanilla ice cream
in the glass. Top the ice cream with more
caramel sauce. Sprinkle the chopped
pecans over the caramel. Cover with
whipped cream.

SERVES 1

Alleyway Parfait

1 scoop chocolate ice cream
3 maraschino cherries, chopped
   Vanilla syrup
6 marshmallows, diced
1 scoop coffee ice cream
   Whipped cream
¼ cup chopped walnuts

Place the scoop of chocolate ice cream in
a parfait glass. Top with maraschino cherries and vanilla syrup. Top with marshmallows. Place the scoop of coffee ice
cream over the marshmallows. Cover with
whipped cream. Sprinkle the chopped
walnuts over the whipped cream.

SERVES 1

Maple Parfait

1 scoop maple ice cream
   Whipped cream
1 tablespoon chopped pecans
2 whole pecans, halved

Place the maple ice cream in a parfait
glass. Cover with whipped cream.
Sprinkle the chopped pecans over the
whipped cream. Garnish with pecan
halves.

SERVES 1

Mint Parfait

1 scoop vanilla ice cream
Whipped cream
1½ teaspoons peppermint extract
Maraschino cherries, sliced

Place the vanilla ice cream in a parfait glass. Cover with whipped cream. Drizzle the peppermint extract over the whipped cream. Garnish with maraschino cherries.

SERVES 1

Nutty Parfait

1 scoop maple ice cream
1 scoop coffee ice cream
Whipped cream
¼ cup chopped walnuts
2 tablespoons butterscotch sauce
¼ cup chopped almonds
2 tablespoons chocolate syrup

Place the scoops of maple and coffee ice cream in a parfait glass. Cover with whipped cream. Top with chopped walnuts. Pour the butterscotch sauce over the walnuts. Sprinkle the chopped almonds over the butterscotch sauce. Top with chocolate syrup.

SERVES 1

Raspberry Parfait

1 scoop raspberry ice cream
½ cup raspberries, puréed
¼ cup chopped walnuts
Whipped cream

Place the raspberry ice cream in a parfait glass. Top with puréed raspberries. Sprinkle the chopped walnuts over the raspberries. Cover with whipped cream.

SERVES 1

Deluxe Diner Parfait

1 scoop vanilla ice cream
½ teaspoon chopped pecans
2 maraschino cherries, chopped
1 scoop chocolate ice cream
3 tablespoons chocolate syrup
Whipped cream

Place the vanilla ice cream in the bottom of a parfait glass. Sprinkle the pecans and the maraschino cherries over the ice cream. Place the scoop of chocolate ice cream over the nuts and cherries. Drizzle the chocolate syrup over the top. Cover with whipped cream.

SERVES 1

DINERS AND FAST FOOD

The beginning of the 1960s saw a dramatic new trend in the eating habits of Americans. Fast-food chain restaurants were cropping up in towns and cities all across America. With restaurants like A & W, Dairy Queen, Foster Freeze, and McDonald's sprouting in suburban neighborhoods, diner owners began to feel the pinch of competition with corporate America.

The 1960s also saw the emergence of themed coffee shops with futuristic interiors, which appealed to families. Drive-in restaurants catered to young people with limited incomes and a passion for cheeseburgers and French fries.

This explosion of competition led to a steady decline in the diner business. Americans were on the move and, it seemed, diners just didn't move fast enough.

To fight back, manufacturers designed new diners more likely to fit the new, more mobile lifestyles of Americans: Paramount produced the Roadking diner, and the Kullman Company tried out the idea of a diner/drive-in combination. Neither of these concepts showed promise as serious competition for the fast-food industry.

Most fast-food restaurants were strategically situated in neighborhoods where hungry customers had easy access to them. Diners, on the other hand, were situated on the outskirts of town, in industrial parks and business districts. To the public, diners became known as dives and greasy spoons that catered to truck drivers and highway patrol officers.

At the same time, fast-food chains spared no expense in advertising their new restaurants. They guaranteed that no matter which franchise one ate in, the quality of food and service would be the same. This was a promise a diner owner could not match.

OVERLEA DINER, BALTIMORE, MARYLAND

Unable to compete with the buying power and advertising clout of the chains, some diner owners closed their doors forever. Many others sold their diners at a loss, while a few managed to relocate or renovate. In time these businesses began to look less like traditional diners and more like small restaurants.

WHAT'S FOR DESSERT?

Apple Spice Cake

½	cup butter
¾	cup sugar
3	tablespoons light corn syrup
½	cup cottage cheese
1	teaspoon grated lemon rind
1	teaspoon fresh lemon juice
1½	cups all-purpose flour
1½	teaspoons baking powder
⅛	teaspoon ground cloves
½	teaspoon cinnamon
¼	cup milk
2	eggs
1	apple, peeled and diced
	Whipped cream

Grease a 9-inch square baking pan. Set aside.

In a mixing bowl blend the butter and sugar. Add the corn syrup and cottage cheese, and mix thoroughly. Add the lemon rind and lemon juice, and mix well.

In a separate mixing bowl sift the flour with the baking powder, cloves, and cinnamon. Add a small amount to the cheese mixture. Blend thoroughly. Add the milk and the eggs, one at a time, alternately with the flour mixture. Beat well after adding each egg. Fold the apples into the batter.

Pour the batter into the prepared baking pan. Bake at 350° for 35 minutes or until a toothpick inserted in the center comes out clean. Cut into squares and top each serving with whipped cream.

SERVES 6

Applesauce Cake

2	cups all-purpose flour
1	teaspoon baking soda
1/4	teaspoon salt
1/4	teaspoon ground cloves
1/2	teaspoon nutmeg
1	teaspoon cinnamon
1/2	cup butter
1	cup sugar
1	egg, beaten
1	cup raisins
1	cup chopped walnuts
1	cup thick applesauce

Grease an 8x4-inch loaf pan. Set aside.

In a mixing bowl sift the flour. Measure 2 cups. Add the soda, salt, cloves, nutmeg, and cinnamon. Sift three times more. In a separate mixing bowl cream the butter and sugar. Add the egg and mix thoroughly. Add the raisins and walnuts. Add the flour to the creamed mixture alternately with the applesauce. Beat until smooth.

Pour the batter into the prepared pan. Bake at 350° for 1 hour and 15 minutes. Let cool.

SERVES 6

Apple-Raisin Rum Cake

1/2	cup butter
1	cup sugar
1/2	cup packed brown sugar
2	eggs
2	cups all-purpose flour

1 1/2	teaspoons baking powder
1/2	teaspoon salt
1/2	teaspoon baking soda
1	teaspoon cinnamon
1/2	teaspoon nutmeg
1	cup evaporated milk
4	tablespoons rum extract
2 1/2	cups peeled and chopped tart apples
1	cup raisins
1	cup chopped walnuts

Grease a 9x13-inch baking pan. Set aside.

In a large mixing bowl cream together the butter, sugar, and brown sugar until fluffy. Beat in the eggs one at a time.

In a separate mixing bowl sift the flour with the baking powder, salt, baking soda, cinnamon, and nutmeg. Add the flour mixture alternately with the milk and rum extract to the sugar mixture. Add the apples, raisins, and walnuts. Pour the batter into the prepared baking pan. Bake at 350° for 40 minutes or until a toothpick inserted into the center comes out clean.

SERVES 6

Raw Apple Cake

2	eggs
2	cups sugar
1	teaspoon vanilla extract
1/2	cup vegetable oil
2	cups all-purpose flour
1 1/2	teaspoons cinnamon
1 1/2	teaspoons baking soda
1	teaspoon nutmeg
1	teaspoon salt
1	cup chopped walnuts
4	cups chopped tart apples

Grease and flour a 9-inch round cake pan. Set aside.

In a mixing bowl beat together the eggs and sugar. Add the vanilla and vegetable oil.

In a separate mixing bowl sift together the flour, cinnamon, baking soda, nutmeg, and salt. Add to the egg mixture. Gently add the walnuts and apples. Pour the batter into the prepared cake pan. Bake at 350° for 45 minutes.

SERVES 6

Banana Cake

2½ cups cake flour, sifted
1⅔ cups sugar
1¼ teaspoons baking powder
1¼ teaspoons baking soda
½ teaspoon salt
⅔ cup butter
⅔ cup buttermilk
1¼ cups mashed bananas
3 eggs
¾ cup chopped walnuts

◆ ◆ ◆

½ cup butter
3 cups confectioners' sugar
1 egg yolk, beaten
¼ cup plus 2 tablespoons light cream
1½ teaspoons vanilla extract

Grease and flour a 9-inch round cake pan. Set aside.

In a mixing bowl combine the flour, sugar, baking powder, baking soda, and salt. Add the butter and half of the buttermilk and beat for 3 minutes. Add the bananas, eggs, and remaining buttermilk. Add the walnuts. Mix thoroughly. Pour the batter into the prepared cake pan. Bake at 350° for 45 minutes. Let cool.

In a mixing bowl combine the butter and confectioners' sugar. Add the egg yolk. Stir in the cream and vanilla. Beat until smooth and creamy. Frost the top and sides of the banana cake.

SERVES 6

LEE'S DINER, YORK, PENNSYLVANIA

Chocolate Cake

2	cups all-purpose flour
1	cup sugar
1/4	cup cocoa powder
2	teaspoons baking powder
1	cup mayonnaise
1	cup brewed rich coffee, chilled

♦ ♦ ♦

1	ounce dark chocolate
2	tablespoons butter
2	cups confectioners' sugar
2	tablespoons warm water

Grease and flour a 9x12-inch cake pan. Set aside.

In a mixing bowl sift together the flour, sugar, cocoa powder, and baking powder. Blend in the mayonnaise and coffee. Mix thoroughly. Spread into the prepared cake pan. Bake at 350° for 30 minutes. Let cool.

In the top of a double boiler over hot water melt the chocolate with the butter. Add the confectioners' sugar. Beat until smooth. Add water until creamy. Let cool. Frost the top of the chocolate cake.

SERVES 6

Black Forest Cake

5	tablespoons butter
8	eggs
1 1/4	cups sugar
1/2	cup cocoa powder, sifted
2/3	cup all-purpose flour, sifted
1 1/4	teaspoons vanilla extract
	Maraschino cherries, sliced
1	ounce semisweet chocolate, grated

♦ ♦ ♦

1/3	cup sugar
2	tablespoons cornstarch
1/8	teaspoon salt
2	cups tart pitted cherries
1/4	cup kirsch
2	drops red food coloring

♦ ♦ ♦

4 1/2	cups confectioners' sugar, sifted
1	cup butter
3	egg yolks

Grease and flour 3 9-inch round cake pans. Set aside.

In a saucepan melt 5 tablespoons butter. Set aside and let cool. In a mixing bowl beat the eggs with 1 1/4 cups sugar until very thick and the batter triples in size.

In a separate mixing bowl sift together the cocoa powder and the flour. Fold in the egg mixture. Blend until well mixed. Add the melted butter and vanilla. Pour an even amount of the batter into each of the prepared cake pans. Bake at 350° for 25 minutes or until a toothpick inserted in the center comes out clean. Let cool in pans for 5 minutes. Loosen the edges and remove the cakes. Let cool completely.

In a saucepan combine 1/3 cup sugar with the cornstarch and salt. Drain the cherries, reserving 1/4 cup of juice.

In a mixing bowl mash the cherries. Add the reserved juice with the kirsch and red food coloring to the saucepan. Cook over medium heat until thick, stirring occasionally. Stir in the cherries. Let cool and chill.

In a mixing bowl blend the confectioners' sugar with 1 cup butter. Blend until smooth. Add the egg yolks one at a time. Beat until light and fluffy.

Frost the top of one cake with one-fourth of the frosting. Cover with half the filling. Top with a second cake layer. Repeat with the second cake layer. Top with the final cake layer. Frost the tops and sides of the cake. Garnish with maraschino cherries and chocolate shavings. Refrigerate overnight before serving.

SERVES 6

Carrot Cake

2	cups all-purpose flour
¼	cup cornmeal
2	cups sugar
½	teaspoon salt
3	teaspoons baking soda
I	teaspoon baking powder
2	teaspoons vanilla extract
3	large eggs
1½	cups peanut oil
I	cup crushed pineapple
1½	cups flaked coconut
½	cup chopped dried apricots
2	cups grated carrots
½	cup chopped walnut

♦ ♦ ♦

¾	cup butter, softened
I	cup confectioners' sugar
I	8-ounce package cream cheese, softened
I	tablespoon fresh lemon juice
¾	cup flaked coconut
½	cup chopped walnuts

Grease and flour a 9x12-inch cake pan. Set aside.

In a mixing bowl sift together the flour, cornmeal, sugar, salt, baking soda, and baking powder. In a separate bowl blend together the vanilla, eggs, and oil until smooth. Add to the dry ingredients. Fold in the pineapple, 1½ cups coconut, apricots, and carrots. Blend thoroughly. Add the ½ cup of chopped walnuts. Pour the batter into the prepared cake pan. Bake at 350° for 60 minutes. Let cool.

In a mixing bowl blend together the butter and confectioners' sugar. Add the cream cheese and lemon juice, and blend until smooth and creamy. Frost the top of the carrot cake. Garnish with the remaining flaked coconut and chopped walnuts.

SERVES 6

MATTAPOISETT DINER, MATTAPOISETT, MASSACHUSETTS

Lemon Cake

2	cups pastry flour
½	teaspoon baking soda
¼	teaspoon salt
⅓	cup butter
1	cup sugar
2	eggs, well beaten
½	cup milk
1½	tablespoons fresh lemon juice

◆ ◆ ◆

	Juice from 1 lemon
	Grated lemon rind
¾	cup water
2½	tablespoons cornstarch
2	tablespoons water
1	egg yolk, slightly beaten

◆ ◆ ◆

1	cup sugar
½	cup water
2	egg whites, stiffly beaten
½	teaspoon vanilla extract

In a mixing bowl sift the flour. Measure 2 cups. Add the baking soda and salt. Sift three more times.

In a separate mixing bowl cream the butter and 1 cup of sugar. Add the eggs and mix thoroughly. Add the flour to the creamed mixture alternately with the milk. Beat until smooth. Add the ½ teaspoon of lemon juice and blend thoroughly. Pour the batter into a loaf pan. Bake at 375° for 45 minutes. Let cool before removing from loaf pan.

In a saucepan combine the juice of one lemon, lemon rind, and ¾ cup of water. Cook over low heat until the mixture begins to boil. Mix the cornstarch with 2 tablespoons of water and add to the lemon juice. Cook over low heat for 3 minutes, stirring constantly. Add a small amount to the egg yolk. Return the egg mixture to the saucepan. Beat thoroughly. Let the filling cool.

In a saucepan combine 1 cup sugar and ½ cup water. Cook until the sugar has dissolved and a candy thermometer registers 235°. Remove the pan from the heat. Pour steadily into the beaten egg whites. Continue beating until peaks form. Add the vanilla. Let the frosting cool.

Spread the filling over the cake, and then frost with the frosting.

SERVES 6

Orange Cake

1	cup pastry flour
¼	teaspoon baking soda
¼	teaspoon salt
6	eggs, separated
¾	cup sugar
½	teaspoon grated orange rind
¼	cup fresh orange juice
1	tablespoon fresh lemon juice

Grease a 10-inch tube pan. Set aside.

In a mixing bowl sift the flour. Measure 1 cup. Add the baking soda and salt. Sift four more times.

In a separate mixing bowl beat the egg yolks until they are thick and the color of lemons. Add the sugar and beat thoroughly. Blend in the orange rind, orange juice, and lemon juice.

Beat the egg whites until stiff. Fold in the egg yolk mixture. Add the flour a little at a time. Mix thoroughly.

Pour the batter into the prepared tube pan. Bake at 350° for 45 minutes. Invert the pan to cool for 1 hour. Remove the cake and serve.

SERVES 6

Sour Cream Cake

3 ounces unsweetened chocolate
2 cups pastry flour
1 teaspoon baking soda
1/4 teaspoon salt
1 cup sugar
1 cup sour cream
1 egg, well beaten
3/4 cup milk
1 teaspoon vanilla extract

♦ ♦ ♦

2 ounces unsweetened dark chocolate
1/4 cup butter
4 cups confectioners' sugar
1/4 cup warm water

Grease 2 9-inch round cake pans. Set aside.

In a saucepan melt the chocolate. Let cool and set aside. In a mixing bowl sift the flour. Measure 2 cups. Add the baking soda and salt. Sift three more times.

In a separate mixing bowl blend the sugar with the sour cream. Add the beaten egg and mix thoroughly. Blend in the melted chocolate.

Add the sour cream mixture to the flour alternately with the milk. Beat until smooth. Add the vanilla and blend well.

Pour the batter into the prepared pans. Bake at 325° for 25 minutes. Let cool before removing from pans.

In the top of a double boiler melt the chocolate with the butter. Add the confectioners' sugar. Beat until smooth. Add water. Continue mixing until the frosting becomes creamy. Let cool. Frost the top of the chocolate cake layers. Place one layer on top of the other. Frost the sides of the cake.

SERVES 6

Pineapple Upside-Down Cake

1/4 cup butter
1 cup packed brown sugar
1 10-ounce can pineapple slices, drained
Maraschino cherries, sliced
4 eggs
1 cup sugar
2 tablespoons water
1 teaspoon vanilla extract
1 cup all-purpose flour
1 teaspoon baking powder
1/4 teaspoon salt
Whipped cream

In a saucepan melt the butter. Add the brown sugar and blend until the sugar has dissolved. Let cool.

Arrange the pineapple slices in the bottom of an 8-inch round baking dish. Place slices of maraschino cherry in the center of each pineapple ring. Pour the sugar mixture over the top.

In a separate mixing bowl beat the eggs until frothy. Gradually beat in the sugar. Add the water and vanilla. In a separate mixing bowl sift together the flour, baking powder, and salt. Add to the egg mixture. Blend thoroughly. Pour the batter over the pineapple rings. Bake at 350° for 45 minutes. Let cool thoroughly.

To serve loosen the cake from the pan. Invert onto a serving platter. Cover with whipped cream.

SERVES 6

Mississippi Mud Cake

2 cups sugar
½ cup butter
4 eggs
1 teaspoon vanilla extract
1½ cups all-purpose flour
⅛ teaspoon salt
½ cup cocoa powder
1 cup chopped walnuts
1 cup marshmallow creme

♦ ♦ ♦

¼ cup butter
1 teaspoon vanilla extract
⅓ cup cocoa powder
½ cup evaporated milk
2 cups confectioners' sugar

Grease and flour a 9x12-inch baking pan. Set aside.

In a mixing bowl cream the sugar with the butter. Beat in the eggs and 1 teaspoon vanilla. In a separate bowl sift together the flour, salt, and cocoa powder. Add the flour mixture to the creamed mixture. Add the nuts. Pour into the prepared baking pan. Bake at 350° for 25 minutes. Remove from the oven. While the cake is still hot, spread the marshmallow creme over the top. Let cool.

In a mixing bowl blend together the ¼ cup butter, 1 teaspoon vanilla, and ⅓ cup cocoa powder. Add the evaporated milk and sugar, and mix well. Frost the cooled cake. Refrigerate any unused portion.

SERVES 6

Angel Food Cake

1 cup cake flour, sifted
1½ cups sugar
1½ cups egg whites
½ teaspoon salt
1½ teaspoons cream of tartar
1 teaspoon vanilla extract
½ teaspoon almond extract

In a mixing bowl sift the flour with ½ cup of sugar four times.

In a separate bowl beat the egg whites and salt until foamy. Add the cream of tartar, vanilla, and almond extract. Continue beating until the egg whites become stiff.

Add the remaining sugar, a little at a time. Fold gently. Sift one-fourth of the flour mixture over the egg whites and mix well. Continue until all the flour is used.

Pour the batter into a 10-inch tube pan. Cut the batter with a knife to remove any air pockets. Bake at 350° for 35 minutes or until the top is golden brown.

Invert the cake and let cool.

SERVES 8

LIBBY'S BLUE LINE DINER

Owner Karen Griffith says Libby's Blue Line Diner, situated outside Colchester, Vermont, was named after her mother. But the diner, a 1953 Worcester Lunch Car with seating for seventy-five, has had a lot of other names—and locations.

"At one time it was the Forest Diner of Auburn, Massachusetts," says Karen. "At another, it was the Casco Diner of Turner Falls, Massachusetts."

Whatever its name and wherever it stood, the old diner has always served a wide variety of customers. Nowadays its patrons range from white-collar professionals to truckers. "We get all kinds, from college students to attorneys, from schoolteachers to travel agents."

Among Karen's favorite customers is Stan, an IBM employee. "He holds an honorary degree in serving," says Karen. "He will come in the morning, make coffee, and pour some for the customers if the waitresses are busy picking up orders. Sometimes he gets up and takes food out of the window to help serve

it. He has taken the time to learn the table numbers and lingo."

Velveteen Cake

6	ounces semisweet chocolate chips
1/4	cup water
2 1/4	cups cake flour
1	teaspoon baking powder
1/2	teaspoon salt
1 3/4	cups sugar
3/4	cup butter, softened
1	teaspoon vanilla extract
3	eggs, room temperature
1	cup water

♦ ♦ ♦

6	ounces semisweet chocolate chips
3	tablespoons butter
1/4	cup milk
1	teaspoon vanilla extract
1/4	teaspoon salt
3	cups confectioners' sugar

Grease and flour 2 9-inch round cake pans. Set aside.

In a saucepan combine the chocolate chips with the 1/4 cup of water. Cook on low, stirring until the chocolate chips have melted. Set aside.

In a mixing bowl sift together the cake flour, baking powder, and salt. In a separate mixing bowl blend the sugar, butter, and vanilla until well blended. Add the eggs to the sugar mixture one at a time, beating well after each one. Pour the melted chocolate into the flour mixture, alternately with the 1 cup of water. Pour even amounts of the batter into the prepared baking pans. Bake at 375° for 30 to 35 minutes or until a toothpick inserted in the center comes out clean. Let cool. Remove from pans.

In a small saucepan melt the remaining chocolate chips with the butter over low heat. Add the milk, vanilla, and salt.

FRAZER DINER, FRAZER, PENNSYLVANIA

FRAZER DINER, FRAZER, PENNSYLVANIA

Mix well. Gradually blend in the sugar. Mix thoroughly so that all of the ingredients are well blended. Frost the sides and tops of the cakes. Refrigerate any unused portion.

SERVES 6

Pound Cake

6	eggs
2¾	cups sugar
1	teaspoon vanilla extract
3	cups all-purpose flour
1	tablespoon baking powder
¼	teaspoon salt
2	cups heavy cream

Grease and flour a loaf pan. Set aside.

In a mixing bowl beat the eggs on high for 5 minutes. Gradually add the sugar and vanilla, and beat until the sugar has dissolved.

In a separate bowl sift the flour, baking powder, and salt. Add the dry ingredients to the egg mixture alternately with the heavy cream. Pour into the prepared loaf pan. Bake at 350° for 60 to 70 minutes or until a toothpick inserted in the center comes out clean. Let cool for 15 minutes. Remove from the pan and place on a wire rack to cool completely.

SERVES 6

Strawberry Shortcake

1	quart fresh strawberries
1	cup sugar
2	cups all-purpose flour
2	tablespoons sugar
3	tablespoons baking powder
½	teaspoon salt
⅓	cup butter
1	cup milk
	Whipped cream

Wash the strawberries under cold running water. Stem the strawberries and cut in half. In a mixing bowl toss the strawberries with 1 cup of sugar. Refrigerate for 1 hour.

Grease 2 8-inch round cake pans. Set aside. In a separate mixing bowl combine the flour with the 2 tablespoons of sugar, baking powder, and salt. Blend in the butter. Stir in the milk and mix well.

Divide the dough evenly between the prepared baking pans. Dot with butter. Bake at 450° for 12 to 15 minutes or until light golden brown.

Place one cake layer upside down on a serving dish. Cover with half of the strawberries. Top with the second cake layer and remaining strawberries. Cover with whipped cream.

SERVES 6

MISS BELLOWS FALLS DINER, BELLOWS FALLS, VERMONT

Chocolate Brownie

2	ounces unsweetened chocolate
1/3	cup butter
3/4	cup all-purpose flour
1/4	teaspoon baking soda
1/4	teaspoon salt
3/4	cup sugar
2	eggs, slightly beaten
1/2	teaspoon vanilla extract
3/4	cup chopped walnuts

Grease an 8-inch square baking pan. Set aside.

In a saucepan combine the chocolate and butter. Cook over low heat until both have melted. Let cool and set aside.

In a mixing bowl sift the flour. Add the baking soda and salt. Sift three more times.

In a separate mixing bowl combine the sugar and the eggs. Beat until light and thick. Add the melted chocolate and blend well. Add the vanilla and chopped walnuts.

Add the flour, stirring until the batter is smooth. Pour the batter into the prepared pan. Bake at 350° for 30 minutes. Let cool. Cut into squares.

MAKES 16 SQUARES

Diner Cheesecake

2	eggs
1/2	cup sugar
1	tablespoon all-purpose flour
1	cup cottage cheese
6	ounces cream cheese
2	teaspoons fresh lemon juice
1	teaspoon grated lemon rind
1	9-inch graham cracker crust
1	cup sour cream
2	tablespoons chopped almonds

In a mixing bowl beat the eggs until they are the color of lemons. Slowly add the sugar and flour. In a separate bowl blend together the cottage cheese and the cream cheese. Add the lemon juice and lemon rind. Add the egg mixture to the cheese mixture. Blend thoroughly.

Pour the batter into the graham cracker crust. Bake at 325° for 30 minutes. Let cool.

Beat the sour cream until smooth. Spread half the sour cream evenly over the cheesecake. Let cool at room temperature for 1 to 2 hours, then place in the refrigerator. Before serving, spread the remaining sour cream over the cheesecake. Garnish with chopped almonds.

SERVES 6

Black & White Cheesecake

2	cups cottage cheese
1	8-ounce package cream cheese, softened
¼	cup plus 2 tablespoons all-purpose flour
1¼	cups sugar
	Pinch of salt
4	egg whites
1	teaspoon vanilla extract
2	tablespoons cocoa powder
1	tablespoon milk
1	9-inch graham cracker crust

In a mixing bowl blend together the cottage cheese and cream cheese until smooth and creamy. Add the flour, 1 cup of sugar, a pinch of salt, egg whites, and vanilla. Blend thoroughly.

In a separate mixing bowl place one-third of the filling. Add the cocoa powder, remaining sugar, and milk. Blend until smooth. Pour the white filling into the graham cracker crust. Spoon the chocolate filling over the top. Swirl the chocolate filling into the white filling.

Place the cheesecake on a baking sheet. Bake at 325° for 50 minutes. Turn off the oven. With the door slightly ajar, leave the cheesecake inside the oven for 1 hour. Remove and let cool completely.

SERVES 6

Strawberry–Cream Cheese Pie

12	graham crackers, crushed
¼	cup butter, melted
	♦ ♦ ♦
1½	cups cream cheese
¾	cup sugar
2	eggs, beaten
½	teaspoon fresh lemon juice
2	teaspoons vanilla extract
	♦ ♦ ♦
1	cup sour cream
½	tablespoon sugar
1	teaspoon vanilla extract
	♦ ♦ ♦
1	cup strawberries, sliced

In a mixing bowl combine the crushed graham crackers with the melted butter. Pat into the bottom of a 9-inch pie tin.

In a mixing bowl combine the cream cheese and ¾ cup sugar, and blend until smooth and creamy. Add the eggs and blend well. Add the lemon juice and 2 teaspoons vanilla. Mix thoroughly. Pour the batter into the graham cracker crust. Bake at 350° for 15 minutes. Remove the pie from the oven. Let cool for 5 minutes.

In a mixing bowl combine the sour cream, ½ tablespoon sugar, and 1 teaspoon vanilla. Blend until the mixture is smooth and creamy. Spread the topping over the pie. Return the pie to the oven and continue baking for 10 minutes. Let the pie cool.

Refrigerate for 4 hours. Top with sliced strawberries before serving.

SERVES 8

SKIP'S BLUE MOON DINER

Once known as the Miss Toy Town, Skip's Blue Moon Diner in Gardner, Massachusetts, was originally situated in nearby Winchendon, not far from a large toy factory. In 1954 it was moved to a lot in Gardner and renamed Blue Moon.

The diner closed, apparently for good, in 1960 when the owner's wife died. It remained closed for sixteen years until a retired Gardner police officer bought it in 1976 and reopened it as Skip's. Dennis Scitione, the current owner, has run the business since 1984.

A 1949 Worcester Lunch Car, Skip's Blue Moon is a traditional diner, and, as such, it attracts all types. "We have longshoremen

sitting next to guys in sharp suits and ties," says Dennis. "People get to know each other here. They meet and talk much the way they would do in an old-time barbershop. And we get to know our customers and their families. Some of the kids that ate here when they were in high school now have kids of their own in college."

But Dennis is the first to admit that running a diner is a tough business. "The first rule is to have the location and keep it clean. We keep this diner immaculate. And you've got to serve good food—well, that is the name of the game, after all."

Apple Pie

6   tart apples, peeled and sliced
1   cup sugar
2   tablespoons all-purpose flour
1   teaspoon cinnamon
3   tablespoons pineapple juice
1/8 teaspoon salt
     Pastry for 1 9-inch double-crust pie
1   teaspoon butter

In a mixing bowl toss the apples with the sugar, flour, cinnamon, pineapple juice, and salt.

Pat half the dough into the bottom of a pie tin. Pour the apple mixture into the center. Dot with butter; top with the remaining pastry. Seal and flute the edges. Cut 4 slits into the top with a sharp knife. Bake at 400° for 35 minutes or until the crust is light golden brown.

SERVES 6

Banana Cream Pie

1   9-inch pie shell, unbaked
2/3 cup sugar
3   tablespoons cornstarch
1/2 teaspoon salt
3   cups milk
3   egg yolks
1 1/2 teaspoons vanilla extract
1 1/2 teaspoons butter
3   large bananas, sliced
     Whipped cream

Prepare the pie shell according to package directions. Set aside.

In the top of a double boiler combine the sugar, cornstarch, and salt. Blend in the milk. Cook over low heat for 1 minute, stirring constantly, until the mixture thickens. Remove from the heat. Set aside.

In a mixing bowl beat the egg yolks. Slowly add 1/2 cup of the milk mixture. Return to the rest of the mixture in the double boiler.

Return the pan to the heat. Bring to a boil for 1 minute, stirring constantly. Remove from the heat. Add vanilla and butter. Arrange slices of banana in the bottom of the pie shell. Pour in half the filling. Layer with the remaining banana slices and filling. Refrigerate for 2 hours. Cover with whipped cream.

SERVES 6

In a mixing bowl combine the sugar, vanilla, salt, and eggs. Slowly pour the melted caramel candies into the sugar mixture. Mix thoroughly. Add the pecan halves.

Pour the mixture into the unbaked pie shell. Bake at 350° for 45 minutes. Let cool until the pie filling is firm.

SERVES 6

Chocolate Chiffon Pie

1	envelope unflavored gelatin
¼	cup cold water
2	ounces unsweetened chocolate
1	cup milk
2	eggs, separated
¼	teaspoon salt
½	cup sugar
1	teaspoon vanilla extract
⅔	cup cream, whipped
1	9-inch pie shell, baked
	Whipped cream

In a cup soften the gelatin in the cold water.

In the top of a double boiler over hot water combine the chocolate and milk. Heat until the chocolate has melted. Beat until creamy. Add the gelatin.

In a mixing bowl beat the egg yolks until they are lemon in color. Slowly add the salt and ¼ cup of the sugar. Blend well. Gradually add the melted chocolate with the vanilla. Mix well. Refrigerate until the mixture thickens.

In a separate mixing bowl beat the egg whites until firm. Add the remaining sugar. Fold into the chocolate mixture with the cream. Pour into the pie shell. Chill until firm. Cover with whipped cream.

SERVES 6

BURLINGTON DINER, BURLINGTON, NEW JERSEY

Caramela Pie

36	soft caramel candies
¼	cup water
¼	cup butter
¾	cup sugar
½	teaspoon vanilla extract
¼	teaspoon salt
3	eggs, well beaten
1¼	cups pecan halves
1	9-inch pie shell, unbaked

In a covered double boiler over hot water melt the caramel candies with the water and butter over low heat, stirring occasionally.

Chocolate Custard Pie

4	eggs
2⅔	cups milk
⅔	cup sugar
⅛	teaspoon salt
	Nutmeg to taste
1	9-inch pie crust
¼	cup semisweet chocolate pieces
1	tablespoon milk
	Whipped cream

In a mixing bowl whisk the eggs with a fork. Add the milk, sugar, salt, and nutmeg to taste. Blend thoroughly. Pour the filling into the pie crust. Cover the edges of the pie with aluminum foil. Bake at 375° for 20 minutes. Remove the aluminum foil and continue baking 25 minutes or until the pie tests done.

In a small saucepan combine the chocolate pieces and 1 tablespoon of milk. Stir over low heat until the chocolate has melted. Drizzle over the cooled pie. Cover with whipped cream.

SERVES 6

Chocolate Cream Pie

1	9-inch pie shell
3	tablespoons cornstarch
½	teaspoon salt
3	cups milk
3	ounces unsweetened chocolate
3	egg yolks
1½	cups sugar
1½	teaspoons vanilla extract
1	tablespoon butter
	Whipped cream

Prepare the pie shell according to package directions. Set aside.

OASIS DINER, BURLINGTON, VERMONT

In the top of a double boiler combine the cornstarch and salt. Blend in the milk. Cut the chocolate into ¼-inch chunks, and add to the milk mixture. Cook over low heat for 1 minute, stirring constantly, until the mixture thickens. Remove from the heat. Set aside.

In a mixing bowl beat the egg yolks. Slowly add ½ cup of the chocolate mixture with the sugar, vanilla, and butter. Pour all back into the double boiler.

Return the chocolate mixture to the heat. Bring to a boil for 1 minute, stirring constantly. Pour into the pie shell. Refrigerate for 2 hours. Cover with whipped cream.

SERVES 6

ChocolateMarshmallow Pie

1	ounce unsweetened chocolate
20	marshmallows, sliced
1	8-ounce package cream cheese
½	cup milk
1	cup whipping cream
1	9-inch pre-baked graham cracker crust
½	cup chopped walnuts

In the top of a double boiler over hot water melt the chocolate, marshmallows, and cream cheese. In a saucepan heat the milk. Add the hot milk to the chocolate mixture and blend thoroughly.

Remove the pan from the heat. Let cool. In a small mixing bowl beat the whipping cream until thick. Fold into the chocolate mixture. Pour the filling into the graham cracker crust. Top with chopped walnuts. Refrigerate for 4 hours.

SERVES 8

Libby's Key Lime Pie

3	cups graham cracker crumbs
½	cup sugar
⅔	cup butter, melted

♦ ♦ ♦

1	14-ounce can sweetened condensed milk
3	teaspoons lime zest
6	eggs, separated
1½	cups lime juice
3	tablespoons cornstarch
4	drops green food coloring
	Whipped cream

In a mixing bowl combine the graham cracker crumbs, sugar, and melted butter. Mix until moist. Evenly press the mixture into the bottoms and sides of 2 9-inch pie tins. Bake at 350° for 10 minutes. Remove from the oven.

In a mixing bowl combine the condensed milk, lime zest, egg yolks, lime juice, and cornstarch, and mix well.

Place the egg whites in a separate bowl. Add the egg yolk mixture and food coloring. Whip until well mixed. Do not over-whip.

Pour even amounts of the filling mixture into the pie crusts. Return them to the oven. Continue baking for 10 minutes. Let cool for 3 to 4 hours. Top with whipped cream.

SERVES 12

Lemon Meringue Pie

1	9-inch pie shell, unbaked
1⅓	cups sugar
6	tablespoons cornstarch
2½	cups cold water
4	eggs, separated
2	tablespoons butter
1½	teaspoons vanilla extract
½	cup fresh lemon juice
	Grated rinds of 2 lemons
½	teaspoon salt
¼	cup sugar

Bake the pie shell according to package directions. Set aside.

In a medium saucepan blend 1⅓ cups of sugar, the cornstarch, and water. Cook over medium heat, stirring constantly, until the mixture begins to boil and is clear. Add beaten egg yolks, butter, and 1 teaspoon of vanilla. Return to a boil. Blend in the lemon juice and lemon rind. Pour into the pie shell. Set aside.

In a mixing bowl beat the egg whites until creamy. Continue beating. Add the salt, ¼ cup sugar, and remaining vanilla, beating until stiff peaks form. Smooth the meringue over the filling. Bake at 250° until the meringue is light brown.

SERVES 6

Lemon Chiffon Pie

4	eggs, separated
½	cup fresh lemon juice
½	teaspoon salt
¾	cup sugar
1	envelope unflavored gelatin
¼	cup cold water
1	teaspoon grated lemon rind
1	9-inch pie shell, baked
	Whipped cream

In the top of a double boiler over hot water combine the beaten egg yolks, lemon juice, salt, and ¼ cup of sugar. Cook until the mixture is the consistency of custard.

In a cup soften the gelatin in the cold water. Add to the double boiler. Add the lemon rind. Let the mixture cool until it becomes thick.

In a mixing bowl beat the egg whites until stiff. Slowly add the remaining sugar. Fold the egg whites into the lemon mixture. Pour evenly into the pie shell. Let chill in the refrigerator until the filling has set. Cover with whipped cream.

SERVES 6

Fresh Peach Pie

1	9-inch pie shell, unbaked
4	cups peeled and sliced fresh peaches
1	cup peaches, mashed
1	cup sugar
¾	cup water
3	teaspoons cornstarch
	Whipped cream

Bake the pie shell according to package directions. Set aside and let cool.

Arrange the sliced peaches in the bottom of the pie shell.

In a saucepan combine the mashed peaches, sugar, water, and cornstarch. Cook until thick and clear. Let cool slightly.

Pour the mashed peaches over the sliced peaches in the pie shell. Refrigerate until the filling has set and cooled. Cover with whipped cream.

SERVES 6

JUDY'S DINER, MALDEN, MASSACHUSETTS

Peach Upside-Down Pie

2	tablespoons butter
¾	cup sliced almonds
	Pastry for 1 9-inch double-crust pie
⅓	cup packed brown sugar
5	cups sliced fresh peaches
½	teaspoon nutmeg
¾	cup sugar
2	tablespoons quick-cooking tapioca
¼	teaspoon cinnamon
¼	cup packed brown sugar
	Milk

Line a 9-inch pie pan with aluminum foil. Let the excess foil drape over the sides. Spread the bottom evenly with butter.

Press the almonds and ⅓ cup brown sugar into the butter. Place the bottom crust in the pie pan over the almonds and brown sugar mixture.

In a mixing bowl blend together the sliced peaches, nutmeg, sugar, tapioca, and cinnamon. Pour the mixture into the pie shell. Sprinkle ¼ cup brown sugar over the top. Cover with the top pie shell. Brush with milk. Slice vents into the top crust. Bake at 450° for 10 minutes. Reduce the heat to 375° and bake 35 minutes more. Remove and let cool.

Serve by cutting and turning the pie upside down onto a plate. Gently remove the aluminum foil.

SERVES 6

MODERN DINER

Nick DeMoos has run the Modern Diner in Pawtucket, Rhode Island, for the past eleven years, but he is only the latest in a line of dedicated owners who have operated this classic—and classy—establishment. A cream-colored Sterling Streamliner, the Modern Diner was built in 1940. Today, it is one of only a handful of diners listed on the National Register of Historic Places.

When the Modern first opened for business, seats were limited to fifty customers at a time. Later another dining room was added, which is fortunate since the diner frequently overflows with customers.

Nick says the Modern has been drawing more and more customers in recent years. The same is true for many other traditional diners. "I think diners are coming back because everything repeats itself eventually," says Nick, who sees a number of reasons for the revival of interest in diners.

"Compared to the large corporate chains, we have to put out a good product," he says. "Our livelihood depends on it. Anyway, people are tired of ordering the same things. We offer a lot of special things you'd never see at the chains."

For instance, at breakfast the Modern serves up Lobster Benedict and Pear and Almond Pancakes. People stand in line to order these and other specialties.

Nick says an important part of the charm of his diner and others is their down-home feeling. "We have a friendly atmosphere with a lot of regulars who keep coming back."

Pecan Pie

Pastry for 1 9-inch pie
3 eggs
1 teaspoon vanilla extract
⅔ cup corn syrup
¼ teaspoon salt
⅓ cup dark molasses
¾ cup packed brown sugar
6 tablespoons butter, melted
1 cup chopped pecans
¼ cup pecan halves

Line a pie tin with the pastry. Flute the edges.

In a mixing bowl beat the eggs. Add the vanilla, corn syrup, salt, molasses, brown sugar, and butter. Stir in the chopped pecans. Mix thoroughly.

Pour the filling into the pie pastry. Bake on the center rack of the oven at 375° for 30 minutes. Let cool. Arrange pecan halves around the top of the pie.

SERVES 6

Peanut Butter Pie

1 8-ounce package cream cheese, softened
1 cup peanut butter
1 cup sugar
2 cups whipped topping
2 tablespoons butter, melted
2 tablespoons vanilla extract
1 9-inch graham cracker crust

In a mixing bowl cream together the cream cheese and peanut butter. Add the sugar. Mix thoroughly. Add the whipped topping, melted butter, and vanilla. Mix thoroughly.

Pour the mixture into the bottom of the graham cracker crust. Refrigerate for 1 hour or until the filling is set.

SERVES 6

MODERN DINER, PAWTUCKET, RHODE ISLAND

Pumpkin Pie

2/3 cup packed dark brown sugar

1 teaspoon cinnamon

1/2 teaspoon nutmeg

1/4 teaspoon ginger

1/4 teaspoon ground cloves

2 eggs

1 cup evaporated milk

2 cups pumpkin

1 9-inch pie shell, unbaked

In a mixing bowl blend together the brown sugar, cinnamon, nutmeg, ginger, and cloves.

In a separate mixing bowl blend together the eggs, evaporated milk, and pumpkin. Add the brown sugar mixture. Pour the filling into the pie shell. Bake at 350° for 50 minutes or until the pie is done.

SERVES 6

Raisin Pie

2 cups raisins

2 cups boiling water

1/2 cup sugar

2 tablespoons all-purpose flour

1/2 cup walnuts, chopped

3 tablespoons fresh lemon juice

2 teaspoons grated lemon rind

Pastry for 1 9-inch double-crust pie shell

In a medium saucepan combine the raisins with the boiling water. Cover and cook for 5 minutes. Set aside.

In a mixing bowl blend together the sugar and flour. Add the cooked raisins. Blend thoroughly.

Return the mixture to the saucepan. Cook on low heat until mixture starts to boil. Blend in the walnuts, lemon juice, and lemon rind. Pour the filling into the bottom of the pie shell. Cover with the top crust. Flute the edges. Cut slits into the top crust. Bake at 425° for 30 to 40 minutes or until the crust is light brown.

SERVES 6

Raspberry Pie

3 ounces raspberry-flavored gelatin

1/4 cup sugar

1 3/4 cups boiling water

1 10-ounce package frozen raspberries

1 tablespoon fresh lemon juice

3 ounces cream cheese, softened

1/3 cup confectioners' sugar, sifted

1 teaspoon vanilla extract

Salt to taste

1 cup whipped cream

1 9-inch pie shell, baked

In a mixing bowl dissolve the raspberry gelatin with the sugar in the boiling water. Add the frozen raspberries and lemon juice. Stir until well blended and the raspberries are no longer frozen. Refrigerate until somewhat firm.

In a separate mixing bowl blend together the cream cheese, confectioners' sugar, vanilla, and salt. Blend in 1/4 cup of the whipped cream. Add remaining whipped cream and blend thoroughly.

Spread half the cream cheese mixture into the bottom of the pie shell. Top with half the raspberry mixture. Repeat once more with the cream cheese and raspberries. Refrigerate until set.

SERVES 6

Custard Pie

4	egg yolks
¾	cup sugar
2	cups milk, scalded
⅛	teaspoon salt
I	teaspoon vanilla extract
I	9-inch pie shell, unbaked
4	egg whites
½	cup sugar

In a mixing bowl beat the egg yolks thoroughly. Add the ¾ cup sugar and continue to beat until the yolks are the color of lemons. Gradually add the scalded milk, salt, and vanilla.

Pour the custard into the pie shell. Bake at 400° for 15 minutes. Reduce the heat to 250° and continue baking until the custard filling is firm.

In a separate mixing bowl beat the egg whites until stiff peaks form. Beat in ½ cup of sugar. Spread the egg white mixture over the custard pie. Return to the oven. Bake at 300° until the meringue turns golden brown.

SERVES 6

BLUE COMET DINER, HAZLETON, PENNSYLVANIA

KEY CITY DINER, PHILLIPSBURG, NEW JERSEY

Apple Cobbler

1/4 cup butter
1/2 cup all-purpose flour
1/2 cup sugar
1 teaspoon baking powder
1/4 cup milk
3 apples, peeled and sliced
1/2 cup packed brown sugar
1 teaspoon cinnamon
1/2 teaspoon nutmeg

In a large saucepan melt the butter. In a mixing bowl blend together the flour, sugar, baking powder, and milk. Pour the flour mixture into the butter, mixing well.

Pour the entire mixture into the bottom of a casserole dish. Place sliced apples over the mixture. Sprinkle the brown sugar, cinnamon, and nutmeg over the top. Bake at 350° for 35 minutes or until the top is light brown.

SERVES 4

Peach Cobbler

1/4 cup butter
1/2 cup all-purpose flour
1/2 cup sugar
1 teaspoon baking powder
1/4 cup milk
2 1/2 cups fresh peaches, sliced
1/2 cup packed brown sugar

In a large saucepan melt the butter. In a mixing bowl blend together the flour with

the sugar, baking powder, and milk. Pour into the butter and mix well.

Pour the mixture into the bottom of a casserole dish. Place the sliced peaches over the mixture. Sprinkle the brown sugar over the top. Bake at 350° for 35 minutes or until the top is light brown.

SERVES 4

Apple Pan Dowdy

1 1/2 cups all-purpose flour
1/8 teaspoon salt
1/2 cup butter
5 tablespoons ice water
1/4 cup butter, melted

♦ ♦ ♦

1/2 cup sugar
1/4 teaspoon salt
1/2 teaspoon cinnamon
1/4 teaspoon nutmeg
10 tart apples, peeled and sliced
1/2 cup light molasses
1/4 cup butter, melted
1/4 cup water
Heavy cream

Grease a square baking dish. Set aside.

In a mixing bowl combine the flour and salt. Blend in 1/2 cup of butter. Using your fingers work the mixture until it becomes the consistency of coarse meal. Sprinkle the ice water, 1 tablespoon at a time, into the dough.

Roll out the dough into a rectangle. Cut in half. Brush melted butter over the dough. Cut in half again and butter all sides. Stack the pieces on top of one another. Refrigerate for 2 hours.

In a mixing bowl combine the sugar, salt, cinnamon, and nutmeg. Add the sliced apples, and mix well.

In a separate bowl combine the molasses with the melted butter and water. Blend until smooth. Roll the dough out once more. Divide in half and line the bottom of the prepared baking dish. Add the apple filling. Pour the molasses mixture over the apples. Cover with the remaining dough and seal all sides. Cut 2 or 3 slits in the top with a sharp knife. Bake at 400° for 10 minutes. Reduce the heat to 325° and continue baking for 1 hour. Serve warm topped with heavy cream.

SERVES 6

Apple Crisp

4	cups sliced tart apples
¾	cup packed brown sugar
½	cup whole oats
¾	teaspoon nutmeg
½	cup all-purpose flour
¾	teaspoon cinnamon
⅓	cup butter

Arrange the sliced apples in the bottom of an 8-inch square baking pan. In a mixing bowl combine the brown sugar, whole oats, nutmeg, flour, cinnamon, and butter. Mix thoroughly. Sprinkle evenly over the apples. Bake at 375° for 30 minutes or until the topping is golden brown.

SERVES 6

ROUTE 66 DINER, SPRINGFIELD, MASSACHUSETTS

Apple Strudel

½	cup chopped walnuts
1½	pounds tart apples, peeled and sliced
½	cup packed light brown sugar
¼	teaspoon cinnamon
½	teaspoon mace
2	tablespoons chopped candied ginger
½	cup raisins
⅛	teaspoon salt
8	ounces phyllo dough
¼	cup unsalted butter, melted
¾	cup breadcrumbs

In a large baking pan toast the chopped walnuts at 375° for 10 minutes. Set aside.

In a large mixing bowl toss the apple slices with the brown sugar, cinnamon, mace, candied ginger, raisins, and salt. Add the walnuts.

Place 2 24-inch sheets of waxed paper on a clean surface. Place the phyllo dough on the waxed paper, one sheet at a time. Brush with melted butter. Sprinkle with breadcrumbs.

Mound the apple mixture into the center of the phyllo dough, leaving space around the edges. Fold the long side of the dough over the apple mixture. Roll into a jelly roll. Place the dough onto a baking sheet that has been covered with parchment paper. Bake at 350° for 45 minutes or until the dough is golden brown.

SERVES 8

Blueberry Strata

2	cups blueberries
1	cup crushed pineapple
1	8-ounce package cream cheese, softened
3	tablespoons sugar
1	tablespoon milk
½	teaspoon vanilla extract
1	9-inch pie shell, baked
¼	cup sugar
2	tablespoons cornstarch
¼	teaspoon salt
1	teaspoon fresh lemon juice
	Whipped cream

Drain the blueberries and crushed pineapple, reserving 1½ cups of juice. In a mixing bowl combine the cream cheese with 3 tablespoons of sugar, the milk, and vanilla. Blend until smooth. Add all but 2 tablespoons of the crushed pineapple to the cream cheese mixture. Spread in the bottom of the pie shell. Refrigerate.

In a small bowl combine ¼ cup of sugar, the cornstarch, and salt. In a saucepan combine the reserved fruit juice with the cornstarch mixture. Cook until thick. Add the blueberries and lemon juice. Let cool. Pour over the chilled cream cheese. Cover with whipped cream and pineapple.

SERVES 6

Blackberry Slump

1	quart fresh blackberries
1½	cups sugar
1½	teaspoons baking powder
1	cup all-purpose flour
½	cup milk
½	teaspoon salt
¼	cup sugar
3	tablespoons butter, melted

Wash the blackberries under cold running water. Stem the berries and slice. Grease a casserole dish. Place the berries in the bottom of the dish. Sprinkle 1½ cups of sugar over the top of the berries.

In a mixing bowl combine the baking powder, flour, milk, salt, ¼ cup of sugar, and melted butter. Mix thoroughly. Pour this mixture over the berries. Bake at 375° for 45 minutes.

SERVES 6

HENRY'S DINER, BURLINGTON, VERMONT

Jell-O

2	packages cherry Jell-O
1½	cups hot water
1	cup crushed pineapple, with juice
1	cup whole cranberries
2	cups sour cream
2	packages raspberry Jell-O
1½	cups hot water
1	cup frozen raspberries
	Whipped cream

In a mixing bowl dissolve the cherry Jell-O in 1½ cups of hot water. Stir until the Jell-O has dissolved. Add the pineapple and cranberries. Pour the Jell-O into a 2-quart mold. Refrigerate.

When layer one is set, frost with sour cream. Return to the refrigerator.

In a mixing bowl dissolve the raspberry Jell-O in the 1½ cups of hot water. Stir until the Jell-O has dissolved. Add the frozen raspberries. Refrigerate until thick but still pourable. Spread over the sour cream. Refrigerate once more until firm. To serve cut into squares. Top with whipped cream.

SERVES 8

Chocolate Pudding

1½ cups milk
2 cups breadcrumbs
¾ cup sugar
2 egg yolks, beaten
2 ounces unsweetened chocolate, melted
½ teaspoon grated orange rind
¼ cup fresh orange juice
¼ teaspoon salt
½ cup chopped walnuts
2 egg whites

In a saucepan scald the milk. Pour into a mixing bowl. Add the breadcrumbs.

In a separate mixing bowl combine the sugar, egg yolks, unsweetened chocolate, orange rind, orange juice, and salt. Blend thoroughly.

Pour the egg yolk mixture into the milk-breadcrumb mixture. Add the walnuts.

Beat the egg whites until stiff peaks form. Fold the egg whites into the pudding mixture. Blend thoroughly.

Pour the mixture into 6 custard cups. Place the cups into a shallow baking pan. Pour hot water into the bottom of the pan. Bake at 350° for 35 minutes or until the pudding is done. Serve warm.

SERVES 6

Lemon Pudding

2 eggs, separated
⅓ cup sugar
3 ounces cream cheese
1 cup sour cream
½ cup fresh lemon juice
1 teaspoon grated lemon rind
½ cup cream
¼ teaspoon cream of tartar
2 tablespoons sugar

In a mixing bowl beat the egg yolks. Add ⅓ cup of sugar, the cream cheese, and sour cream. Blend until smooth. Add the lemon juice and lemon rind.

Pour into a double boiler. Stir over hot water until the mixture becomes thick. Let cool.

Whip the cream. Add to the lemon mixture. Pour the pudding into a shallow casserole dish. Beat the egg whites until foamy. Add the ¼ teaspoon cream of tartar and 2 tablespoons of sugar, and continue beating until the egg whites are stiff and form peaks. Drop by tablespoonfuls, forming small mounds, onto the top of the lemon pudding. Bake at 425° for 6 minutes. Let cool.

SERVES 6

LINDSY ROSE DINER, HAVERHILL, MASSACHUSETTS

Rice Pudding

4	cups milk
½	cup uncooked long-grain rice
¼	teaspoon salt
½	cup raisins
I	cup evaporated milk
2	eggs, slightly beaten
I	cup sugar
½	teaspoon vanilla extract
⅛	teaspoon cinnamon
⅛	teaspoon nutmeg
	Whipped cream

In a saucepan scald the milk. Add the rice, salt, and raisins. Simmer for 20 minutes, stirring occasionally.

In a mixing bowl blend together the evaporated milk, eggs, sugar, and vanilla. With a wire whisk, whip the mixture. Add to the rice. Cook for 5 minutes, stirring constantly, until the pudding is thick.

Pour into serving dishes. Top with cinnamon and nutmeg. Cover with whipped cream.

SERVES 4

Custard

2	cups milk
2	eggs
¼	cup sugar
⅛	teaspoon salt
½	teaspoon vanilla extract

In a saucepan over high heat scald the milk. Reduce the heat.

In a mixing bowl beat the eggs. Add the sugar and salt. Add the hot milk. Return the custard mixture to the saucepan. Cook over low heat, stirring constantly, until the mixture thickens. Remove and let cool. Add the vanilla and blend. Serve in custard cups.

SERVES 4

CASEY'S DINER

Casey's in Natick, Massachusetts, is one of the oldest—and tiniest—continuously operated diners in the country. Casey's has been serving customers for more than a hundred years and has been run by the same family for most of that time. Fred Casey Jr. is a third-generation owner.

A ten-stool Worcester Lunch Car, Casey's Diner was built in 1922. It replaced an earlier car, with only four stools, which had already operated at this location for decades.

Casey's has always been a small business. "We're more of a lunch car, not a full-service diner," says Fred. "We do a lunch menu only."

Fred says he enjoys working in the diner, but he adds that it is a lot of hard work. "We do everything ourselves," he says. "We don't buy anything preprepared. We chop our own onions and make our own salads."

The hard work pays off. On an average day, Fred may pass up to five hundred orders through the take-out window at Casey's.

"It's our hot dogs and hamburgers," says Fred, who also thinks the diner's longevity contributes to its success.

Like the business itself, the interior of Casey's has stood the test of time. "The mahogany finish of our counter is cracked from all the polish over the years," says Fred.

Casey's is listed on the National Register of Historic Places.

Tapioca

1 egg, separated
2 tablespoons sugar
2 cups milk
3 tablespoons tapioca
1/8 teaspoon salt
1/2 teaspoon vanilla extract

In a mixing bowl beat the egg white. Add 1 tablespoon of the sugar. Continue beating until peaks form.

In a saucepan add the egg yolk to a small amount of milk. Add the tapioca, remaining milk, remaining sugar, and salt. Cook over medium heat until the mixture reaches a full boil. Remove the pan from the heat.

Add a small amount of the tapioca to the egg whites. Blend well. Add remaining tapioca, stirring constantly. Add the vanilla. Let cool for 10 minutes. Stir to blend. Refrigerate.

SERVES 4

Chocolate-Banana Tapioca

3/4 cup sugar
1/3 cup cocoa powder
3 tablespoons quick-cooking tapioca
1 egg
2 3/4 cups milk
1 teaspoon vanilla extract
4 chocolate wafers, crushed
2 large bananas, sliced
1/2 cup heavy cream, whipped
Chocolate sprinkles

In a saucepan blend the sugar with the cocoa powder, tapioca, egg, and milk. Set aside for a few minutes.

Place the pan over medium heat. Cook for 12 minutes, stirring occasionally, until the mixture comes to a boil. Remove the pan from the heat. Add the vanilla. Let cool. Stir the mixture. Place in a mixing bowl, cover, and refrigerate.

To serve place even amounts of crushed chocolate wafers in the bottom of a parfait glass. Add sliced bananas. Fill with half the tapioca mixture. Add a small amount of the whipped cream. Top with more tapioca. Garnish with chocolate sprinkles.

SERVES 4

BLUE STAR DINER ☕

The Blue Star in Newport News, Virginia, is just a regular, old diner, according to the owner, Fannie Blenston. "This diner is just like any other diner," says Fannie. "We can seat around forty-nine people."

But this 1950s homemade diner represents much more than that to the people who eat here. They love the place and love the food, and Fannie's house specialties keep them coming back for more. "I make three homemade specials every day," says Fannie. "Everything is made fresh."

On Mondays customers can choose between the beef stew, meat loaf, or Salisbury steak. "On other days I will make chicken and dumplings, corned beef and cabbage, baked chicken with rice, barbecue beef, or roast pork with dressing and stuffed peppers."

With a variety of home-cooked goodies like that to offer, it is no wonder that Fannie and her crew are kept busy in the kitchen. The Blue Star, situated at 9955 Warwick Avenue in Newport News, Virignia, is open from 6:00 A.M. to 10:00 P.M. daily.

INDEX

MISS NEWPORT DINER, LYNDONVILLE, VERMONT

WHITE MANNA HAMBURGERS, HACKENSACK, NEW JERSEY

CHARLIE'S DINER, WORCESTER, MASSACHUSETTS

continued on page 259

GLOSSARY OF DINER SLANG

To feed a crowd of hungry customers, diner waitresses had to work fast. Shouting instructions to the short-order cooks behind the counter, they could spare no time for immaculate diction. To speed things up, they invented a salty verbal shorthand that changed hot chocolate to "hot cha," baked beans to "bullets," and hamburgers to "grease spots." Known as diner slang, this sort of talk made little sense to most customers, but cooks and waitresses understood it perfectly.

A.C.: Any sandwich made with American cheese.

Adam and Eve on a raft: Two poached eggs on toast.

Adam's ale: Plain water.

All the way: A sandwich made with lettuce, mayonnaise, onion, and butter.

A Pie: Apple pie.

Axle grease: Butter.

Bailed hay: Cole slaw.

Bird seed: Cereal.

Blonde: Coffee with cream.

Bossy in a bowl: Beef stew. "Bossy" is a common name for a cow.

Bottom: Ice cream added to a drink.

Bowl of red: A bowl of chili con carne.

Bow wow: A hot dog.

Break a cowboy: Western omelette.

Break it and shake it: To put a raw egg in a drink, especially a milk shake.

Brown bellies: Baked beans.

Bucket of cold mud: Dish of chocolate ice cream.

Bucket of hail: A small glass of ice.

Bullets: Baked beans.

Bun pup: A hot dog.

Burn it and let it swim: A float made with chocolate syrup and ice cream on top.

Burn one: Put a hamburger on the grill.

Burn one all the way: A chocolate milk shake with chocolate ice cream.

C.B.: Cheeseburger.

Chopper: A table knife.

City juice: Water.

C.J: A cream cheese and jelly sandwich.

Clean up the kitchen: Hash.

Cold spot: A glass of iced tea.

Cowboy: A western omelette.

Cowboy on a raft: Western omelette on toast.

Cow feed: A salad.

Creep: Draft beer.

Cup of mud: Coffee.

Deadeye: A poached egg.

Dough well done with cow to cover: Buttered toast.

Draw one: Coffee.

Echo: Repeat the order.

Eighty-one: A glass of water.

Eighty-six: Do not sell to the customer.

Eve with a lid on: Apple pie.

Fifty-five: A glass of root beer.

Fifty-one: Hot chocolate.

Five: A large glass of milk.

Forty-one: Lemonade.

Gentleman will take a chance: Hash.

G.A.C: Grilled American cheese sandwich.

George Eddy: A customer who doesn't leave a tip.

Go for a walk: Take-out order.

Gravel train: Sugar bowl.

Graveyard stew: Milk toast.

Grease spot: A hamburger.

Groundhog: A hot dog.

Hamlette: An omelette made with ham.

High and dry: A sandwich without butter, mayonnaise, or lettuce.

Hold the hail: No ice.

Hops: Malted milk powder.

Hot cha: Hot chocolate.

Hot top: Hot chocolate.

Hounds on an island: Franks and beans.

Houseboat: A banana split.

Ice the rice: Add ice cream to rice pudding.

In the alley: To serve as a side dish.

In the hay: A strawberry milk shake.

Java: Coffee.

Jerk: An ice cream soda.

Joe: Coffee.

L.A: To serve an item with ice cream.

Lead pipes with rounded cows: Spaghetti and meatballs.

Life preservers with a hot top: Doughnuts with hot chocolate.

Lumber: A toothpick.

Mama: Marmalade.

M.D.: Dr. Pepper.

Mike and Ike: Salt and pepper shakers.

Mud: Black coffee or chocolate ice cream with chocolate syrup.

Nervous pudding: Jell-O.

No cow: Without milk.

Oil: Butter.

Pair of drawers: Two cups of coffee.

Pig between two sheets: Ham sandwich.

Pipes: Straws.

P.T.: Pot of tea.

Put out the lights and cry: Liver and onions.

Sand: Sugar.

Seaboard: Item wrapped for take-out.

Sea dust: Salt.

Shingle with a shimmy and a squeeze: Toast with jelly and orange juice.

Shoot one from the south: To make an especially strong cola soda.

Sidearms: Salt and pepper.

Sinkers and suds: Doughnuts and coffee.

Splash of red: Tomato soup.

Squeeze one: Orange juice.

Twenty-one: Limeade.

Two cows make them cry: Two hamburgers with onions.

Wrecked hen with fruit: Scrambled eggs with orange juice.

Yum-yum: Sugar.

Zeppelins in a fog: Sausages in mashed potatoes.

KIMBERLY DINER, MILFORD, CONNECTICUT

A NEW POPULARITY

Diners have been a part of the American landscape for more than a century and have played a major role in the developing American culture. While it faced an uncertain future twenty years ago, the diner is gaining new popularity today. Old diners are being renovated and rebuilt, and newer models coming off the assembly line are opening for business almost daily in towns and cities across the nation.

Food and atmosphere have always been the key to a diner's success.

Ironically, fast-food chains now find themselves in fierce competition with what once was viewed as an outdated industry. The chains cannot match the varied menu and relaxed, homey feeling of the local diner. Apparently, on the theory that "if you can't beat 'em, then join 'em," some franchises are trying to adopt the diner concept.

Imitation diners may look the part, but the resemblance stops at the door. Waitresses don't greet customers by their first names, nor do they remember how the regulars take their coffee. No one behind the counter of a chain restaurant understands diner slang (see Glossary of Diner Slang on page 256).

Some diners are so revered that they have been listed on the National Register of Historic Places. Among these are the Modern Diner in Pawtucket, Rhode Island, Casey's Diner in Natick, Massachusetts, and Miss Bellows Falls Diner in Bellows Falls, Vermont.

However, today's diner is more than a historical artifact. It's a thriving business. The industry that began more than one hundred years ago in Province, Rhode Island, still flourishes today. Having survived wars, the Great Depression, and even the onslaught of corporate chains, America's diners are still there to welcome hungry customers who want a home-cooked meal at a reasonable price, served in the friendliest place in town.

WEBBIE'S DINER, LYNN, MASSACHUSETTS

DINER PLACE INDEX